To the memory of my sister

May W. Van Staaveren Stark

An
American in Japan
1945–1948
A Civilian View
of the Occupation

An
American in Japan
1945–1948

A Civilian View
of the Occupation

JACOB VAN STAAVEREN

Introduction by Akira Iriye

UNIVERSITY OF WASHINGTON PRESS

Seattle and London

This book was published with the assistance of a grant
from the Japan Foundation.

Library of Congress Cataloging-in-Publication Data

Van Staaveren, Jacob.
  An American in Japan, 1945–1948: A Civilian View of the
Occupation / by Jacob Van Staaveren : introduction by Akira Iriye.
    p. cm.
  Includes bibliographical references and index.
  ISBN 0-295-97363-3
  1. Yamanashi-ken (Japan)—History. 2. Japan—History—Allied
occupation, 1945–1952. I. Title
DS894.59.Y3485V36   1994
952'.164044—dc20   94-5717
                                                              CIP

The text paper used in this publication is acid-free and recycled from 10%
post-consumer and at least 50% pre-consumer waste. The text and insert
papers meet the minimum requirements of American National Standard for
Information Sciences—Permanence of Paper for Printed Library Materials,
ANSI Z39.48–1984.

Contents

Preface

In the growing body of historical literature on the American and Allied occupation of Japan from September 1945 through April 1952, relatively little has been published on the contribution of military and civilian personnel who served in military government, working to effect occupation reforms at the grass-roots level among ordinary Japanese citizenry. Their activities were conducted under the supervision of Eighth Army headquarters in Yokohama and implemented by its subordinate organizations, consisting of two U.S. Army corps, eight military government regions (which included the special district of Hokkaido, commonly considered a prefecture) and military government units reorganized into forty-five "teams" in July 1946. The number of military and civilian personnel assigned to military government during the occupation ranged from a minimum of 1,888 to a maximum of about 2,800.

A number of reasons can be ascribed to this gap in the written histories. One was the constant turbulence created by U.S. postwar personnel policies enabling officers and enlisted men with sufficient service points from World War II to take early discharges from the Army and Navy. Some took their discharges in Japan and continued to work as civilians in military government, but many opted to return to the United States to resume their schooling or careers. Among their replacements, some like myself did manage to put pen to paper and write several articles about the occupation shortly after we returned home. But at that time we were less wont to write about our personal experiences than to describe with a broad brush the problems and progress of one or more facets of the occupation.

Certainly one can also point to the sheer volume of military government records. In the early months of the occupation, Eighth Army headquarters required from its many units in the field frequent periodic reports focusing heavily on details of Japanese compliance with demilitarization directives designed to reform every facet of the body politic—social, educational, religious, and economic. In addition, these reports contained data on the local economy, black-marketing, unemployment, the homeless, repatriation, public health, the status of crops, fishing, lumbering, mining, and so on. Any historian who wished to read and analyze these mountains of records of varying quality would face a most daunting task.

Another reason has been the continuing perception, correct during most of the first year of the occupation, that the primary task of military government was surveillance. Early on, this was to ensure that the Japanese abided by all of the demilitarization directives issued by General Douglas MacArthur, Supreme Commander for the Allied Powers, whose Tokyo headquarters bore the acronym "SCAP." In fact, most of the surveillance task was accomplished relatively early, and military government personnel, especially civilians, increasingly began to advise and assist Japanese officials and the populace at the prefectural and local level on how to implement SCAP's wide-ranging reforms. These local efforts went largely unnoticed. Scholars, journalists, and other writers understandably focused, then and now, on events in Tokyo, where the Supreme Commander and his large military and civilian staff made the decisions and crafted the multiple directives, guidance papers, and even laws, including a new Constitution, designed to convert Japan into a western-style democracy. In consequence, most published accounts describe and analyze the occupation "from the top."

What follows here, however, is an autobiographical account of the occupation of Japan "from below." It describes the experiences of an American civilian "civil information and education officer" on the Yamanashi Military Government Team from late 1946 to September 1948. My specific duty was to advise and assist prefectural officials and citizens of Yamanashi Prefecture on how to democratize their educational system, adult organizations, and labor unions, and how to maintain a separation of religion and the state in conformance with SCAP's many reform directives and the Japanese government's new postwar legislation.

My personal background in 1946 included a master's degree from the University of Chicago in philosophy and history, including studies in the religions and cultures of Asia. In addition, I had completed a year of doctoral studies in history and political science. I had also amassed a fair amount of administrative, research, and writing experience. My two years in Japan were followed by a thirty-year career as a professional historian with various United States agencies.

The book is based largely on the voluminous letters, notes, and reports I wrote while in Japan, to which I refer by date throughout the text. These materials are in my personal files. In addition, I have used many documents of the Yamanashi Military Government Team, including letters from Japanese citizens, which are presently in my files or housed in Archive II of the Washington National Records Center in College Park, Maryland, as well as the *Japan Year Books* of the occupation period.

I hope this account will enable the reader to understand better what it was like to try to bring about fundamental changes in a Japanese province in the wake of the nation's defeat. I recount in detail the life of occupationaires in Tokyo and the prefectures as well as my observations of the everyday reactions of ordinary Japanese toward the occupation and its personnel. Certainly I encountered many examples of sincerity of purpose as both Americans and Japanese sought to change the country in constructive ways.

Several individuals contributed greatly to my efforts to document my experiences in occupied Japan some four and a half decades ago.

Hosaka Chushin, late professor emeritus of English Literature at Yamanashi *Gakuin* University, whom I first met in 1947, provided very useful information and also explained in his many letters to me facets of Japanese culture germane to the documentation I possessed on education and religious reforms in Yamanashi Prefecture. Regrettably, Professor Hosaka's untimely death in 1991 precluded his reading the manuscript.

I am also greatly indebted to Maurice Jakofsky, M.D., of Mission Viejo, California, who served as the medical officer on the Yamanashi Military Government Team from July 1946 to January 1948. Not only did Dr. Jakofsky refresh my memory of many events of that period but he read and critiqued the finished manuscript.

In addition, my late sister, May W. Van Staaveren Stark, sent to me numerous invaluable books and articles on Japanese history and culture while I was serving in occupied Japan.

Finally, I wish to extend my deep appreciation to Elizabeth, my wife, for reviewing the manuscript as it evolved chapter by chapter. Her editorial questions and suggestions as well as her computer expertise contributed substantially to my completion of the narrative.

Jacob Van Staaveren
Alexandria, Virginia

Introduction

by Akira Iriye

This book recounts in great detail the life of an American "civil information and education officer" in Yamanashi Prefecture during 1946–1948. Based mostly on letters, notes, and reports he wrote at that time, his account enables the reader to understand what it was like to try to bring about fundamental changes in a Japanese province in the wake of the nation's defeat.

Almost from the beginning of the war, American officials had determined that in order to prevent Japan from ever again menacing the peace of Asia and security of the United States, it would be of crucial importance to reform Japanese politics, society, economy, and culture. The war was seen not merely as one between two more or less interchangeable powers, but one that pitted one type of nation against another—or, as many pointed out then, as "a war of ideas." Unless Japan, and its ally, Germany, were fundamentally altered, the war would not have solved anything. During the war, therefore, the Department of State as well as the armed forces of the United States paid special attention to what was called "postwar planning"—to prepare for the occupation of defeated enemy countries in such a way as to transform them into peaceful, liberal societies. In order to carry out such a task, it would of course be necessary for the United States to train military and civilian personnel, and both the army and the navy established schools and institutes in various parts of the country to teach their officers everything from the history and languages of Japan and Germany to principles of democracy and liberalism. In the meantime, the State Department coordinated its postwar planning with the military agencies to formulate specific policy guidelines for the occupation of these countries.

From the beginning, the occupation of Japan was considered to be America's primary responsibility. Unlike Germany and Austria, where the occupation would be coordinated with the European allies, in Japan the United States would have a free hand, although it would consult its allies, especially China and Britain, in the task. This, of course, was because the United States had shouldered the major burden of fighting in the Pacific, whereas in Europe it had been shared with the European powers.

It should also be noted, however, that within the United States government there was a greater degree of cohesiveness about planning for the treatment of postwar Japan than of Germany. Whereas toward the latter, serious divisions of views persisted until the very end (it is well known that some Americans wanted to turn Germany into a pre-industrial, agricultural society, while others vehemently opposed such a proposal), regarding Japan, there was essential agreement on certain key points.

The Japanese militarists responsible for aggression would have to be punished, of course, and the nation must be deprived of lands it had acquired in its aggressive wars of conquest. But the Japanese people would not be penalized. Rather, they would be encouraged to change. Thus, they would enjoy the benefits of modern civilization that they had deserved, but of which they had been deprived for so long. They should be taught to think for themselves, act independently, and overcome feudalistic tendencies in interpersonal relations. Reforms in land systems, labor organization, and education would be particularly important. But the key to American wartime planning was the belief that the Japanese people were capable of appreciating and undertaking such reform measures, if only given a chance. That was what the occupation was going to be about, to give the Japanese a chance to free themselves from their feudal and militaristic restrictions and join other peoples in establishing a civil, peaceful, democratic community.

The Potsdam declaration, issued on 26 July 1945 by the governments of the United States, Great Britain, and China, calling on Japan to surrender, clearly expressed the same philosophy. "The time has come," the declaration stated, "for Japan to decide whether she will continue to be controlled by those self-willed militaristic advisers whose unintelligent calculations have brought the Empire of Japan to the threshold of annihilation, or whether she will follow the path of reason." The occupation forces, it continued, "shall be withdrawn from Japan as soon as . . . there has been established in accordance with the freely expressed will of the Japanese people a peacefully inclined and responsible government." In other words, the nation would be occupied in order to ensure the emergence of such a government. It should also be recalled that one month before the Potsdam declaration was announced, the wartime allies had met in San Francisco and adopted a new charter for the United Nations, which was envisaged as the key framework for the postwar world order and which Japan would be invited to join once the occupation ended. The preamble enumerated certain principles that would guide the national and international affairs once peace was restored: "fundamental human rights . . . dignity and worth of the human person . . . the equal rights of men and women . . . fundamental freedoms for all without distinction as to race, sex, language, or religion." All these principles would constitute the basis of occupation-initiated reforms in Japan.

By not responding immediately to the Potsdam declaration, the Japanese leadership in effect invited the atomic bombings of Hiroshima and Nagasaki as well as Soviet entry into the war. These developments led to a belated decision on the part of the Emperor and his advisors to end the war, and a formal ceremony of surrender took place on the battleship *Missouri* in Tokyo bay on 2 September 1945, thus paving the way for the occupation of the country.

Jacob Van Staaveren's story can be read in such a context. He played an important role in the remaking of Japan. He was involved in many of the changes envisaged in wartime planning—in education, political affairs, religious, and other civic activities. The book thus helps one to understand what happened when lofty objectives of national transformation were tried out at the local level. To what extent did the reform measures penetrate the surface of Japanese society and touch the masses? How did the citizens understand the meaning of democracy, for instance, in their daily life? What aspects of reform worked well, and which less so? How was it possible that a handful of American occupation officers (some of whom, like Jacob Van Staaveren, were barely thirty years old) were able to carry so much authority and that their orders and wishes were, if one is to judge by this book, apparently obeyed by the Japanese? These and many other questions about postwar Japanese transformation under the aegis of the U.S. occupation can now be better explored, thanks to the rich first-hand material contained here.

Today, after the lapse of almost fifty years, it is easy to take a cynical view of the alleged transformation of Japan under the occupation. After all, can a few years of reform induced from above really be expected to alter significantly the ingrained habits and attitudes of a people?

Were not the Japanese, and even the American occupiers themselves, merely going through the motions, both of them anticipating that once the occupation ended, things would go back to their traditional ways? Didn't the Cold War, in any event, bring about the cancellation of most of the reforms? Does today's Japan have the remotest resemblance to what the Americans at that time visualized as a consequence of their efforts? How did the United States attempt as impossible a task as the democratization of another country to begin with?

To such skeptics and cynics, this book will present a wholesome antidote, for it contains ample evidence of the earnestness with which both Americans and Japanese sought to change the country. At least one occupation official went about his task with utmost seriousness and sincerity, and it would seem that most Japanese with whom he came into contact responded in kind. It is an amazing fact, in retrospect, that a young man should have, almost single-handedly and without the overt use of force, undertaken the task of implementing the policies of the occupation administration, and that so many Japanese seem to have cooperated with him. Perhaps this is the most important thing we should remember, the author seems to be saying—that at least initially, both sides took the task of transforming Japan extremely seriously.

As one who was at the receiving end of many of these reforms, I can say that what the author writes about is genuine and authentic. I was a schoolboy in Japan during the occupation, and Jacob Van Staaveren accurately conveys the atmosphere of those days. I was very much part of one critical change he chronicles in detail, the institution of the new 6–3–3 structure of education. This replaced the prewar system, in which a compulsory six-year primary education ended schooling for most Japanese, and only a tiny minority went on to middle and higher schools. I was going to be in seventh grade in April 1947 when the new system was supposed to go into effect, and I still remember the anxiety felt by pupils of my generation as well as our parents as to the nature of the change. Under the new system, social studies curricula were introduced, and we studied democratic thought and government from teachers for whom these were also novel concepts. Other aspects of educational changes the author describes—coeducation, textbook revision, teacher unionism, abolition of morals education, demolition of *hôanden* (little buildings containing the Emperor's picture)—I had also witnessed at first hand while I was in grade school, and here again, the descriptions in this book match what I still remember very vividly.

As the author says, many of the reforms—including the 6–3–3 system of schooling—have survived to this day, while others were given up as soon as the occupation ended. Some of the more intractable problems he faced, such as the treatment of the Korean minority in Japan or the separation of church and state, still exist, and the chapters that deal with these issues are among the most interesting. But ultimately what makes the book unique and important is Mr. Van Staaveren's description of how the two nations, until recently bitter wartime foes, undertook their postwar cooperation at the local level. The young "civil information and education officer" who was sent to Yamanashi was neither a Japan nor an education specialist. He had a strong background in Western political and religious history. The letters and reports he wrote at that time suggest a less expert knowledge of Japanese history or educational philosophy. Because of this very fact, however, his eagerness, his lack of self-consciousness, and his genuine faith in what he was doing come through. This is the most refreshing thing about the book, as well as the reason why it should be read widely by both Americans and Japanese. Today, in very different circumstances, we are apt to be critical of the occupation-initiated reform of Japan and to forget the genuineness and uniqueness of that experiment, when America was full of confidence, good will, and sense of mission, and when Japan, while prostrate, was also eager to do anything to overcome the sense of grief and shame over the defeat. As the two nations, nearly fifty years after the end of World War II, grope for new ways of cooperating with one another to define a post–Cold War Pacific order, it will not be too much to ask that their leaders and people go back to the spirit of those early postwar years and recall the sense of fresh excitement about their cooperation.

An
American in Japan
1945–1948
A Civilian View
of the Occupation

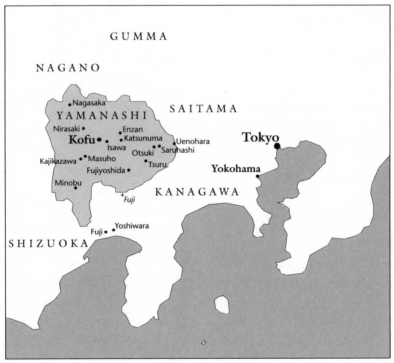

Yamanashi and surrounding prefectures

1

Assignment to Japan

Departure from Seattle

It was autumn 1946. World War II had been over for a year, and the difficult work of shaping the peace had begun. In the Pacific theater, American and other Allied personnel, both civilian and military, were heading to Japan for occupation duties.

Seattle, Washington, on September 10 was cool and breezy. Shortly after noon two U.S. Army buses pulled up to the New Richmond Hotel, a faded and slightly seedy hostelry near the city's main railroad passenger terminal. About fifty Department of the Army civilians (DACs) clambered aboard the buses for the short ride to one of Seattle's many quays for ocean-going commerce. I was among them. Upon arrival, we marched up the gangplank and onto the upper deck of a drab troopship, the *Cape Cleare*, named after the southernmost tip of the Republic of Ireland. A relatively small 8,000-ton vessel, it had provided heroic transport service in the Pacific theater during World War II which ended officially when a Japanese government delegation signed the Allied Terms of Surrender on the battleship USS *Missouri* in Tokyo Bay on September 2, 1945. A crew member guided us to our "staterooms" where we quickly dropped our bags and joined about a hundred Army officers, who had boarded earlier, at the ship's rail to watch longshoremen hoist cargo into the ship's hold.

The occasion was festive. Flags, banners, and balloons fluttered along the quay, and hundreds of enlisted men crowded the lower decks and hung from every porthole, some holding crudely drawn signs appropriate for the hour: "Tokyo or Bust," "Tokyo Here We Come," and "Gotta See a Geisha Girl." Near the gangplank, a United Service Organization (USO) all-girl band led by Carmen de la Vega, formerly of New York City, belted out the popular tunes of the day. Carmen, an outstanding guitarist and singer, was a favorite performer at Seattle's USO center and other military clubs and at the New Richmond Hotel where she and her troupe resided. Clad in a fiery red dress and blessed with dark, flashing eyes and a beguiling voice, she was popularly known as "The Latin from Manhattan." Whenever Carmen and her musical partners completed a melody, accompanied by spirited body gyrations, the thousand or more troops aboard the *Cape Cleare* cheered lustily, waved, blew kisses, and shouted invitations to them to come aboard and stow away for the voyage to Japan. The band members responded enthusiastically, returned the waves and kisses, and then struck up another tune.

It was a common postwar dockside ritual. Unlike World War II when ships with servicemen left American ports by stealth at night to fight Japan throughout the Pacific area, and Germany and Italy in North Africa and Europe, peace now assured those who embarked for these distant lands a cheery farewell. Most military and civilian personnel on the *Cape Cleare* would see duty in Japan and Okinawa; the rest were destined for South Korea, the Philippines, or the small islands of Guam and Wake.

An hour and a half elapsed before the last cargo was hauled aboard and the crew began pulling in the ropes that secured the ship firmly to the quay. Then as the gangplank was withdrawn, the *Cape Cleare's* engines revved up, creating a foamy wash astern. Several blasts of its horn signaled the beginning of the journey to Yokohama. Carmen and her band launched into "My Bonnie Lies over the Ocean," with the ship's passengers singing along in discordant but exuberant attempts at harmony. As the army transport slowly eased into Puget Sound bay, the band played a mournful "Auld Lang Syne" amid the final cheers, shouts, and whistles from the troops. Carmen's music was quickly out of earshot as the vessel picked up speed and began to roll with the swells of the sea. Seattle receded from view, but the shoreline along the bay's great length remained visible for several hours. Dusk fell, then night. Flickering lights of distant towns and homes surrounding the bay pierced the growing darkness until a grey mist finally enveloped the *Cape Cleare* in total darkness.

Thus began a thirteen-day journey to Japan, where only a year earlier thousands of American and Allied troops had arrived to disarm and demilitarize the populace. Under the command of General Douglas MacArthur, these troops supported a professional military-civilian staff headquartered in Tokyo and numerous military government units throughout Japan which were set up for the purpose of democratizing the nation's institutions. All of the *Cape Cleare's* passengers had waited two, three, or more weeks for this embarkation day. A maritime union's dispute with Seattle's port authorities over wages and other matters had led first to a labor slowdown. This was followed, beginning September fourth, by a nationwide maritime strike, the largest in U.S. history. The strike immediately tied up dozens of commercial vessels in Puget Sound ports. Although military transports were exempt from the shutdown, their loading nonetheless was delayed considerably. For us fifty civilians, the enforced layover in Seattle was tantamount to a vacation at government expense. Upon the receipt of our Army travel orders to entrain to an embarkation port, we drew our full federal salaries plus per-diem for hotel, meals, and other living expenses. We were instructed only to "keep in touch" with the Army's personnel-processing office in the New Richmond Hotel which would inform us of the day and hour of our departure to Japan. Otherwise we were free to visit friends and relatives, patronize Seattle's movie houses and other theatrical offerings, sail on Lake Washington, or dine at any of Seattle's many fine seafood restaurants.

The pleasant memories of the lengthy holiday in Seattle were erased abruptly on our first night at sea. After the *Cape Cleare* left Puget Sound and steamed into the rougher waters of the mighty Pacific Ocean, the ship bobbed like a bottle and lurched rather than swayed. Many of us, overcome by nausea, headed for the ship's rail where we lost our last meal. "The damned tub doesn't have enough ballast," moaned an Army major. "I hear it's only half loaded because of the maritime strike." No one disputed his assessment of what caused so much misery to so many.

The *Cape Cleare's* accommodations did nothing to alleviate the frequent *mal de mer* of its many passengers. "Our so-called staterooms are jammed to capacity with triple-decker bunks," I recorded, "with no less than eight in one small room and twenty-seven in another. There are no chairs. The ventilating system cooks us in daytime and freezes us at night." To reach the "dining room," sparsely furnished with long tables and hard benches, we had to pass through a narrow corridor where a kitchen-exhaust pipe spewed perpetually foul odors. The bathroom was typical of a troopship, with a dozen or more toilet seats abreast and not a single door to assure a few moments of privacy. Although the *Cape Cleare* reportedly had been reconverted from wartime to peacetime use, those passengers who were veterans of ship travel during World War II swore that the reconversion was not discernible. There was only minor consolation in the knowledge that, below decks, about 1,000 Army enlisted men were jammed together in quarters more spartan and unpleasant than ours.

Our austere accommodations were not unusual in 1946. In early postwar Japan I would encounter other Americans who had journeyed to the Far East in military transports bereft of any amenities. There was gradual improvement. Later ships carrying the wives and children of military and civilian occupationaires were considerably more luxurious. By 1948 wartime vessels like the *Cape Cleare* had ceased to be used for carrying American personnel to and from the Pacific area.

Whatever the nature of ship facilities in this era, the journey from the United States to the Far East was a long one. Most voyages from Seattle to Yokohama took thirteen to fifteen days; from San Francisco, seventeen to nineteen. A few military transports brought civilians, officers, and enlisted men directly from the East Coast. One, the *Wisteria*, in late 1946 steamed for fifty-three days from Brooklyn, New York, to Yokohama via the Panama Canal. According to some of its passengers, they needed a week to recover their land legs.

Large-scale air service to the Far East was not yet cost-effective or practical. All military and civilian passenger aircraft were still nonjet. They were relatively small and possessed limited range. The Great Circle route via Alaska was still too hazardous for most planes, and those flying from San Francisco had to refuel in Hawaii and again at Guam, Wake, or the Philippines. The air journey consumed at best two days and frequently three or four because of the need for en-route plane maintenance and repairs. Generally, air travel was reserved for "very important persons" (VIPs), usually fairly high ranking military and civilian personnel or those whose skills were needed urgently. As many Americans still regarded a Pacific flight as dangerous, it was not uncommon for some VIPs, including several on the *Cape Cleare*, to refuse a proffered opportunity to fly.

Our passage to Japan in September 1946, while rough and occasionally stormy, was unnoteworthy. There was only a brief, misty view of an outermost island of the Aleutian chain. The overcast weather was often interspersed with rain, drizzle, or fog, typical of the Great Circle route. Each day's routine was broken only by meal calls and an occasional shipboard safety drill. Civilians and officers whiled away their time by reading, playing cards, walking around the deck, or "shooting the bull," there being no recreational or other facilities on board to do anything else.

We civilians were a notably diverse group, representing many of the skills sought by General MacArthur's headquarters in Tokyo and Lieutenant General Robert L. Eichelberger's Eighth Army headquarters in Yokohama. The passenger list included a veterinarian, an auto mechanic, an administrative assistant, an economist, a historian, a radar specialist, public school teachers, clerks, a language anthropologist, an attorney, and an ex-commissioner of corrections from New York State. Some knew precisely the nature and location of their pending jobs. The ex-commissioner of corrections would serve in Tokyo as an adviser on penal reform in Japan; the language anthropologist would concentrate and advise on the possible reform of the Japanese language; the attorney would be assigned to a special tribunal charged with reviewing the records of Japanese accused of war crimes, and the public school teachers would conduct educational courses for servicemen under the aegis of the army's Information and Education Program, but would learn the name of their military units or bases only after they reached Japan.

Cape Cleare's civilians had volunteered to work in the Far East for varying reasons: to obtain more professional experience; to swell thin bank accounts (all civil service positions paid twenty-five percent more than in the United States); to fulfill a spirit of adventure; and, for some married men, to give themselves and their wives and children, who would follow soon, the experience of living in a totally different culture. A handful seemed to have less positive reasons for going abroad: to escape unhappy marriages or because they were near-alcoholics. At least three appeared to be in the latter category as they imbibed constantly from bottled spirits in their satchels. They were eager to live in an area where, according to very reliable reports, tax-free liquor could be purchased in unlimited quantities and flowed abundantly in the bars of all American and Allied billets, hotels, and clubs.

Arrival in Yokohama

September 24, 1946, marked the *Cape Cleare's* arrival at Yokohama after thirteen days at sea. As it entered the breakwater, we noted large red and black letters on the outer jetty—KILROY. The always-anonymous adventurist, the American enlisted man of World War II, had long preceded us into Japan's home waters. As our ship chugged slowly towards port we saw the protruding, rusting hulks of remnants of the once-powerful Japanese Navy. Our first glimpse of the Japanese people came when the small crew of a harbor launch pulled up alongside the *Cape Cleare* to discharge a Japanese harbor pilot, who then steered our ship through the last few miles of the channel waters to its berth.

We docked precisely at 1:00 P.M. The quay was a beehive of activity. Scores of Japanese dock workers, shabbily attired, milled about waiting to unload the ship's cargo. Parked nearby were numerous American Army buses and trucks, all with Japanese drivers, waiting to bring the military and civilian passengers to their quarters in the Tokyo-Yokohama area. What were the workers thinking? It was impossible to know.

Nearly an hour elapsed before passenger disembarkation began. Once on the dock, we civilians were directed to board certain buses and we set out immediately on a 24-mile ride to downtown Tokyo. As in England, all traffic moved on the left rather than on the right side of the roadway. Upon departing, we saw many Japanese on adjacent wharves fishing with poles, some holding up umbrellas to ward off a light drizzle. Then as we turned onto the main highway we saw acres and acres of rubble everywhere interspersed with many small huts and hovels patched together with whatever useful debris Japanese families could find. Rising above the desolation were occasional gaunt smokestacks and the walls and rusty girders of former factories and buildings.

Everyone on my bus appeared transfixed by the enormity of the destruction on both sides of the highway as far as the eye could see.[1] Thus had American airpower wreaked vengeance on the Japanese homeland, especially the Army Air Force's B-29 Superfortresses, which flew a small number of destructive missions beginning June 14, 1944, from an air base near Chengtu, China, against the island of Kyushu, then from the conquered island of Saipan in the Marianas beginning November 24, 1944, against targets in Tokyo, Yokohama, Nagoya, and other cities. Soon the Superfortresses were flying from other recently conquered islands in the Pacific. The single most devastating attack of the war was launched against Tokyo on the night of March 9, 1945 when about 330 low-flying B-29s from air bases on the islands of Guam, Saipan, and Tinian dropped incendiary bombs on a heavily populated and industrialized area. About sixteen square miles of the city were totally destroyed. More than 100,000 Japanese were killed and many thousands more were wounded.[2] Although we could observe easily from our bus scores of men and women cleaning up the rubble, a year after war's end it appeared the task had barely begun.

As we neared Tokyo's center, the traffic, mainly Japanese, increased markedly. Thousands of old cars, trucks, and taxicabs, many fueled by charcoal burners wired to their rears, honked their way through the streets. In their midst were scores of cyclists along with hand-pulled carts and other conveyances. On the sidewalks and street intersections hundreds of citizens, most carrying bundles, were hurrying in every direction. I did not expect to see such vitality in Japan's severely battered capital city, so soon after peace was declared.

Our bus soon reached "MacArthur Boulevard," which took us through an unbombed sector of Tokyo and past the very modern *Dai Ichi* building, the headquarters of a former Japanese insurance company which now served as General MacArthur's office and main headquarters as Supreme Commander for the Allied Powers (SCAP). Along the same boulevard were several blocks of other fairly modern office buildings, hotels, and billets, all inhabited by military and civilian officials and other employees of the American and Allied occupation forces. After winding around the picturesque Imperial Palace grounds and moat, our bus reached the Ichigaya section of the city and dropped many of us off at a billet located across the street from the still-intact former headquarters of the Japanese War Ministry. The latter was presently the site of the International Military Tribunal for the Far East, formally established by General MacArthur on January 19, 1946, to try twenty-eight of Japan's former top military and civilian leaders for war crimes.[3] We checked into the billet, a temporary hostelry for new civilian arrivals from the States, where happily I was assigned to a double room. Compared with the "staterooms" on the *Cape Cleare*, our temporary quarters were sheer luxury. After some unpacking, most of us partook of an early dinner in a nearby army "mess" or dining room.

While dining, we encountered several fellow Americans, all "old Japan hands" by virtue of their two-, three-, or four-months' residency in the country and employment in SCAP headquarters. Two offered to take us on a quick evening tour of MacArthur Boulevard. A few of us accepted the offer. We boarded a U.S. Army bus (with a Japanese driver) which then stopped at the Imperial Hotel, designed by American architect Frank Lloyd Wright, now filled with only the highest-ranking American and Allied occupation officials. After leaving the bus we strolled along MacArthur Boulevard, past the *Dai Ichi* building where General MacArthur labored seven days per week, then along the Imperial Moat. There was no rubble to be seen. American bombing crews had been given strict orders during the war not to strike the Imperial Palace and the area immediately adjacent to it. We encountered hundreds of Japanese citizens. Most passed by in silence but some smiled, returned our waves, and exchanged greetings with a *kamban wa* or "good evening." We tried out other Japanese words from our small Japanese-language phrase books, acquired before leaving the States, with modest success. I wondered: How long will this peaceful attitude of the populace continue?

The next day several of us new arrivals managed a tour of the unbombed section of the *Ginza*, Tokyo's famed shopping street lined with numerous large, western-style department stores and scores of smaller shops, half Japanese, half western, all selling a wide assortment of items, from crystal jewelry, postcards, and trinkets to fruits and vegetables. With the official exchange rate of fifteen *yen* to the dollar and inflation rampant, everything was very costly. Fortunately for occupationaires, there was no need to patronize the stores and shops. Nearby was a large U.S. Army post-exchange or "px" where basic necessities were available at reasonable prices. Along the *Ginza* we again witnessed the comings and goings of hundreds of smoking, charcoal-burning vehicles, cyclists, ox-pulled and hand-pulled carts, and thousands of Japanese pedestrians, many if not most carrying shopping bags and bundles. The throbbing scene included a few human-pulled rickshaws, transporting off-duty military and civilian occupationaires. In a heavily bombed area near the *Ginza*, workmen were stacking rubble in neat rows, some ten feet high along the curb. "No one is sleeping in this city", I noted. "Everyone is doing something or going somewhere". I spent the remainder of the day unpacking a footlocker and small trunk and getting acquainted with a booklet on army regulations for personnel in occupied Japan.

The next morning I entrained for Yokohama, riding in a special military coach reserved for authorized American and Allied personnel and "off limits" to Japanese citizens. Attached to virtually every passenger train, these clean, uncrowded military coaches contrasted sharply with the ones used by the Japanese. At each station during the 35-minute ride, hundreds of passengers, many carrying bags filled with vegetables, fruit, and other foodstuffs, pushed, pulled, or clawed their way into and out of coaches. A few entered or left the coaches through open windows. I would witness this human turmoil on railroad station platforms frequently in the ensuing months. At Yokohama, a waiting army bus brought me and some fellow Americans to our destinations. I left the bus at Eighth Army's personnel office.

Processing for Duty

I had an important matter to discuss with Eighth Army's personnel officials. About three months earlier I had signed a two-year contract in Washington, D.C., to serve as an economic analyst with SCAP's Economic and Scientific Section (ESS). The job description also contained, however, some fine print permitting personnel offices in Japan to assign me, in the event of "unforeseen circumstances," to another position for which I was "reasonably qualified." During the month or more needed for the requisite security background check before my papers could be processed and my travel orders cut, I entrained to Oregon for an extended visit with my family. Travel orders arrived by surface mail (air mail was still not commonly used) at least two months later. These indicated that unforeseen circumstances had indeed arisen and I had been reassigned to an administrative position in Eighth Army headquarters in Yokohama. A long-distance call to Washington, D.C., elicited no explanation for the change except that the job situation in occupied Japan was always fluid. The recipient of my call assured me I would be able to make a satisfactory adjustment upon arrival.

Thus it was that I found myself conferring with a member of Eighth Army's personnel office. He was cordial and friendly and solicitous of my disappointment over the loss of my expected position. The explanation was simple. With some exceptions, a lag of six weeks to two months occurred between the receipt of a job-request in Washington and the arrival of a civilian in SCAP or Eighth Army headquarters. A three-month delay was not unusual. Only small numbers of highly essential civilians arrived by air. Because of the time lag, SCAP and Eighth Army offices were inclined to hire "in-theater" civilians, former officers and enlisted personnel who elected to take their service discharges in Japan, provided they were reasonably qualified for a particular assignment. Ofttimes, men and women officers and enlistees eligible for service discharge merely took off their uniforms and continued to perform the same duties in newly civilian positions. In consequence, civilians who had been recruited in the United States weeks or months earlier would be placed upon arrival in another position compatible with their education and training.

For some of us newly arrived civilians, one of the personnel officials continued, there was another reason why some job vacancies in occupation offices had vanished. On August 10, 1946, President Harry S. Truman had imposed for fiscal reasons a six-month hiring freeze in the federal government which extended, with some exceptions, to American occupation forces in Japan, Okinawa, South Korea, and elsewhere. Only positions categorized as "critical" could be filled. As the processing of my papers was completed shortly after the president's freeze order, it was very likely that a communication from SCAP headquarters to Washington had voided my original position shortly before my travel orders were mailed to me in Oregon.

Quickly perusing my Civil Service Form 57, which contained my *vita*, the personnel officer noted I possessed B.A. and M.A. degrees, had taken some courses towards a doctorate in history and political science, and also had gained fairly broad work experience: in a bank; at the University of Chicago where I was employed first as an administrative assistant in the bursar's office and then as an assistant in the office of the dean of students; as an administrative assistant for the National Labor Relations Board in Chicago; and successively as a research assistant for the Council of State Governments and the U.S. Municipal Finance Officers Association, both agencies affiliated with the Public Administration Clearing House headquartered adjacent to the campus of the University of Chicago, where I had studied as a graduate student. Agreeing that I was overqualified for an administrative post with a logistic unit (listed in my travel orders) and that I could readily assume a more responsible position, the officer introduced me to his supervisor, who also leafed through my personnel file. The two of them suggested that I immediately contact Eighth Army's Internal Affairs Office, which was hiring civilians for prefectural military government teams for positions not subject to the hiring freeze. In any event, I had to report for duty the next day, as civil servants could not be unemployed in occupied Japan.

With time of the essence, I went immediately to the Internal Affairs Office where I was at once ushered into the office of its chief, Lt. Col. Amel T. Leonard, an articulate and brisk officer who quickly informed me that he was a graduate of the U.S. Military Academy in New York at West Point. Scanning my education and work-experience papers, he confirmed that his office was recruiting civilians with professional backgrounds for forty-five prefectural military government teams (including those in large urban areas). As the occupation of Japan promised to be peaceful, he explained, it was essential for prefectural teams to become more civilianized, so as to carry out more effectively SCAP's many social, educational, religious, political, economic, and other reforms. The majority of the officers on the teams did not possess college or university degrees and, in addition, the hiring of civilians would reduce the personnel turbulence occasioned by the departure of many officers each month who had acquired sufficient service points to make them eligible for discharge from military duty.

The most immediate need, he continued, was for civilians who could work in the area of civil information and education. Their duties were not only to exercise surveillance over the enforcement of SCAP's directives requiring the demilitarization of education and religion but also to assist prefectural education officials, school principals, and faculties in instituting SCAP's democratic school reforms, adult education organizations such as youth associations and women's groups and, since the abolition of State Shintoism, to explain the importance of the separation of state and religion. The military officers and the few civilians already in the field received ample guidance from SCAP's directives and other instructions from SCAP's Civil Information and Education Section (CI&E). In addition, Eighth Army headquarters also sent implementing directives and guidance as necessary.

Although public school teachers with B.A. degrees and teaching experience were considered especially well suited to serve as civilian CI&E officers on prefectural military government teams, other qualifications were taken into account. Colonel Leonard noted I had an above-average educational, administrative, and research background. Some of my graduate courses on the religions and cultures of Asian nations, including Japan, provided good "expertise" on Asian affairs, and I had served as a student counselor. Especially valuable, he said, was my former employment with the U.S. National Labor Relations Board in Chicago, where I had monitored regional labor elections and helped draft reports to assure that voting was free and unfettered. This experience appeared most timely now that thousands of Japan's teachers and other workers were organizing their own unions.

Thus I could qualify readily for the CI&E program. Presently there were five or six vacancies on prefectural military government teams, none subject to the hiring freeze, as civilians usually replaced a departed or departing officer. Before I could proceed, however, I needed to obtain a special Form 78 releasing me from my current assignment, a sometimes troublesome task.

I was elated. Nonetheless, I was still curious to know the status of the position of economic analyst in SCAP's Economic and Scientific Section (ESS). With a half day to spare, I returned to Tokyo and found my way to the ESS personnel office. There I was greeted by an overwrought Army Major who proclaimed immediately he was new in his task, his predecessor having left suddenly for the United States, leaving personnel files "in a mess." He was at a loss where to look for a three-month old request for an economic analyst and, in any event, all spaces were frozen temporarily. "Try the Government Section," he suggested. This I did, where a less harried personnel officer, after looking at my Form 57, said my services could be used, but that obtaining a waiver from the job freeze would take some time. He offered no assurance a waiver request would be approved.

This settled the matter. My best option was to transfer to a military government team. As it was late Friday and offices would be closed over the weekend, it was the following Monday before I conferred again with a member of Eighth Army's main personnel office, underscored Colonel Leonard's offer to me to join the CI&E program, and requested the requisite Form 78 authorizing a transfer from the logistic unit. The personnel officer said it would have to be approved by a "higher authority" in his office. Another day elapsed before I was promised the coveted Form 78. I was then informed it might take a week or more to "process" the document.

Meanwhile, I had learned that a number of my shipmates aboard the *Cape Cleare* had also found, upon arrival in Japan, that their positions had been canceled or filled by "in-theater" civilians (i.e., former uniformed officers or enlisted men). In addition, some who expected to be located in the Tokyo-Yokohama area had been instructed to transit to Sendai, Kyoto, or to more distance places such as Okinawa, Guam, and South Korea, their employment agreements with the Department of the Army, as in mine, permitting a change in job assignments or locations. The howls of protest were loudest from a few ordered to go to South Korea which, deservedly or not, had the reputation of being the occupation's "Siberia" because of the political and economic chaos in that country following Japan's official surrender. The surrender ended thirty-five years of Japanese rule in Korea, creating a political vacuum American forces were trying to fill. (The Soviet Union, in accordance with the Potsdam Agreement of July 1945, had occupied North Korea down to the 38th parallel.) Several of the unhappy transferees were former public school teachers who were destined to teach in the Army's Information and Education Program for enlisted men.

No civilian who accepted duty with American forces in Japan, South Korea, or other areas of the Pacific was compelled to fulfill his or her two-year working agreement. Anyone refusing the proffered alternate job or location could return to the United States on pain of reimbursing the U.S. Government $400 for the cost of transportation (or $200 after remaining only one year). I never encountered any civilians who exercised this option, but I heard of a few who did. The reimbursement penalty was waived only for unusual extenuating circumstances.

Inexplicably, almost a fortnight elapsed before I received a Form 78 releasing me from the Eighth Army logistical unit listed on my travel orders. Meanwhile, I had to carry out whatever duties its civilian chief assigned to me. He was a congenial fellow but was understandably reluctant to give me any long-term task once he was apprised of my plan to transfer to Eighth Army's military government program. After two or three days, he asked me to conduct an "analysis" of the number of Japanese employees in Tokyo's numerous hotels and billets filled with American and occupation personnel.

My findings, some of which I retained, proved interesting and enlightening about the life style of occupationaires in Tokyo a year or so after war's end. The small former Philippine Embassy was home to 26 officers and civilians and had a staff of 43; the Mitri Hotel, housing 48, had a staff of 86; the Tokyo Kaikan, with 100 or so residents, made do with a staff of 400; and the Imperial Hotel, inhabited by only 60 of SCAP's highest ranking military and civilian officials, maintained a staff of 432 to keep things shipshape. In partial extenuation, the Tokyo Kaikan and the Imperial Hotel frequently hosted large official receptions, and their dining rooms were available to hundreds of nonresidents in SCAP's bureaucracy. In any event, these two favorite occupation "watering places" had staffs that far exceeded in numbers the Ritz Hotel in Paris, which then boasted a ratio of two employees for each of its esteemed guests. As a prostrate Japanese government was forced to underwrite most of the labor costs, there was no incentive for managers of these hostelries to economize on Japanese employment.4

In the Imperial Hotel dining room I quickly discovered what were probably the world's largest and most luscious Japanese-cultivated strawberries, their flavor doubtless enhanced by the architecturally unique ambience. I had never seen such strawberries in America.

After completing the analysis of Japanese employment in SCAP's principal hotels and billets, my temporary boss asked me to report officially for duty each morning by telephone to determine if there might be another very short-term task or two that I could undertake. This novel charade left me free to engage in considerable sightseeing during the ensuing days in and around Tokyo. I would return briefly to his office only twice more to shuffle a few papers.

During the first interregnum in my temporary duties, I visited the Education Division of SCAP's Civil Information and Education Section which was responsible for developing policy for reforming Japan's educational and religious institutions and for encouraging the growth of democratic adult organizations, such as youth associations and women's groups. I conferred first with Dr. Abe M. Halpern, a language anthropologist with whom I had shared quarters on the *Cape Cleare* from Seattle. Halpern was studying the feasibility of requiring the Japanese to replace gradually their very difficult writing system (this included the indigenous *hiragana* and *katakana* alphabets plus *kanji* character-writing) with a totally romanized writing system called *romaji*. Halpern introduced me to Mark T. Orr, chief of the Education Division, William K. Bunce, chief of the Religions Division, Russell M. Durgin, chief of the Youth Organizations and Student Activities Branch and two or three other officials who were specialists in primary, secondary, or higher education.

Orr described to me very briefly the thrust of pending reforms in Japan's educational system. He cited a SCAP directive of October 22, 1945: "Administration of the Education System in Japan." This banned "militaristic" or "ultranationalistic" activities in Japan's schools and specifically prohibited the teaching of existing courses on morals, history, and geography. It also set forth a number of precepts of a "democratic" education. Orr also mentioned new and impending Japanese educational laws that would require the establishment of a 6–3–3–4 educational structure, and the work of the Civil Information

Division in informing the Japanese public of many new, occupation-imposed reforms. Orr's comments were highly informative, as were my short conversations with several other members of his division.

By pre-arrangement, I received yet another briefing on my upcoming duties on a military government team in Eighth Army's Internal Affairs Office, this time by a Miss Emily. A former school teacher, prim and energetic, Miss Emily had taken her discharge from the Women's Army Corps (WAC) some months earlier to serve as a civilian in the same position she had held as a uniformed officer. She expressed surprise that I had already talked to several members of SCAP's Education Division, hinting darkly that perhaps I had gone "out of channels." From her comments, I divined SCAP and Eighth Army were quite separate organizations. She expounded on the duties of an education officer and also stressed the importance of the "civil information" task in implementing educational, religious, political, and other reforms. The two duties were normally combined on a military government team, hence the title of "Civil Information and Education (CI&E) officer."

As my papers were nearly processed (why their processing was such a protracted task remained mystifying), she suggested and I agreed that I would join the Yamanashi Military Government Team headquartered in Kofu, Yamanashi Prefecture, about 100 miles southwest of Tokyo. There an overburdened but very able team adjutant was also serving part-time as a CI&E and a Public Affairs officer. I surmised he would leave the team shortly. At the end of Miss Emily's discourse, I inquired if she had visited many military government teams. Except for the one in Tokyo, she confessed she had not, but intended to do so soon.

"Captive" of IXth Corps Headquarters

It was near mid-October 1946 before my Form 78 and other papers assigning me to the Yamanashi Military Government Team were in order. There now arose another unexpected delay. I would have to travel to IXth Corps headquarters in Sendai in northern Japan for final approval of my assignment. This headquarters possessed administrative oversight of fourteen military government teams through two military government regions/districts plus a special military government region/district for the large island of Hokkaido. Final approval, I was assured, would be perfunctory. A train with military coaches and sleepers left each evening for Sendai. My travel orders would be ready in a day or two. (Occupationaires on official duty were not free to travel without "orders".) Actually, three days elapsed before the travel orders were "cut" and I departed from Tokyo's teeming central railway station for the 10-hour, 240-mile overnight journey to Sendai.

There was no rest. My sleeping berth was designed for small-statured Japanese citizens, not a six-foot, two-inch American, so I was forced to curl up in the form of a half-pretzel. The train made many stops. At each station, the air vibrated with the shouts and conversations of throngs of food-short Japanese entering and leaving the coaches with knapsacks and bundles filled with vegetables and other items, the incessant cling-clang of station bells, and the clamorous toot-toot of the train's horn. I was bleary-eyed at daybreak, but the picturesque rural scene of small villages, cultivated fields, and the thatched roofs of homes and barns offered some compensation for a night spent without the restful presence of Morpheus. At the Sendai railway station shortly after sunrise, a U.S. Army bus transported me and several other officers who had also spent the night on the train to IXth Corps headquarters.

Upon arrival, I was escorted to the corps' CI&E office where an affable and intelligent Army Major greeted me. We established an easy rapport. He described briefly the administrative military government function of the corps in northern Honshu and Hokkaido. He then led me to the office of the civilian chief, who would provide me with more information on my duties. Beginning with his limp handshake, I was dismayed by the latter's appearance and demeanor. He was well into his fifties. It was difficult to believe his assertion he was a college graduate and had once taught in a private school. He boasted of his experiences as an "old Japan hand" who had worked for twenty years prior to World War II for an American oil company in Japan, Korea, and Manchuria, the latter two areas once part of Japan's "Greater East Asia Empire." He claimed to know the Japanese well and said he could speak the language. Explaining the role of CI&E officers on military government teams, he emphasized the need to follow SCAP's education and religious directives to the letter in order to rid schools and other educational institutions of "militarists" and "ultranationalists."

It was not an edifying discussion. He manifested little interest in the sweeping reforms planned for Japan's educational system which had been underscored during my briefings in SCAP and Eighth Army headquarters. His attitude towards the populace was harsh. I had already encountered this among some of the military and civilian personnel I had met in Tokyo and Yokohama. It was understandable throughout World War II, especially among American and Allied servicemen who had bitter memories of Japanese military atrocities against civilians and prisoners of war. Nonetheless, the war was over and, in my judgment, it was now in the vital interest of the United States and its allies to assist Japan in the tasks of reconstruction and to democratize its institutions as much as possible. The comments of the IXth Corps' civilian education chief indicated he had arrived early in Japan with the occupation forces, had asserted his credentials, and was promptly given his ranking CI&E sinecure. In sum, the substance of his advice was that CI&E officers should be "tough" toward the defeated enemy. I chose not to argue with him.

Meanwhile, my return to Tokyo was delayed for several days as the officers at IXth Corps debated whether I should be reassigned, either to IXth Corps headquarters or to a team other than Yamanashi. I had stated my wish to go to Yamanashi, where the CI&E program had made a creditable start. So once again I had extra time on my hands. After checking into temporary quarters, I took a walk through a bombed part of Sendai. This city too had suffered major destruction and, as in Tokyo and Yokohama, men and women were still stacking the rubble. It was a depressing scene. The late October weather was overcast and cold. I wondered how the workers and other citizens kept warm.

Three days elapsed before I was told there would be no change in my status, so I was free to leave. My return to Tokyo by train was a reprise of my trip to Sendai: ten hours in a cramped sleeper without sleep. Fortunately, I reached my temporary quarters on a Saturday morning, October 26, permitting me to recuperate over the weekend. Surely, I thought, I would depart for the Yamanashi Military Government Team on Monday, October 28. It was not to be. In Yokohama early that morning, I learned that Colonel Leonard, the head of Eighth Army's Internal Affairs Office, would be gone for a couple of days. Somehow, only he could sign a document permitting the cutting of my travel orders. His assistant, Miss Emily, was in, however, seemingly anxious to hear about my trip to Sendai. After hearing me out, she credited herself and Colonel Leonard with "saving" my original assignment to Yamanashi and then declaimed once more in wearying detail on my forthcoming CI&E duties. Upon Colonel Leonard's return, another day elapsed until my travel orders were ready. It would be early November before I finally entrained for Kofu, the capital of Yamanashi Prefecture.

Tokyo: The Occupationaire's Utopia

By the end of October 1946 I was no longer perplexed as to why the processing of my papers had taken an inordinate time, and why offices in Yokohama, Tokyo, Sendai, and presumably elsewhere seemed to lack a sense of urgency to get things done. The explanation, for me at least, was simple. A long and bloody war had been fought and, except for the highest officials in SCAP and Eighth Army headquarters, most military and civilian employees viewed the occupation as an opportunity to relax. Working discipline, by all accounts, was not very severe. My personal experiences and observations in Yokohama and Tokyo showed lunch hours to be uncommonly long. The midday break was also the favorite time for scores of employees to "run over to the PX." There were other emoluments for occupationaires. Living expenses were remarkably low. Meals in the regular Army messes cost twenty-five cents or seventy-five cents per day, although they were priced somewhat higher at the numerous clubs and grills scattered downtown and in unbombed Tokyo, including the most fashionable place of all, the Imperial Hotel. Room charges were a mere four to six dollars per month and were only a few dollars more in the more modern hostelries such as the *Dai Ichi* Hotel. The billets and hotels were staffed with a surfeit of Japanese maids to make the beds, houseboys to sweep the rooms, waiters and waitresses to serve meals or drinks in the Army messes, clubs, and bars. In addition, they featured a wide assortment of Japanese billet and hotel clerks, record keepers, elevator operators, door attendants, drivers of jeeps, cars, and trucks, and mechanics at motor pools to keep the vehicles running.

The mostly youthful Japanese men and women who worked for the occupation forces were, with few exceptions, very friendly and cooperative. The women appeared especially appreciative of the deference accorded to them by western men, a trait notably absent in most Japanese males because of their culture. On Sundays and Japanese holidays, the women shed their western attire and donned brightly colored kimonos, making cheerful the most drab army billets and mess halls. They all dressed modestly. "No sweater girls in this country," I recorded. All of the Japanese employees seemed to study English assiduously and were delighted with opportunities to test their vocabularies and their pronunciation of American words and phrases.

For occupationaires with a day off or with time on their hands, there were sightseeing tours sponsored by the American Red Cross. At the onset of my many free days, I joined two tours. The first was to Kamakura, a city about forty miles south of Tokyo. As the seat of government for a series of strong and wealthy military shoguns from about A.D. 1185 to A.D. 1333, the city had witnessed a great flowering in literature, art, architecture, sculpture, and religion, much of it still visible in various structures and Buddhist temples. Most awesome is a giant bronze Buddha, cast in A.D. 1252, towering more than forty feet high and measuring almost one hundred feet in girth, with a face measuring eight feet wide from ear to ear.[5] Another tour was to the picturesque island of Enoshima, barely off the coast and not far from Kamakura. Traveling to and from both tourist spots, I noted that "the hills, rice paddies, and vegetable groves were all very colorful and every square foot of land was cultivated," and also, that "the Red Cross tours were free, included a box lunch, and an accompanying Japanese interpreter who explained the historical importance of many things we saw." (Oct. 9, 1946)

Occupationaires with a sense of history could attend the International Military Tribunal for the Far East, now occupying the former headquarters of the Japanese War Ministry, a complex of buildings and billets renamed "Pershing Heights" in honor of General John J. Pershing, commander of the American Expeditionary Forces in Europe during World War I. The Tribunal, consisting of eleven judges representing the victorious Allied Powers, listened gravely to testimony regarding twenty-eight of Japan's highest military and civilian officials, categorized as "Class A" war criminals, who "planned, prepared, and initiated aggressive war," according to the indictments. Many occupationaires attended the proceedings, although during my two visits I observed that about 80 percent of the spectators in the visitors' gallery were Japanese. We American and Allied visitors focused most closely on General Tojo Hideki, Japan's premier at the time of the December 1941 attack on Pearl Harbor which brought the United States into the war. Tojo would glance up occasionally at the visitors with what appeared to be a look of puzzlement.

Newsmen were wont to describe the trial, which had been under way for five months, as a "boring spectacle." In a sense it was, as all testimony had to be translated laboriously from Japanese into English and English into Japanese. During both of my visits, attorneys for the prosecution and the defense were debating the relevance of prewar documents that led to the formation by Germany, Italy, and Japan of the "Tripartite Pact," signed in Berlin on September 27, 1940. Boring or not, I viewed the trial as a significantly poignant proceeding and "a wonderful lesson in diplomacy and international intrigue."

For the several thousands of American and Allied military and civilian personnel residing in the Tokyo-Yokohama area, most of whom were in their twenties, thirties, and forties, there was no lack of entertainment. The very modern Ernie Pyle Theater in Tokyo (named after the famous U.S. war correspondent, killed by enemy fire on April 19, 1945, during a battle on Ie Shima, a small island near Okinawa), housed a huge concert hall with a revolving stage, two movie theaters, a library, and other facilities. There were also many other opportunities for SCAP's and Eighth Army's young employees to work off their energies after office hours. In a letter to a friend, I described the recreational opportunities in Japan's capital:

I have already attended an opera and two concerts by the Nippon Philharmonic Orchestra in Hibya Hall. One of the orchestra's performances featured Beethoven's Ninth Symphony, parts of which were sung by a 450-voice Japanese chorus. Another orchestra holds concerts in the Ernie Pyle Theater. A 10-day ballet season has just opened at the Imperial Theater. There are also tea-time concerts here and there featuring music from the sweet and sentimental to "jive" and "jitterbug."

It is possible to go dancing every night of the week in any of several Red Cross, officers, or enlisted men's clubs or in the large occupation-run hotels. One Red Cross club features four different Japanese dance bands a week. There must be two dozen or more dance bands around the city. If one fancies variety shows, there is a dog and monkey show and a family bicycle act—both are absolutely amazing! For most occupationaires, Tokyo appears enveloped in a perpetual Roman Holiday. (Oct. 9, 1946)

"Most of this entertainment," I further noted, "is free or costs very little. Presumably, the Imperial Japanese Government is paying for most of it."

As October 1946 neared its end, I was still on my enforced vacation in Tokyo, awaiting the cutting of my travel orders in Yokohama. The free days enabled me to take a few more Red Cross tours, including one to the Japanese Diet building, to attend another concert by the Nippon Philharmonic Orchestra, and twice to watch General MacArthur arrive or depart from his office in the *Dai Ichi* building. I also visited again the Education Division of SCAP's CI&E section, where I was introduced to several officials I had not met earlier. As during my previous visit, a few generously gave their time explaining the problems already encountered and others expected in revamping Japan's entire educational system. These officials met frequently with their counterparts in the Japanese government's Ministry of Education. I promised to send to Abe Halpern data on the teaching of *romaji* in primary and secondary schools in Yamanashi Prefecture. These brief contacts with SCAP's policymakers in the area of education and religious reform would prove invaluable in the ensuing months.

Sunday, November 3, 1946, found me still in Tokyo, although I now had my travel orders in hand. It was a historic day for two reasons: the birthday of the Emperor Meiji, Japan's first modern sovereign, who ruled from 1868 to 1912 and during whose reign the nation adopted its first Constitution, and the decision of the postwar Japanese government to promulgate a new, largely SCAP-authored, democratic Constitution. Newspapers reported that the present Emperor, Hirohito, who had renounced his divinity on January 1, 1946, would make a brief public appearance to announce officially the adoption of the document, slated to take effect six months hence. With several friends, I went to the Imperial Plaza outside of the palace grounds to witness the ceremony. We managed to obtain an excellent view of Hirohito and the Empress, who arrived dramatically in a horse-drawn carriage. During their appearance they acknowledged the cries of "*Banzai*!" (variously translated as "10,000 years!," "Long life!" or "Long live the Emperor!") from an admiring throng of 100,000 or more. Prime Minister Yoshido Shigeru then gave a speech in Japanese, which we occupationaires could not, of course, understand but could read the next day in local English-language newspapers.

That same evening several of us attended a performance of Giacomo Puccini's famous opera *Madame Butterfly* in the Tokyo Theater. Prior to World War II, *Madame Butterfly* and also Gilbert and Sullivan's *The Mikado* had been banned by government authorities, as both treated too lightly Japanese customs and the Emperor. "Whether *Madame Butterfly* was sung in Japanese or Italian," I recorded, "I do not know, being unfamiliar with both tongues." I adjudged the opera to be "highly colorful, superbly staged, and marred only by the perfume of too many unwashed bodies in a poorly ventilated theater." It was remarkable that there could be so much vitality among Japanese actors, actresses, dancers, musicians, singers, and other artists so quickly after the end of a devastating war. Remarkable, too, was their knowledge of and ability to perform western popular and symphonic music and to stage western ballet and opera.

It was my last evening in Tokyo before entraining to my assignment in Yamanashi Prefecture.

2

The Yamanashi
Military Government Team

Reporting for Duty

Early Monday morning, November 4, 1946, an Army jeep with a Japanese driver brought me to the Shinjuku station in Tokyo where I would entrain for Kofu, the capital of Yamanashi Prefecture. Shinjuku, I had been informed, was the largest and busiest railway station in Japan. Upon my arrival there, I saw no reason to challenge this judgment. Its platforms were a sea of humanity as thousands of Japanese of all ages boarded or rushed out of coaches, often through open coach windows. Trains arrived or departed constantly. The scene was familiar: men, women, and youngsters leaving the city carried knapsacks, baskets, boxes, nets, and other containers primarily to forage for food in the countryside; those arriving from the countryside were laden with vegetables, fruits, rice, and other necessities purchased, according to conventional wisdom, from farmers and villages, largely at black-market prices.

I had no difficulty finding my train with a special military car attached to the rear. Seated inside were several Army officers and civilians. We introduced ourselves. No one else was traveling as far as Kofu, about one hundred miles southwest of Tokyo. In contrast with the trains between Tokyo and Yokohama, where occupationaires were a familiar sight to the Japanese, at Shinjuku and especially at stations beyond, I became sharply aware, uncomfortably so at times, of the curiosity with which the populace viewed us "foreigners." Scores of young boys and girls waved or smiled at us. Their elders, however, were more inclined to stare at us for a moment and then move on. Were they envious of our comparative luxury and near-empty coaches? As none of us Americans could speak or understand Japanese, what our onlookers were saying to one another was a mystery.

After a short wait, several blasts from the train's horn signaled our departure. We chugged immediately through a section of Tokyo I had not seen previously, although the landscape resembled that between Yokohama and Tokyo: acres of rubble from air bombings were interspersed with tall smokestacks, remnants of buildings or factory walls, piles of concrete, bricks, and twisted metal; then suddenly, randomly, there were clusters of homes, stores, and other enterprises that had escaped fire and destruction. The countryside beyond was speckled with unpainted small farmhouses and sheds, most with thatched roofs, surrounded by meticulously tilled fields. Here and there a man or women was hoeing a plot by hand, plowing a small field with an ox, or riding in an ox-drawn cart on a narrow road. The rice and other crops had been harvested, and farming families were readying their land for another planting. All the while, I chatted with several of my fellow passengers who, after relatively short distances, left the train for their respective offices at or near the headquarters of the Army's First Cavalry Division, an all-combat unit that was always on alert in its assigned area to deal with any resistance to the occupation.

As the train steamed into a mountainous region, we passed through many tunnels, some of considerable length. I recalled a recent conversation with an Army captain serving with an engineering unit in Yokohama who had been impressed with Japan's railway system, tunnels, and bridgework. The Japanese Army, he said, had used this engineering proficiency with considerable effect in digging and fortifying its bunkers on many Pacific islands during the war.

The number and length of rail tunnels, I would soon learn, was a favorite issue among some officers and enlisted men of the Yamanashi Military Government Team. They would debate vigorously as to the number of tunnels between Shinjuku station in Tokyo and Kofu. The arguments, occasionally acrimonious, led to an uneasy consensus that there were forty-one. Never settled was the question of the longest tunnel. Some had clocked the train's passage through it down to the minute and second, but the tunnel's exact length remained unknown as no one was privy to the train's speed.

After three and a half hours and numerous stops, the train reached Kofu. A Japanese station attendant greeted me and said in halting but fairly good English that he would assist me with my baggage. He led me to the station's exit where an Army corporal was loading mail and supplies for the team onto a small truck. He was surprised to see me, not having been alerted to the possible arrival of a civilian from Tokyo. I accompanied him for the short drive to team headquarters, which was housed in a very attractive, modern two-storey structure, conspicuous for the large American flag flying from the top. "It's the former city library, built just before the war," the corporal volunteered. "The large older building across the street is where the prefectural governor and other officials keep busy." Not many yards from team headquarters was a smaller two-storey building. "That's the bachelor officers' quarters (BOQ)," the corporal added, "and the quonset huts below are where we enlisted men stay; below that is the motor pool."

Leaving my baggage with the corporal, I entered team headquarters and a Japanese employee escorted me to the adjutant's office. There a captain, age twenty-six, also greeted me with surprise. Yes, he was aware a civilian was being recruited for the team's CI&E program, but he had received no advance notice of the arrival date. This was understandable, he explained, as Eighth Army's administrative command chain from Yokohama went through several offices; it often took ten to twelve days for correspondence to arrive. After scanning my travel orders and other papers, he described briefly the makeup of the Yamanashi Military Government Team. As he talked, I noted a pair of gloves and a riding crop on a corner of his desk.

Upon completion of our short conversation, the adjutant led me to the office of the team commander, Lt. Col. Burton E. Stetson, who greeted me cordially if stiffly. He then introduced me to four other officers who were at their desks. Two others were away making inspections or on some other business. I met them the next day. I had wondered how an all-uniformed group would react to the presence of a civilian in their midst. Within forty-eight hours I was gratified to note all were quite friendly, albeit at least three, I gathered, had reservations about Eighth Army's plan to "civilianize" some of the uniformed spaces on military government units. This change had begun slowly and had gained impetus after the initial military government units in Japan were reorganized into "teams" on July 1, 1946.

Recalling the assertion of Colonel Leonard in Yokohama that most officers serving on military government teams were not endowed with degrees from institutions of higher learning, I was naturally curious about the educational background of my new colleagues. I had an answer shortly. Of the team's eight officers, consisting of a lieutenant colonel, one major, five captains, and one first lieutenant, three had attended a college or university: The medical officer had graduated from a medical school, the adjutant possessed a B.A. degree and had attended an army civil affairs school, and the labor officer had gradu-ated from a two-year junior college. The other five were not without additional military schooling, however. All had attended or graduated from various army training schools prior to or during World War II. Six came from the ranks of the U.S. National Guard in their home states or had been members of the U.S. Army Reserve Forces.

During a second discussion with the adjutant, I was surprised to learn that the team possessed only six enlisted men, although more would be assigned soon. I wondered how the team could accomplish its various missions. The answer lay in the team's large Japanese staff of nearly forty translators, interpreters, typists, phone operators, administrative assistants, and custodians with varying degrees of proficiency in the English language. In addition, substantial numbers were also employed in the BOQ, the enlisted men's quarters, and the motor pool.

The Japanese staff supporting the team's official activities, I soon discovered, was an unusually able one. Two women staff members had studied in a Methodist Mission school in Canada, a third at Duke University in Durham, North Carolina, and a fourth had been well educated in Japan. A male staff member was also educated in the United States. The English proficiency of all five made them indispensable to the team. Of the four women, one served as interpreter for the adjutant in his CI&E and political affairs work, a second as interpreter for the medical officer, a third headed the team's administrative staff, and a fourth served as a librarian and assembler of educational exhibits sponsored periodically by the team. The male staff member had the dual responsibility of supervising the team's fifteen-member translation section and serving as the translator for the team commander. The latter and the adjutant appeared to assume that the presence of several Christians on the staff, all in key positions, would facilitate in varying ways the inculcation of western democratic concepts in Japanese citizens.

Also serving on the team at the time of my arrival was a Nisei. He and many hundreds of other American-born Japanese were studying or visiting in Japan at the onset of the war and thus had been unable to return home after war began. Because the loyalty of some to the United States was suspect (all had to support the home front in Japan, and some males were impressed into the Japanese Army), they had to undergo a protracted security review before receiving permission to leave for the States. Meanwhile, most were able to serve with the occupation in non-sensitive positions until their clearances were granted. Even after being cleared, many elected to remain in Japan and continue to work for and enjoy the many perquisites of a Department of the Army civilian. Being bilingual (although usually not as fluent in the Japanese language as western-educated Japanese citizens), their services were, in fact, essential. The team's Nisei worked with an officer on procurement matters.

I was assigned to live briefly in temporary quarters and then moved into the BOQ. The rooms were amply furnished and the second floor included a glass-enclosed, spacious, and well-stocked cocktail lounge, comfortable chairs, and a modern record player. On clear days we could see through the windows the upper part of famous Mt. Fuji, which bisected the prefectures of Yamanashi and Shizuoka.

The BOQ's manager was an attractive, fortyish, well-dressed Japanese woman, also with a good command of English, who maintained a taut rein over numerous cooks, dishwashers, room cleaners, and bar boys. Enlisted men had been promised, as their numbers increased, replacement of their quonset huts with better accommodations. They too enjoyed the services of numerous attendants. As in Yokohama and Tokyo, there appeared to be a surfeit of employees, well over two dozen to look after the personal needs of Yamanashi Prefecture's small contingent of officers, civilians, and enlistees. There was often much to do as the team's personnel roster was augmented frequently and temporarily by official visitors from SCAP, Eighth Army, and IXth Corps headquarters, the Kanto Military Government Region, the First Cavalry Division, and other units, all of whom were entitled to bed and board in the BOQ or the enlisted men's quarters.

Team officers and enlisted men displayed considerably more discipline than I had observed in Tokyo and Yokohama. To underscore the importance of the function of the Yamanashi Military Government team, the commander, upon his arrival in Kofu in October 1946, decreed that military personnel should wear Class-A uniforms at all times. Furthermore, officers should always conduct their official duties with Japanese prefectural government and other officials with gloves and a riding crop in hand, the symbols of "a military officer and a gentleman." Although this edict appeared to serve a useful purpose in Kofu and nearby towns, in the ensuing months it would be obeyed sometimes more in the breach than in the observance by some officers making long and arduous inspection trips to Yamanashi's more remote areas.

Following another discussion or two with the team commander and the adjutant, I was assigned an office on the first floor of the team's headquarters building next to a library reading room that displayed a collection of English language magazines and books. The room also occasionally housed educational exhibits for school students of all ages and adults.

The adjutant, who had been responsible for the prefectural CI&E and political reform programs as additional duties, had in previous months managed to assemble a small but capable Japanese staff to assist him in the area of education: Miss Enomoto Aiko, a former student and later a teacher in the *Eiwa Jo Gakko* or Christian girls' school in Kofu, who had once attended a Canadian Methodist college; Miss Aramaki, who organized the educational exhibits and performed other administrative duties; and Mr. Ito Sukefumi, a retired middle-school teacher and principal in Yamanashi Prefecture. Mr. Akaike Hajime, who had studied in America in his youth and served many years with the Japanese Young Men's Christian Association (YMCA), would join my staff in March 1947. All four proved to be outstanding employees, devoted to bringing about a more democratic Japan.

The Team Evolves

The military government team I joined early in November 1946 had been established only four months earlier. Previously, there had been only a small military detachment in Kofu, the capital of Yamanashi Prefecture. For an explanation, it is necessary to describe briefly the manner in which American and Allied forces entered Japan at the end of World War II.

Immediately after Japan signed the Allied Terms of Surrender in September 1945, elements of the U.S. Sixth and Eighth Armies, plus a corps of British Commonwealth troops from Great Britain, New Zealand, Australia, and India began to arrive in the country. American forces, at their maximum, totaled about 250,000 men. Meanwhile, in November 1945, small combat-type U.S. military government groups and companies began to arrive from the Philippines. These had been assembled hastily and staffed partly by personnel trained in U.S. Army civil affairs schools after most of the original groups and companies were sent, along with other tactical forces, to South Korea, where Japan's abrupt surrender had created a serious political vacuum.[1]

Troops of the Soviet Union, as noted earlier, had quickly moved into North Korea down to the 38th parallel in accordance with American and Allied agreements reached in Potsdam, Germany, in July 1945.

The abrupt end of World War II threw into disarray the Allied plan for occupying Japan's four main islands. The existing organizational system within the occupying armies subordinated the commanders of military government groups and companies to the commanders of tactical units. This made sense in the immediate aftermath of the war, when no one knew whether the Japanese would resist their former enemies or cooperate with them. Before year's end, however, the verdict was in: the Japanese had chosen to be peaceful. This permitted a major reduction in tactical military strength. At the end of 1945, the U.S. Sixth Army withdrew completely, leaving the U.S. Eight Army as the principal occupying force along with elements of the British Commonwealth units, which occupied parts of south-central Japan, including the island of Shikoku.[2] Despite a strong rationale for permitting available military government units to assume the responsibilities for which they were trained, no official action towards this end was taken until July 1, 1946.

There were several reasons for the delay. Many Eighth Army commanders of tactical units were loathe to relinquish the important duty of surveillance of the populace. No doubt they enjoyed the emoluments and prestige of early occupiers, but they were disinclined to surrender without specific orders all of their authority over personnel whose training was in civil affairs (now called military government), but whose combat experience was nil and whose abilities were unknown. Some tactical commanders believed these personnel might not be sufficiently strict either to assure the complete demobilization of the Japanese or to exercise the surveillance mandated to reform their institutions as required by SCAP. Further muddying the organizational problem was the absence of clear instructions from Eighth Army headquarters in Yokohama as to how commanders of tactical and military government units should coordinate their activities.

There was also another difficulty, namely, the inadequate size and number of military government units that reached Japan in the early months of the occupation. They comprised only six groups and twenty-nine companies. This contrasted with the fifteen groups and fifty-one companies planned originally to maintain surveillance in Japan's forty-six prefectures (including large cities). The shortfall was caused, as already noted, by the dispatch of many groups and companies in the Phillipines to South Korea. Those military government units that did reach Japan were handicapped by major distortions in officer and enlisted strength, possessing in some instances too many of the former and too few of the latter. Furthermore, shortly after the end of the war many of the oldest and often the best-trained officers were lost to attrition because they had sufficient service points to take their military discharges. The maximum number of personnel assigned to military government units was reached in the first few months of the occupation, when they totaled about 2,800.[3]

The problem in establishing a reasonably strong military government presence in numerous prefectures in Japan can be illustrated by describing how a very small unit was established in Kofu, Yamanashi Prefecture, in December 1945. The detachment comprised only three officers and five enlisted men of the 32d Military Government Headquarters and Headquarters Company, a reorganized unit from the Philippines with surveillance responsibility over both the Tokyo metropolitan area and Yamanashi Prefecture. The detachment was part of the 99th Field Artillery Battalion, a tactical unit stationed at Tamaha Airfield, about six miles from Kofu although its personnel worked in several requisitioned rooms in the prefectural government building in the city.

With manpower limited to a major, two first lieutenants, and five enlistees, the detachment's duties were daunting. It was expected to maintain surveillance over and report on the same range of activities as those of the 32d Company for Tokyo. The latter, with far more manpower, possessed eight staff sections and ten divisions. Staff sections consisted of administration, services, economics, finance, labor, law, public safety, and public affairs. These, in turn, were subdivided. The Economic Section, for example, encompassed natural resources, industry and manufacturing, trade and commerce, and utilities; the Public Affairs Section included public administration and education. The other six sections were similarly subdivided.[4]

Obviously, the detachment could perform only a bare minimum of its manifold duties. It summarized its activities (as did all military government units in Japan) in weekly reports and, beginning March 1, 1946, in semimonthly, monthly, and special reports as necessary. The requisite data about Yamanashi Prefecture was provided mostly by the various offices of the prefectural government through a central liaison office. All detachment data requests and replies flowed through this office and were translated by a team administered initially by the prefectural government and then by the detachment. In addition to translating official reports, letters from local citizens, and other correspondence, the translators—all residents of Yamanashi—also rendered from Japanese into English the highlights of the prefecture's three daily newspapers and a few magazines. The translations were in "dictionary" English, reasonably accurate but quaint to American readers (there were no Americans, including Nisei, who were more proficient in translating). The detachment, upon its establishment, had also ordered prefectural authorities to provide all of the labor and materials necessary to convert the city's main library building into a military government headquarters, convert another nearby building into a BOQ, and erect accommodations for enlisted men, the motor pool, and other facilities. Additional military government personnel were, of course, expected to arrive later.

The few detachment officers and enlistees did more than sit at their desks, however. In compliance with SCAP and Eighth Army directives and guidance requiring the demobilization of Japan, they oversaw with tactical personnel the confiscation of firearms, swords, and other weapons, the search for stored war matériel, and the inspection of industrial plants to make certain they were no longer producing airplane fuselages, engines, spare parts, and other war goods. They also earmarked plants and equipment suitable for reparations demanded by the Philippines, Indonesia, China, and other countries occupied or victimized by Japan prior to or during World War II. They looked for food caches which, if found, were distributed among the most destitute prefectural citizens.

In addition, during the 1945–46 winter, detachment members monitored in Yamanashi Prefecture a SCAP-ordered vaccination campaign against typhus and smallpox. The highest priority was given to vaccinating preschool and school-age children, although this public health effort included other measures for the entire populace, such as requiring officials to clean up the prefecture's highly unsanitary prisons. Fortunately, these and other SCAP-directed programs prevented any major epidemics in Japan during the first harsh, postwar winter.

The Yamanashi Military Government Detachment's activities in December 1945 and January 1946 were difficult and frustrating because of undermanning and the necessity for billeting its personnel at the

COMMAND CHANNELS FOR MILITARY GOVERNMENT TEAMS AS REORGANIZED 1 JANUARY 1947

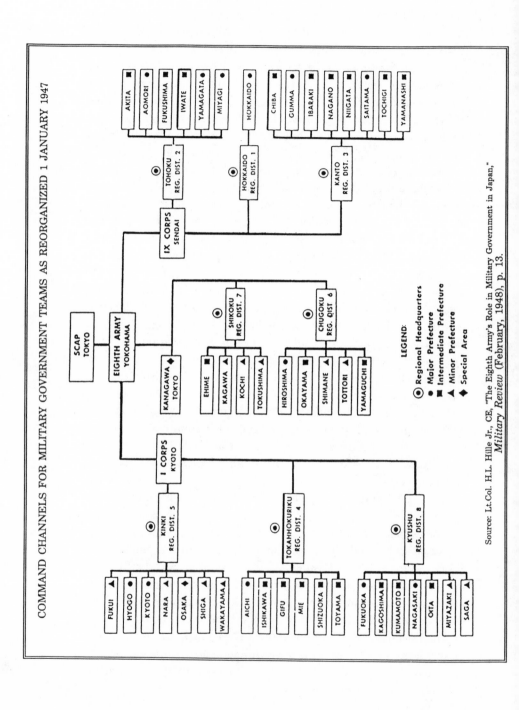

Source: Lt.Col. H.L. Hille Jr., CE, "The Eighth Army's Role in Military Government in Japan," *Military Review* (February, 1948), p. 13.

99th Field Artillery Battalion at Tamaha Airport, six miles from Kofu. This required extensive commuting twice a day over a partially bombed and rutted road, an ordeal that ended, happily, in February when Japanese laborers completed work in Kofu on a BOQ, enlisted men's huts, and a motor pool. The task of converting the city's library building into a military government headquarters with an American flag atop, giving the headquarters a separate and distinct identity in Yamanashi Prefecture, was not completed, however, until August 1946.[5]

The Structure of Military Government in Japan

A gradual resolution of the major personnel and organizational problems besetting the military government units in Japan was put in motion on 1 July 1946. Effective this date, the Eighth Army directed the conversion of existing military groups, companies, and detachments into forty-five prefectural and eight regional/district "teams" with an overall strength of 2,624 officers and enlisted men. (The island of Hokkaido officially was a district but, as will be seen, it was commonly considered to be one of the forty-five prefectural teams.) In Kofu, a "Yamanashi Military Government Team" was established. During July and August, four more officers arrived, and three more in October. Of the seven new arrivals, two replaced officers and others replaced enlisted men, so that the total of five or six assigned to the detachment since its formation in December 1945 remained at first unchanged. Additional enlistees began to join the team near the end of 1946 and early in 1947.[6]

Meanwhile, another reorganization in August 1946 divided prefectural military government teams into four categories according to the size of the population under their jurisdiction: minor, intermediate, major, and special. Minor teams, numbering eleven, were authorized five officers and twenty-three enlisted men; intermediate teams, numbering twelve, seven officers and twenty-six enlisted men; and major teams, numbering twelve, eight officers and thirty-nine enlisted men (the Yamanashi Team, initially a minor team, was redesignated as intermediate in December 1946). Special military government teams were established in the two largest urban areas. Osaka was authorized forty-five officers and 125 enlisted men, and Kanagawa-Tokyo, sixty-five officers and 150 enlisted men. Hokkaido, considered a prefecture but officially a region/district, also was authorized a sizeable contingent of military personnel.[7]

The eight military government regions/military districts with administrative oversight of the prefectural teams also possessed different levels of personnel strength, ranging from seven officers and thirty enlisted men for the smallest, to eighteen officers and forty-one enlisted men for the largest. At the top of the military government structure was, of course, the Eighth Army headquarters in Yokohama, which administered fourteen prefectures, one region/district (Hokkaido), and two military government regions/districts in northern Japan through IXth Corps headquarters in Sendai; twenty prefectures and three military government regions/districts through I Corps headquarters in Kyoto; and directly nine prefectures and two military government regions/districts in south-central Japan plus the special Kanagawa-Tokyo area.[8] The south-central area was occupied by British Commonwealth forces, although most of the personnel on prefectural teams and the two regions/districts were Americans.

The recruitment of civilian professionals (i.e., graduates of colleges or universities who possessed teaching, public health, information, labor, administrative, or other experience) for military government teams and regions/districts began slowly in the last half of 1946. The greatest need was for qualified workers in educational and religious reform. Male civilians with the requisite education and experience were assigned as Civil Information and Education (CI&E) officers; their aides were assistant CI&E officers or Education Specialists. Qualified females specializing in adult women's education were designated Women's Affairs officers.

The high point of professional civilian presence on the Yamanashi Military Government Team was reached in the months after June 1947 when the following four job specialties were represented: education and religion, labor-union education, public welfare, and information. Throughout the team's existence, in addition, the staff included one medical officer with an M.D. degree as well as two to four nonprofessional civilians, three of them Nisei, who were engaged in administrative, clerical, typing, and procurement activities.

Some military government teams made do for months with a single CI&E officer, military or civilian, who had no assistants. On the Yamanashi Military Government Team, I assumed sole responsibility for the CI&E program upon the departure of the adjutant for the United

States in December 1946, very shortly after my arrival. Except for a seven-month period, I had only one civilian assistant. He was converted immediately into a labor education officer and worked under my supervision. Consequently, I relied heavily on my small but excellent Japanese staff. After the arrival of more enlisted men beginning in late 1946, I persuaded the team commander to assign two or three of the most capable to my office. In the spring of 1947, I began to receive periodic professional civilian assistance from an unexpected source: the Kanto Military Government Region, which exercised, albeit very perfunctorily, administrative oversight of the eight military government teams in the region, including Yamanashi Prefecture. One such assistant was a women's affairs officer, and the other was a highly experienced former public school principal and superintendent who served as the Kanto Region's CI&E officer.

Civilian professionals provided additional expertise for military government teams and regions, and they augmented SCAP's efforts in carrying out its far-reaching reforms. They also could be relied upon, with few exceptions, to remain a minimum of two years, offsetting the manpower turbulence among military personnel, who were transferred frequently to other teams or units or received sudden discharges from military duty. Some civilians would remain on the teams until their deactivation on November 30, 1949.

The basic structure of military government in Japan remained unchanged until 1949. In May of that year the descriptive "military government" became "civil affairs." Then in September, because of financial constraints and to signal a phasing down of the occupation, Eighth Army announced that all prefectural civil affairs teams would be deactivated on November 30, 1949, and their functions transferred to the eight remaining civil affairs regions, the staffs of which would be augmented. The eight regions remained operative until near the end of the occupation of Japan in April 1952.[9]

About the relationship of civilians to uniformed officers on military government teams, my own experience can serve as commentary. Several officers on the Yamanashi Military Government Team had reservations at first about my presence because Japan was under a "military occupation," which called initially for a stern attitude towards the Japanese. Soon, however, I was on very friendly terms with all of my colleagues except Colonel Stetson, the team's commanding officer. His attitude toward me, albeit polite, was cool. Then one day at lunch he mentioned that his favorite military general was Napoleon Bonaparte, about whom he had read extensively. Because I too had read about Bonaparte's career in my studies on the French Revolution and its aftermath, our relationship warmed immediately. In the ensuing months, we would discuss from time to time in the BOQ cocktail lounge or in the dining room the exploits of France's legendary general and political leader.

Colonel Stetson was one of two officers still with the Yamanashi Military Government Team when I departed for the United States in August 1948. The other was the labor officer, Captain John Kopke. The medical officer, Captain Maurice Jakofsky, remained with the team until early 1948. Kopke and Jakofsky were, in my judgment, the two most capable and conscientious officers on the team. Other officers either departed the team shortly after I arrived or came and went after a brief duty tour. Usually they were transferred to another understaffed military government team. In instances where an officer was not capable of performing his assignment, he was transferred to a nonmilitary government unit. The team's executive officer, a major, was ordered in the spring of 1947 to serve temporarily as a judge for the ongoing Class B war-crime trials in Yokohama, but he never returned to the team.

Early in 1947 our small American community in Kofu, numbering then about thirty-two officers, civilians, and enlistees, was enlarged slightly when the wives of three officers arrived to reside in several newly constructed American-style or renovated large Japanese homes on the outskirts of Kofu. The cost of this housing was borne, of course, by the Japanese government. The transfer of three officers to "dependent housing" greatly relieved the chronic overcrowding of the BOQ caused by the many visiting officials each month from Eighth Army headquarters, SCAP, IXth Corps, and other organizations. Several additional American-style homes and/or duplexes for military and civilian personnel had been constructed by mid-1947.

Life was fairly circumscribed for our small American community. Recreation facilities were limited. Enlisted men, however, soon had access to a small gymnasium (fashioned from a former prefectural courthouse), a small athletic field, and a hall where they could dance occasionally with Kofu's damsels eager to meet young Americans and polish their halting English. Although team officers and civilians could also work out in the gymnasium, most preferred to take long walks, invariably trailed by friendly youngsters, until they reached Kofu's outskirts. Because they took so many tiring field trips or traveled elsewhere in the performance of their duties, officers and civilians preferred to spend most of their leisure hours in the team's attractive cocktail lounge, where windows framed a view of Mt. Fuji's summit. Abetted by freely flowing liquid spirits, the officers would discuss vigorously their early military training or the battles of World War II. The famous "Battle of the Bulge" in Europe during the winter of 1944–45 was a favorite subject for two former participants. Sports, hunting, and politics were also lively topics.

Watching movies was another recreation option. New films were shown in the enlisted men's mess hall three or four times per week, but the best American and British films were often featured in one of Kofu's five unheated theaters. Hastily built after most of Kofu was destroyed by an American B-29 bombing on July 6, 1945, they were all of very rudimentary construction. Each theater had set aside a reserved section for team members consisting of straight-backed chairs, whereas local citizens sat on long wooden benches. In winter or on cold evenings, moviegoers had to be well bundled to watch a two-hour film.

For news, team members depended on the Army's *Stars and Stripes* and the English-language *Nippon Times*. Many also subscribed to *Time*, *Newsweek*, and other publications. For radio news and entertainment, there was the Armed Forces Radio Network. Beginning in the spring of 1947, late at night on personal radios, if the electric voltage was adequate, one could hear an excellent half hour of world news from an American broadcaster based in Nanking, China. Radio Moscow also featured each evening a one-hour English-language program of news and commentary—essentially propaganda. The two commentators, a man and a woman, always presented a very negative exposition of political, economic, labor, and social developments in America, Europe, China, and occupied Japan and South Korea, clearly for the purpose of undermining the morale of Americans and their Allies.[12] The Soviet Union's "worldwide peaceful policies and its superior system of national government" were always stressed. Thus was the Cold War dramatized over the air waves for American listeners in Yamanashi Prefecture and elsewhere in Japan shortly after the end of World War II.

The term "Cold War" was used more frequently after the spring of 1948, when the Soviet Union gradually imposed a blockade of all surface traffic into and out of West Berlin, thus triggering the famous eleven-month U.S. airlift, beginning in July of that year, to resupply the citizens and American and Allied forces in that part of the city. With the outbreak of the Korean War on June 25, 1950, the term gained common currency.

3
The Team's Task:
Demilitarization and Education

Yamanashi's Geography and Population

My first three days on the Yamanashi Military Government Team in November 1946 were spent getting acquainted with my team colleagues, numerous members of the Japanese staff, Mr. Yamaguchi Konosuke, chief of the prefectural government's Education Section, and the specifics of my CI&E duties. The last were hastily summarized by the always-busy adjutant, who would leave soon for the United States. He repeated in essence what I had learned from Miss Emily in Yokohama and members of SCAP's Education Division, adding what he himself had done and learned in previous months when inspecting the requisite five schools per month and meeting occasionally with prefectural government officials, school principals and faculties, and leaders and members of adult education groups. My most immediate need, however, was to familiarize myself with Yamanashi Prefecture and its citizens. Fortunately, much of the data was contained in a War Department Civil Affairs handbook dated September 24, 1945. A section on geography stated that:

[Yamanashi is] divided into four zones, the Chichuba Mountains in the east and northeast, the Central Rift Valleys in the northwest, the Akaishi Mountains in the west, and the Fuji volcanoes in the southeast. . . . The Chichuba Mountains to the west of the Kanto Plain constitute a compact group of mountains forming a difficult barrier between the Kanto Plain and southwestern Honshu. The Chichuba Mountains extend 70 miles north-south and have a maximum width of 50 miles. This region contains parts of seven prefectures: Yamanashi, Tokyo, Saitama, Gumma, Nagano, Shizuoka, and Kanagawa.[1]

The famous snow-covered Mt. Fuji towers 12,388 feet and bisects Yamanashi and Shizuoka Prefectures. It last erupted in 1707, depositing a layer of ash as far away as Tokyo.

The civil affairs handbook, written in bureaucratic style, failed to capture the grandeur of the Kofu basin surrounded by mountains. I tried to describe it in a letter: "This beautiful area is called 'Shangri-la' by my fellow Americans. Outside of the BOQ and other billets, Mt. Fuji rises in majestic splendor. Surrounding mountains are blanketed by the winter's first snow, which glimmers against the blue and purple mountain ranges. It is an artist's paradise." (Nov. 11, 1946)

Yamanashi's population, according to the handbook, was 663,026 in 1940 although by late 1946 the prefectural government's estimate was about 850,000. The majority of its citizens depended upon agriculture for their livelihood. The main crops were rice, barley, and soybeans. The prefecture also produced much fruit, with grapes and persimmons leading the list. Animal husbandry consisted of poultry, rabbits, and cattle. Among the various industries, silk production played a major role along with such related activities as sericulture, weaving, and spinning. There were dozens of small textile mills. In addition, lumbering and mining operations gave rise to associated factories, such as those engaged in the manufacture of crystal items.[2]

Kofu, Yamanashi Prefecture's capital, in 1940 had a population of only 106,579. During World War II, however, citizens from the Tokyo-Yokohama area crowded into the city, believing its rural location would not make it a target for American bombers. The assumption proved valid until the night of July 6–7, 1945, when 120 B-29 Superfortresses bombed the city's center, the nearby town of Isawa, and twelve villages. Of Kofu's 26,000 homes, about 18,000 were destroyed and 230 were badly damaged by the bombs and accompanying firestorms. Also destroyed or badly damaged were scores of shops and other business establishments and important educational institutions, including the men's and youths' normal schools, the agricultural, technical, and medical schools, and two schools for the deaf and blind. Human casualties were heavy, with 750 killed, 345 seriously injured, 894 slightly injured, and 35 missing.[3]

Accompanied by a team member and numerous friendly boys and girls, I walked through parts of the city on my first evening in Kofu. Although much of the destruction was still in evidence, the pace of rebuilding was notably swift. Following a second walk the next evening, I wrote: "The city is being restored very rapidly. I dare say that in another year or two, the greater part of the bombed area will no longer be visible."

A few days after I began my duties, my interpreter related an interesting story about Kofu and Yamanashi Prefecture. As the American bombings of Japan's major industrial areas intensified in late 1944 and early 1945, thousands of citizens in the Tokyo-Yokohama area fled to the countryside, especially to Yamanashi Prefecture. Among this exodus were 7,000 to 10,000 young, unmarried girls and women. After a brief stop in Kofu, they traveled to relatively isolated small towns and villages in Yamanashi's mountain regions. They were sent there by their families who believed the propaganda of Japan's militaristic government that their daughters would be ravished by American and Allied troops should they land on Japanese soil. When these fears proved unfounded shortly after war's end, they all returned to their families.

Presently, all cities, towns, and villages in Yamanashi and throughout the nation were trying to cope with a major influx of population—the millions of demobilized Japanese military and civilian personnel who had fought or lived in Japan's former Greater East Asia Empire, including China, South Korea, Formosa, the Philippines and other parts of Southeast Asia, and the Pacific islands. General MacArthur had ordered their immediate return to Japan's home islands. At the peak of this effort, from September 1945 to June 1946, an enormous fleet of nearly 400 ships of all types and sizes, about half American and half Japanese, were marshalled to conduct this largest and fastest repatriation in history. Most of the approximately 6.6 million returnees were returned to Japan by the end of 1946. Concurrently another 1.2 million Chinese, Koreans, Formosans, and Ryukuans, who had been brought forcibly to Japan in the prewar and wartime years to work in mines and factories, were ferried back to their homelands. About 600,000 Koreans, many of long residency in Japan, chose not to return permanently to either South or North Korea.4 Among this number were many who returned briefly to South Korea immediately after war's end only to find life too difficult in their native country.

To move forward on the POW issue, the Soviet Union, during its short war against Japan in August 1945, found about 2,726,000 civilian and military Japanese in Manchuria, Dairen/Port Arthur, North Korea and the Sakhalin and Kurile Islands. Of this number only 575,000 were taken to the USSR. The Soviets refused to repatriate any of its captives until near the end of 1946 and then released initially only those who had become—or appeared to have become—fervent Marxist-Leninists and promised to work on behalf of the Japan Communist party. A few whose homes were in Yamanashi eventually found their way to my office and told me of their harsh experiences in labor camps. By 1956, though 2,379,00 had been repatriated, many remained unaccounted for.

A final accounting years later by the Japanese government showed about 254,000 confirmed deaths plus 93,000 missing but presumed dead for a total of 347,000. The majority of the dead were civilians. Most perished in Manchuria from severe cold, disease, malnutrition and neglect during the harsh winter of 1945–46. In April 1991, during a visit to Tokyo, Soviet President Mikhail Gorbachev provided the Japanese government with additional details about those who never returned, including the names and burial locations of 60,000 Japanese who died in Siberia.5

Indispensable Documents

To return to the subject of briefing documents, two were indispensable for military government CI&E officers. One was a short history of Japan's educational system with emphasis on the period after 1937. Titled *Education in Japan* and dated February 15, 1946, it was issued by SCAP's Education Division and was sent to all existing Eighth Army tactical and/or military government units. It described the structure of Japan's Ministry of Education until war's end. It also described the current college and university systems, both public and private, and contained six of SCAP's most important education directives to the Japanese government through January 17, 1946. In addition, it included the Ministry of Education's implementing directives and instructions to all prefectural, city, town, and village governments, and a copy of the Imperial Rescript on Education of October 30, 1890, during the Meiji period, 1868–1912.

The second document was titled: *Report of the United States Education Mission to Japan,* dated March 30, 1946. Prepared at the request of General MacArthur by a select 27-member committee which included some of America's most distinguished educators who visited Japan, the report offered a philosophical and structural outline for democratizing the nation's pedagogical and adult-education systems and for ensuring the separation of religion and state. SCAP's endorsement made it a veritable "bible" for all military and civilian officials, whether they were engaged in the civil education task in Tokyo or on military government units and teams. "Our first recommendation," said the authors of the report, is that a new philosophy, new procedures, and a new structure be adopted for the schools of Japan. This should be done in a manner as to recognize human personality as of paramount importance and the State as a means to this end. As the first step in that direction, we approve the discontinuance in the public schools of partisan teaching, political or religious.[6]

The second recommendation called for a drastic decentralization of education. "The Ministry of Education has been the seat of power for those who controlled the minds of Japan. Consequently, we propose that its administrative controls be reduced." The authors also urged the extension of compulsory education to nine years, adoption of coeducation in the schools, complete reform of the curricula and teaching methods, and equal-education opportunities for all students regardless of economic backgrounds. In another landmark recommendation, the authors urged the creation of an entirely new educational structure consisting of six years of primary school, three years each of junior and senior high school, and a system of higher education centered around four-year colleges and universities—in short, a 6–3–3–4 system of education. Further, they recommended improved salaries and professional training for teachers, and a radical reform in the use of the Japanese language, preferably the adoption of *romaji*, a romanized version of Japanese writing.[7]

Finally, the American educators recommended the creation of a strong and independent national adult-education department within a "revitalized" and "democratized" Ministry of Education.[8]

Also indispensable for all personnel on military government teams engaged in CI&E work was a compilation of all of SCAP's sixty or more educational and religious directives issued since the onset of the occupation in September 1945. Most of them required in various ways the "demilitarization" of Japan's entire educational system. Individual directives banned temporarily the teaching of traditional courses in morals, history, and geography (the morals course was soon banned permanently), or placed specific prohibitions on the operation of public, private, and religious schools and on the hiring of former members of the armed services as teachers or education officials. They also restricted the content of school radio broadcasts and delimited adult education activities. These directives were designed to clear the way for democratizing Japan's educational and religious institutions and citizen organizations.

Early Demilitarization Activities

During the early weeks and months of the occupation, officers assigned to the demilitarization task in education and religion conducted
a wide assortment of inspections. For example, they spot-checked
schools to verify that school faculties and students had ceased periodic
readings of the 1890 Imperial Rescript on Education, in which the Emperor was accorded a hallowed status; that courses temporarily banned
were not being taught; and that students no longer paid obeisance to
the Emperor's portrait in a *hoanden* shrine, which stood at or near
the entrance of every school. (Eventually, SCAP ordered all of these
shrines removed from school premises.) They also checked schools to
verify that semi-militaristic sports such as *kendo, karate*, and *ju jitsu*
had been abolished, and that school faculties and students no longer
made organized visits to Shinto shrines and Buddhist temples.

Another important demilitarization task affected education. Officers
were to exercise oversight of a SCAP purge of citizens whose backgrounds were deemed too militaristic or ultranationalistic. A SCAP directive of January 4, 1946 ordered removal from high office of all those
who, in the words of the Potsdam Declaration of July 1945, "have
deceived and misled the people of Japan into embarking on world
conquest." These comprised seven categories of personnel from public
office such as war criminals, certain career military and naval personnel,
influential members of the highly nationalistic Imperial Rule Assistance
Association (IRAA), and the like. In the ensuing weeks, about 550,000
personnel, including 116,000 educators, holding high or reasonably
high public offices who believed they would fall under the directive
resigned their positions.9 In Yamanashi Prefecture, an estimated 1,000
educators resigned.

Understandably, some educators in Yamanashi and throughout
Japan were uncertain if their prewar or wartime activities or associations
met the purge criteria. Others met the criteria but, desiring to remain
employed, they hoped their fellow citizens and occupation authorities
would not notice them. Aware of this particular problem, SCAP ordered the Japanese government to take additional measures to screen
educators. In compliance, the Ministry of Education early in 1946
directed the establishment of thirteen-man committees at national,
regional, and prefectural levels to eliminate from employment "militarists, ultranationalists, and individuals hostile to occupation policies."

The ministry also called for "the preferential reinstatement of persons previously dismissed for anti-militarism or similar reasons." In every jurisdiction, each committee would consist of seven representatives of the Japan Education Association and six officials chosen by the prefectural governor from other educational, industrial, and religious bodies.[10] The ministry's instruction spelled out how this additional screening should be done at the levels of primary and secondary schools and colleges and universities. Again, officers assigned to the education demilitarization task exercised surveillance over this special screening process.

In light of the foregoing tasks, plus others, it was nearly spring 1946 before most education officers throughout Japan could devote much time to the positive work of assisting prefectural education officials, school faculties, and citizen leaders in democratizing, in accordance with SCAP directives, all educational and religious institutions and citizen organizations.

Early Educational Activities

From December 1945 to June 1946 the Yamanashi Military Detachment numbered only three officers and five or six enlisted men. Nonetheless, once the major demilitarization tasks were completed, it managed to perform a few constructive educational activities by June 1946 and more after it became a team in July of that year, in support of SCAP's wide-ranging educational and religious reform objectives. Before describing them, the size and composition of Yamanashi's educational system a few years before Japan struck Pearl Harbor, should be noted: (1) Primary schools—a total of 314 consisting of 26 six-year and 288 eight-year schools with 118,674 students; (2) Secondary schools— a total of five boys' middle schools with 2,883 students and six girls' schools with 2,719 students—also three industrial, five agriculture, and three commercial schools with 2,568 students, mostly boys, a few girls; (3) Special schools—one school for deaf only, and one school for deaf, dumb, and blind with 37 students; (4) Normal schools—one regular mens' school and one regular women's school with a combined enrollment of 398 students, and one youth normal school with a lesser enrollment; (5) Youth schools—a total of 233 with 23,643 students; (6) Private schools—a total of 21, mostly for boys but several for girls, one of which was sponsored by the United Methodist Church of Canada, for a total of 2,442 students.

Among Yamanashi's principal cultural institutions were three Shinto shrines plus the remnants of an old one; two Buddhist temples, a complex of buildings, a museum, and the headquarters of the Nichiren Buddhist sect near the town of Minobu; and three libraries in Kofu with the newest one, the Kofu Municipal Library, constructed in 1927 (requisitioned by the Yamanashi Military Government Detachment in late 1945—remodeled and used as a military government headquarters)[11]

Throughout Japan, the end of a disastrous war had left the educational system in considerable disarray and had created extreme poverty. In Yamanashi Prefecture, a report prepared in May 1946 by the Yamanashi Military Government Detachment underscored two of many serious problems:

> One difficulty facing all schools is the shortage of essential supplies. On a recent inspection of Masuho Primary School, it was learned that students and teachers lacked paper, pencils, and other essential items. In addition, some teachers had sixty or more students in their classes.
>
> To alleviate partially the lack of school supplies, approximately 25,400 notebooks which had been printed during the war for the use of the Japanese Army were made available to the prefectural Education Section for use in the schools. The notebooks had lain unused for many months in a warehouse.[12]

Not surprisingly, new freedoms under the occupation also created problems. With the lifting of many former rigid controls on the Japanese school system by the Ministry of Education, most teachers were uncertain how to use their new liberties. In some parts of Yamanashi Prefecture, a detachment member recalled, schools initially were closed because teachers did not know what to teach without three temporarily banned textbooks (specifically those used for courses on morals, history, and geography). In May and June 1946 a detachment member participated in two large prefectural teachers' conferences to explain salient parts of the *Report of the U.S. Education Mission to Japan*. He also met with prefectural school inspectors, all middle-aged or elderly gentlemen whose traditional task was not only to inspect periodically school facilities but also to make certain that principals and teachers abided by the strict prewar and wartime instructions issued by the Ministry of Education. Their ability to adjust to the precepts of the New Education appeared doubtful.[13]

Despite the compliance of Japan's educators and public officials with SCAP directives in the early months of the occupation, Eighth Army headquarters in Yokohama nonetheless instructed all U.S. and Allied military government or tactical units to inspect, beginning March 1946, a minimum of five schools per month in each prefecture. An inspection form, modified and lengthened several times until it contained more than 300 questions about individual schools and their compliance with SCAP education directives, was submitted monthly. Although a broad consensus soon emerged among education officers, uniformed and civilian, that the form was unnecessary, it continued to be required past mid-1948.

Nationally, from mid-1946, one facet of the demilitarization of education required special oversight for many months. This was the screening of educators by 13-member Teachers' Qualifications Committees. Initial appointments to these committees by prefectural governors often left much to be desired. After the Yamanashi Military Government Detachment became a "Team" in July 1946, the adjutant, who served as acting CI&E officer, discovered that no less than eight of the thirteen members of the committee in Yamanashi were former members of the nationalistic IRAA.[14] All were former school principals, and a few had served as school inspectors in Japanese-controlled Manchukuo (now Manchuria). Their average age was fifty-two. The adjutant dissolved the old committee, replacing it with a new committee of six women and seven men, all with verifiable nonmilitaristic credentials and with an average age of thirty-seven.[15]

By the time I began my duties in November 1946, fifty-one principals and teachers had been removed from Yamanashi schools by three Ministry of Education directives (upon SCAP's instructions). Twelve educators remained in the "doubtful" category, but in subsequent months new names were added to the list requiring screening, usually on the basis of information provided by citizens and sometimes students.[16]

In the area of adult education, the adjutant met in July 1946 with prefectural education officials to discuss the feasibility of establishing a training center to acquaint parents and teachers with the functioning of American-style Parent-Teacher Associations (PTAs). Traditionally, Japanese parents maintained a respectful distance from school faculties, meeting with them only two or three times a year, and then only to listen to reports by the principal and head teacher on a school's activities. The training center proposal proved premature. A few weeks later the adjutant addressed two newly organized democratic women's groups, one in Yoshida, where he talked about the history of women's suffrage in America, and the other in Uenohara, where he described the American public school system.[17]

Meanwhile, in August 1946, to celebrate the opening of the new Yamanashi Military Government headquarters opposite the prefectural government building, the adjutant and the team's Japanese staff prepared three separate exhibits in the headquarter's large reading room for viewing by Yamanashi's citizens of all ages. These consisted successively of photographs of German Nazi atrocities in Europe during World War II, photographs of American life, and paintings by Mr. Yamamoto, a local artist. SCAP's Civil Information Division in Tokyo provided the photos for the first two exhibits, which were shown widely throughout Japan. In October, the reading room became available in daytime to prefectural students and adults with sufficient proficiency in English who wished to peruse an excellent, SCAP-donated collection of 400 English-language volumes on American and western education, literature, history, political science, and other subjects plus a modest assortment of American news and other magazines.[18]

Because of its proximity to Tokyo, the Yamanashi Military Government Team, after its establishment in July 1946, found itself playing host to many more SCAP and other military and civilian officials than most other teams throughout Japan. In October, for example, three members of SCAP's CI&E section made separate official visits to Kofu. They were C. F. Gallagher of the Religions Division, who inspected several prefectural Shinto and other shrines to determine the state of their physical condition, Philip C. Keeney of the Libraries Division, who examined Kofu's library facilities, and Russell L. Durgin, chief of Youth Organizations and Student Activities, who conferred with prefectural youth leaders and addressed two newly formed democratic youth associations. (As mentioned earlier, I had met Durgin, who had been active in the Japanese YMCA movement before World War II, shortly before I joined the team). As was customary, official visitors would discuss their findings with the team commander and the officer or officers responsible for a particular program before returning to Tokyo.[19]

Knowledge of the foregoing activities facilitated considerably the assumption of my CI&E duties in November 1946. Having spent several days reading pertinent documents about Yamanashi Prefecture and SCAP's directives and other guidance materials on the educational and religious reform programs, I was prepared to make my first field trip. My first priority was to inspect a Japanese school. The adjutant agreed to accompany me. I was especially curious to know if faculty and students would accept a civilian in place of a uniformed officer. I had my answer before the day ended.

4

The First School Inspections

The Ichikawa Primary School

Shortly after ten o'clock on Thursday, November 7, 1946, the adjutant, with gloves and riding crop in hand, the interpreter Miss Enomoto, a Japanese driver, and I departed for a primary school not far from Kofu. We rode in the team commander's black, four-door, 1940 De Soto sedan, requisitioned many months earlier from its prefectural owner, and available for the use of team members if the commander had no travel plans for the day. Upon our arrival, we parked on the edge of the school playground. Our reception was unforgettable:

Our unannounced appearance created pandemonium. Hundreds of students bounded out of their classrooms and surrounded us. Amidst their chatterings in Japanese were scores of shouts of "Hello!" "Hello!" Wading through the throng were the principal and head teacher who, upon greeting us with several bows, invited us to come to the teachers' room for tea. For lack of time, we declined.

We proceeded immediately to stroll through the school, which housed, according to the principal who accompanied us, about 1,000 students and a faculty of twenty-six. It was a rambling, one-storey, unpainted structure with several wings that had been added periodically. Nearly half of the windows were broken or missing, which increased the draftiness of the school. There was no central heating. Classrooms were furnished sparsely, with only desks and chairs, most of them marred from extended use. An isolated light bulb hung from the ceiling in each classroom to provide additional light on dark winter days. (Nov. 1946)

We looked for but found no violations of SCAP directives prohibiting any manifestations of "militarism" or "ultranationalism" in the school, such as the display of the 1890 Imperial Rescript on Education, or the use of the traditional morals textbook (now totally banned), or improperly censored textbooks on history and geography (for the latter we had to rely solely on our interpreter). We paused in one classroom to observe a young woman instructing her pupils by rote, i.e., in response to each question, her pupils shouted the answer in unison. American educationists considered this pedagogical method as a mind-numbing exercise that stifled creative thinking. They believed it contributed significantly to the susceptibility of students in the prewar and wartime period to government propaganda about Japan's "destiny" and the importance of its "Greater East Asia Co-prosperity Sphere." Thus all military officers and civilians on military government teams assigned to the CI&E task had been counseled, as had been noted earlier, to discourage, if possible, the practice of learning by rote.

As this inspection was primarily for my benefit, the adjutant said he would demonstrate how he had tried in previous weeks to inculcate a more democratic method of instruction in Japanese schools:

He assumed the role of teacher. Then with Miss Enomoto (the interpreter) at his side, he asked the students to be quiet. He posed a question from a textbook and asked those who knew the answer to raise their hands without shouting. He called on one student to reply. He repeated this technique several times with several other teachers in nearby classrooms now present. Did all of the teachers understand this better teaching method? All murmured their assent. Were there any questions? There were only two or three. It was a very stilted meeting. (Nov. 1946)

Next, we inspected hastily the school lavatory or *benjo*. It was a highly odorous structure—and "coeducational":

Boys used one side, where there was a wall-length urinal, and girls used the other side, which contained toilet seats badly shielded with numerous cracked or broken doors. There was nary a sign of toilet tissue, as most citizens in Japan, young and old, had to provide their own. The *benjo* was uncommonly perfumed, according to the principal, because of the late harvest season, with the result that the human waste or "night soil" had not been removed by a farmer for some time. The principal was instructed to tell the farmer to remove the night soil as quickly as possible. (Nov. 1946)

The inspection of school *benjos* was an optional CI&E duty performed at the request of the team's medical officer to improve the health of students and teachers.

Thus ended my only on-the-job orientation for my CI&E duties on the Yamanashi Military Government Team. The always-busy adjutant, with many pressing administrative matters on his desk, was impatient to return to his office. As we ended our forty-five minute stay, I informed the school principal and head teacher I would return after the lunch hour to meet with the entire faculty. We then took our leave and, with hundreds of boys and girls again crowding around the De Soto sedan—now shouting "Goodbye!" "Goodbye!"—we returned to Kofu.

Lunch over, I returned to the school with Miss Enomoto. We were greeted again by throngs of friendly students and by the principal. This time we accepted his invitation to meet in his office, as I wished to assess his knowledge of the New Education and to inquire about any administrative problems. He was surprisingly candid. Over tea and tangerines he cited the major difficulties confronting all primary schools in Yamanashi Prefecture: overcrowded classrooms, the shortage of teachers, especially good ones, the absence of new textbooks and other reference materials, and the lack of many school supplies. I asked him about a photograph on his wall. Who was the Japanese officer in full military regalia? He replied that it portrayed the late Meiji Emperor, and he assumed it was permissible to keep it in his office. I asked him to remove it, as it was the intent of SCAP's directives to eliminate all military symbols in schools. Nervously, he placed the picture in a drawer of his desk. I assured him it was not a serious violation and said we had observed no others during the morning visit.

I then asked the principal to call a one-hour recess as I desired to meet with the entire faculty, but without his presence, lest it inhibit individual responses to my questions. The faculty assembled quickly in a large classroom while the temporarily leaderless students crowded as closely as they dared to watch the civilian "Americano." I gave a short talk on the purposes of the New Education and the new Constitution, which had been promulgated by the Emperor only four days earlier. When I solicited questions, several teachers said they felt very uncertain how to apply the precepts of the New Education. In the past they knew exactly what to teach and how to control their students. Most difficult was how to present a lesson to allow students to "think for themselves." They had also tried to use a recommended group discussion method but this made it very difficult to maintain class discipline. All appeared to agree they needed more specific guidance on how to teach in a more democratic way. As for the new Constitution, they had been studying it and teaching it to their students, but the meaning of some of the articles remained unclear despite the explanations in newspapers and radio broadcasts. (Nov. 1946)

I tried to persuade the teachers that, with practice, it would become easier to teach in ways other than by rote. I also explained that more democracy in classrooms did not mean an absence of discipline. Students should remain under control, especially those who were constantly noisy or unruly, so the others could study and recite when called upon. With the issuance of some new textbooks and guidance materials, all teachers would soon be able to adjust to the New Education.

Before adjourning the meeting, I asked the teachers if they had joined a local teachers' union. Uncertain, apparently, of my views on union membership, they delayed their response to the question. Finally, one said that most had joined or were contemplating doing so. Had they participated in union meetings? The same teacher replied they had not, as the union leaders "knew best what should be done." I urged them to participate in any decision-making, as this was the democratic thing to do. My listeners did not appear enthusiastic, either about the union or about my counsel not to let a handful of union leaders make all of the decisions for them. I then bade the group farewell and, after one more short conversation with the principal and head teacher, departed in the De Soto sedan, again amid a schoolground chorus of "goodbyes." For me, the afternoon had been exhilarating.

After returning to my office, I composed a brief summary of my observations. Boys and girls in the first three grades were taught in the same classroom, usually by very young women; those in the fourth grade and beyond were taught in separate classrooms, mostly by men. The attire of teachers and students bespoke their severe economic straits. The men wore frayed shirts, faded trousers and jackets, or parts of their former military uniforms; most of the women wore the traditional *mompei* trousers, but some were attired in pantaloons, kimonos, and skirts and blouses. Student clothes likewise suggested a spartan life. Teachers and students left their *getas* or sandals outside of the classrooms, and many who were suffering from head colds wore masks to avoid contaminating others. The last was a common practice in Japan. Throughout the school, several upper-grade girl students carried babies on their backs, brothers or sisters who needed care while their mothers labored in the fields. One girl carried the baby of a teacher, a duty shared during the day by several other girls. Boys never carried babies, a task considered demeaning for the young male species. The only warmth in the drafty school building flowed from scores of colorful, mostly crayon-drawn local scenes that hung on the walls of every classroom—homes, fields, village streets, fellow-students, family members, and the incomparable Mt. Fuji.

Through their earlier briefings, I had been alerted to the extreme youthfulness of the women teachers in the first three grades. Because the wartime years had created a severe shortage of public-school teachers, the Ministry of Education had given thousands of provisional teaching certificates to young women who had not attended a normal school or had not completed their studies while enrolled. Many were only middle-school graduates.

During my afternoon visit to the primary school, the teachers appeared more animated and less hesitant to reply to questions than during the morning visit with the adjutant. Miss Enomoto had the answer. I was a civilian. It had been her experience, after interpreting for many months for uniformed team officers and visiting nonuniformed officials from SCAP headquarters, that Japanese officials and citizens usually spoke more frankly when talking to civilians. Although American military officers generally comported themselves far more democratically than had their former Japanese counterparts, this could not dispel the legacy of many years of militaristic governments and the authoritarian behavior of most Japanese police. Uniforms still bore an inhibiting presence.

In accordance with an Eighth Army directive, the findings of my inspection of the school were summarized on a 15-page inspection form. The data submitted was mostly statistical. But I recorded one facet of the day's activity privately. This was the highly impressive performance of my interpreter Miss Enomoto, who translated without hesitation English into Japanese and vice versa. I soon concluded she was the best interpreter, among several able ones, on the staff of the Yamanashi Military Government Team.

The Hatta and Tamamura Primary Schools

Because of other pressing duties, more than a week elapsed before I inspected more schools. It was already evident I would have to husband my time and could not afford to spend a full day at only one school. Thus on my second inspection outing, I went to the Hatta and Tamamura primary schools.[1] My arrival with my interpreter in a jeep again triggered considerable jubilation, with scores of boys and girls crowding around us shouting friendly greetings. A principal met me at one school and a head teacher at the other (principals, I learned quickly, were often away performing other official functions in their communities).

I walked down the corridors of each school, noting their physical condition, stopped in several classrooms where my interpreter checked history and geography textbooks to make certain that militaristic and ultranationalistic statements had been deleted with heavy black ink, and then met briefly with the faculties in the teachers' rooms. The youthfulness of many women teachers at the two schools once more was manifest. After explaining briefly the purposes of the New Education to the teachers at each school, I asked them to respond. As at the first primary school, numerous teachers expressed uncertainty as to how to apply the democratic precepts of the New Education and to interpret some of the articles in the new Constitution. They remained perplexed over how to teach more "creatively," encouraging students to think for themselves, without sacrificing classroom discipline.

I encouraged the teachers to keep trying, suggesting that the arrival of better textbooks and more clearly written instructions would enable them to adapt to more democratic teaching methods. Then after conferring with the principal and head teacher respectively at the two schools, and after a quick reconnaissance of their *benjos*, which I suggested should be kept cleaner, I returned to my office. I had found no violations of SCAP directives. By now, I wondered whether the excessive number of students in most classrooms in the three primary schools visited thus far would seriously impede the adoption of the New Education.

The Nirazaki Boys' Middle School

For the next inspection, I selected a boys' school in Nirazaki. This was one of Yamanashi's eleven prestigious middle schools, of which there were five for boys and six for girls. Unlike the turbulent reception at the primary schools, only the boys exercising on the large playground greeted me and my interpreter as we arrived by jeep; the rest remained in their classrooms. Those surrounding us chorused "Hello," but a few asked "How are you?" or said "Welcome to school," indicating they had been receiving instruction in English. Again, a somewhat elderly principal and a head teacher hastened to greet us and escorted us to the office of the former, where we quickly indulged ourselves in a cup of proffered tea. The principal knew, of course, the purpose of my visit.

I explained I wished to walk through the school, after which I would talk first with him then with some of the faculty.[2]

The middle school contrasted sharply with the primary schools we had visited earlier in the month. It was of much more solid construction and appeared to have fewer broken windows. Classroom chairs and desks were more sturdily made, and the school was quite clean. It possessed a large auditorium and a small library. Classroom walls were more barren, unlike those of the primary school where student art was copiously displayed. The school's large outdoor *benjo,* however, left much to be desired. By the time we completed our stroll through the school and the premises, the initial brief display of school discipline had partially vanished as a large group among the approximately 1,300 students, wearing dark and somewhat frayed uniforms, crowded as close as possible to get a good look at a CI&E officer in civilian attire. On the playground I stopped abruptly and asked a group of about ten if they were receiving any military training. They all said no. Do you like your teachers? They all said yes. What is your favorite sport? "Baseball!" they replied in unison. Can you name a famous American baseball player? "Babe Ruth!" they replied. After another minute or two of bantering, one student invited me to come to their school and speak to the entire student body. I thanked him for the invitation and said I would consider doing so later. It was evident all were proud of their school.

Having observed no evidence of militarism or ultranationalism in the school (I expected any violations of SCAP directives to be minor by this date), I conferred briefly with the principal and then with the head teacher and a number of the all-male faculty who clearly were somewhat older and better educated than those in the primary schools. Not surprisingly, they said their school suffered from a paucity of essential supplies, albeit the shortages did not appear to be as severe as I had found at the first three schools. Other handicaps were censored textbooks and the poor quality of paper in all of the hastily published, postwar middle-school texts.

I then explained briefly the purpose of the New Education and the recently promulgated new Constitution, and how the proposed 6–3–3–4 educational reform promised to increase greatly the learning opportunities for all young students, female as well as male. No one expressed opposition to the reforms, although I had been amply briefed that virtually none of the principals, faculties, and students in Japan's boys' middle schools—nor the majority in girls' middle schools—looked forward to having their cherished and traditional institutions reduced in rank to only three-year upper secondary schools beginning with the 1947–48 school year. Nor did a brief exposition on the democratic benefits of coeducation receive any audible approbation. A universal and understandable concern expressed by both the principal and some faculty members was how to accommodate the sizeable influx of new students as the new educational structure gradually went into effect. I then departed with scores of boys shouting cheery farewells, with a few adding "Come again!" The friendliness of the students and faculty was invigorating, although my interpreter diplomatically reminded me that their warmth probably stemmed more from curiosity than from the popularity of a military government official.

An Unpleasant Visitor from IXth Corps

Upon returning to my office I learned that the civilian CI&E chief at IXth Corps headquarters in Sendai, who had made a poor impression on me during my visit in October, would arrive in Kofu late in the afternoon. He was undertaking a hurried review of the work of CI&E officers in several prefectures in the Kanto Military Government Region. Upon his arrival he first made a perfunctory courtesy call on the team commander, then informed me he wished to make a quick visit to several schools, including Yamanashi's school for the handicapped. The next morning, after fortifying himself with spirits in the BOQ, we departed very early for the town of Minobu.3

I expected my interpreter to accompany us. He declined to take her along, reminding me he "could speak the language." It proved to be a most distressing day. En route to our first destination in the team commander's De Soto sedan, the chief delivered a monologue on the chicanery of the "Japs" based on his "business experience" with them before World War II, and as further evidenced by their attack on Pearl Harbor on December 7, 1941. Thus it was necessary to "keep a close eye on them." Unfortunately, his attitude was still shared by many civilian and military occupationaires. In my judgment, the negative phase of the occupation had ended and the primary objective was to assist and advise the Japanese in instituting educational and other reforms.

The Minobu Girls' Middle School was the most outstanding school I had seen thus far in Yamanashi Prefecture. Both there and at the Minobu Primary School we were offered tea and an opportunity to talk with their respective principals and head teachers. The IXth Corps CI&E chief gruffly declined as it became quickly clear that his claim of fluency in the Japanese language withered in the face of necessity. In fact, his fractured Japanese ruled out even a short meeting with the school officials, let alone their faculties.

I sensed that a primary objective of the chief was to find a violation of a SCAP directive. While walking through the Minobu Primary School, we paused in a fifth- or sixth-grade classroom to watch a teacher conduct a geography class using a heavily deleted textbook. Suddenly my visitor growled, "This fellow is talking about Japan's Greater East Asia Co-prosperity Sphere. I heard him. He also has a drawing of it on the blackboard." I looked at the blackboard but failed to discern the outlines of Manchuria, North China, Korea, and Southeast Asia. In an angry voice he asked the teacher why he was teaching about the Co-prosperity Sphere in violation of a SCAP directive.

The ensuing few minutes descended into a contretemps between my guest and the teacher, whose astonishment was exceeded only by his bewilderment as the two engaged in an exchange of broken Japanese and English. When the teacher seemed to grasp the nature of the accusation, he denied it vigorously. Scores of students from other classrooms crowded around us to see what the rumpus was all about. The principal and head teacher appeared and momentarily joined the debate.

Clearly, the chief's own language deficiency plus his visceral suspicion of the Japanese had led him to misconstrue what he had seen and heard. To me, it was inconceivable a teacher would deliberately discuss Japan's former empire while two military government officials were inspecting his school. I finally intervened, tugged at his arm and said I would have the teachers' record reviewed by the prefectural Teachers' Qualification Committee. This mollified him sufficiently to enable us to complete our tour of the school, trailed by several hundred boys and girls.

We had a final, very brief visit with the principal, and my guest attempted to underscore in his uncertain Japanese the seriousness of the teacher's offense. The former, obviously shaken, responded mostly with a series of "Ah so's." We then headed for the De Soto sedan and, amidst a large crowd of students chanting "Goodbye," we drove off, leaving the teacher and the principal pondering no doubt the bizarre incident and the disparate behavior of two inspecting military government officials.

As we motored back to Kofu it took utmost restraint not to tell the chief he had played the fool and, in my judgment, had undermined the authority of and respect for the Yamanashi Military Government Team. Having served in my post less than a month, I decided not to cross swords with him. All the while he grumped with satisfaction that he had caught a "Jap" red-handed violating a SCAP directive. "Gotta keep an eye on these fellows," he warned me.

In Kofu, we stopped very briefly at the building housing temporarily the school for the handicapped, where the principal was obviously most pleased to see us. He escorted us past the classrooms where we could observe teachers working with those unable to speak, hear, or see. In passable English he asked for our assistance in placing the students in a school with better facilities (the original two structures had been destroyed by the July 1945 bombing raid). Although prefectural authorities, at the urging of the team, were already engaged in rehabilitating another building to house the handicapped students, I promised to do what I could be expedite their effort.[4]

We reached team headquarters near the end of the working day. While the IXth Corps' education chief hurried into the BOQ to refresh himself with a favorite stimulant, I informed the adjutant of what had occurred at the Minobu Primary School, asserting it had been a serious error not to have taken an interpreter with us, as our visitor's claim to proficiency in the Japanese tongue had proved ridiculous. In addition, his demeanor had not been that of an educator.

As it turned out, the chief's subsequent unprofessional behavior in the BOQ and his brief official conversations with the adjutant and team commander indicated to both he was ill-suited for his CI&E post at IXth Corps, certainly so when compared with the quality of most military and civilian officials from Eighth Army and SCAP headquarters who had visited the Yamanashi Military Government Team recently.

Unfortunately, I had to suffer our visitor's association once more. Early the next morning, prior to his departure by train to another prefecture, I had to perform an unofficial team rite, accompanying him (as did other team officers when they had an official visitor) to two of Kofu's best crystal-manufacturing shops. There he was able to use his limited Japanese vocabulary to make several purchases. We then drove to the railway station where he boarded a military coach.

I would meet him again at several subsequent CI&E conferences. He was obviously ill at ease at these gatherings, which were attended by increasing numbers of civilian military government CI&E officers and SCAP officials who were all better educated and more experienced than he and very serious about reforming Japan's educational and religious institutions. Eventually he was shunted off to Hokkaido and was replaced at IXth Corps by a more qualified civilian.

Needless to say, I did not refer the geography teacher's name to the Yamanashi Teachers' Qualification Committee.

5
Other Initial Duties

Obtaining Educational Films

In addition to making several school inspections in November 1946, I dealt with other CI&E matters during my first thirty days on the Yamanashi Military Government Team. One arose unexpectedly. A member of SCAP's Civil Information Division in Tokyo phoned team headquarters to offer the temporary use of two special documentary education films if they were picked up immediately, since only a few copies were available for the forty-five military government teams in Japan. No enlisted man was available at the moment to get them, there still being only five on the team, all busy procuring supplies, manning the motor pool, or engaging in other essential support duties. With time of the essence, I decided to bring the films to Kofu.

There were two other reasons why I wished to go to Tokyo. First, it would give me an opportunity to learn more about the activities of SCAP's Civil Information Division, which I had not visited previously. Second, the supply of stationery items for my office—and for the team—was woefully low, and it was uncertain when the special post-exchange railway car, which serviced numerous military government teams periodically throughout Japan, would return to Yamanashi Prefecture. Some of the most essential stationery items, I was assured, could be picked up in SCAP headquarters.

Thus I entrained for Tokyo the morning after my first school inspection. The journey to and from the nation's capital was similar to the previous train trip. I was in a military coach attached to the end of the train. The other coaches were filled with hundreds of Japanese citizens, the majority going to or returning from the countryside with foodstuffs. I was a conspicuous solitary traveler, the object of stares and occasional waves of a remarkably friendly citizenry, until a few occupationaires stationed at the Army's First Cavalry Division near the capital joined me for the last hour or so of the train ride.

Upon arrival I went immediately to the Motion Picture and Theatrical Branch of SCAP's CI&E section. There I had the good fortune of meeting briefly with David W. Conde, the branch chief, who explained SCAP's current practice of using both regular American motion pictures with educational content in Japanese motion picture theaters, and special documentary films for viewing in schools or in motion picture theaters. He said his branch was also working with the Japanese motion-picture industry to produce a variety of Japanese films with constructive educational themes. The use of films in the CI&E program, Mr. Conde continued, began in April 1946, and the current inventory consisted of nine feature-length films, two short subjects, and nine special documentaries, all with dubbed-in Japanese dialogue.

Two of the best American films for purposes of the CI&E program were *Abe Lincoln in Illinois*, and *Watch on the Rhine*. The former showed how a largely self-taught American backwoodsman was able, in America's democracy, to become President of the United States in 1861 and, during the nation's great Civil War from 1861 to 1865, to achieve a victory that abolished slavery and saved the Union. He became thereby one of America's most revered Presidents. The second film underscored the evil and cruel nature of Adolf Hitler and Naziism in Germany. The two documentary films I received from Mr. Conde told how young students in the United States lived, played, and studied, and presented the "democratic" teaching methods used in their schools. Several mobile motion picture crews were also showing a few feature films and documentaries in the more isolated sectors of Japan. Because Japan's movie theaters were so profitable, according to Mr. Conde, their owners had been instructed by SCAP to show the documentaries in cities and towns without cost to students and adults as a public service.

In response to my questions about Japan's wartime films, Mr. Conde explained that 236 of the most militaristic propaganda films produced in Japan in the immediate prewar and wartime period had been collected and destroyed by Eighth Army in the spring of 1946 except for one negative and four prints of each film which were sent to Washington for study.[1] Concluding, he wished me success in my CI&E work and asked me to send whatever reactions I might pick up from the citizens of Yamanashi prefecture after they had viewed the films and documentaries. I promised to do so.

From Mr. Conde's office, I went to the Tokyo PX, where I purchased an assortment of stationery supplies sufficient to fill a large briefcase. I remained in Tokyo overnight. The next morning, a Saturday, I went to SCAP's Education Division where I found several conscientious members at their desks. While talking briefly with several of them, I asked if they had any stationery supplies to spare. They responded generously, giving me enough to fill a large shopping bag. Upon my return to Kofu, I distributed to the team's administrative staff and to several of my colleagues such necessities as notebooks, writing pads, carbon paper, and typewriter ribbons. My colleagues dug into their pockets to help defray the cost. The team commander dropped by my office to say thanks, and he expressed no objection to my going out of military channels to procure these essentials.

I gave the two documentary films to the prefectural Education Section, informing its chief they were to be shown free in theaters throughout Yamanashi Prefecture. This was done, and soon students in primary and secondary schools and their teachers were trooping in the day time to whatever theater was showing the films. Their reactions were not as I had hoped. All students agreed that the two documentaries were "interesting" and "helpful," but most seemed to remember most vividly how "rich" and "prosperous" American students were compared with themselves. Japanese teachers appeared to recall best the small American classes compared with those in Japanese schools. Politely, they said the documentaries enabled them to understand better the nature of a democratic education but, as I soon discovered, most teachers, especially the younger ones, remained uncertain how to teach more democratically and still retain discipline in their classrooms. I sent Mr. Conde a brief report describing these student and teacher reactions.

Addressing the First Youth Association

During my first thirty days on the team, I accepted an invitation to address a recently organized youth association in the town of Funatsu. As noted previously, I had been well briefed on Japan's postwar youth by Russell L. Durgin, SCAP's chief of Youth Associations and Student Activities. But first a word from my notes about the colorful journey to Funatsu in mid-November 1946:

The surrounding ranges were in their best autumn attire of brown, red, and yellow between evergreens. We ascended a small mountain and at the summit we looked down several thousand feet upon glittering Lake Kawaguchi. Beyond was another bluish mountain range, its size diminished somewhat by the presence of Mt. Fuji, its upper reaches shimmering with fresh snow. It was a marvelous view. The scene erased from my mind momentarily the physical aches incurred from bouncing on a rugged seat in a jeep over a twisting washboard road.

After a lengthy ride, we reached the grounds of the Funatsu Primary School, where the meeting was scheduled to be held. As usual, we were surrounded immediately by scores of young boys and girls who greeted us cheerfully. The principal escorted me and my interpreter to a large classroom where about 200 members of the Funatsu Youth Association had gathered and where I was introduced to its president, who did not appear very youthful, and several officers. The president then called the meeting to order and, after some preliminary remarks, I was formally introduced. I had assumed my audience would consist of young men mostly below the age of twenty-one but observed quickly that many attendees were in their late twenties with some appearing to be well into their thirties.

I spoke on "Discipline for Democracy," stealing the title from a book by one of my favorite political philosophers at that time, T. V. Smith, a professor at the University of Chicago. I addressed the need for Japanese citizens to understand their new Constitution and, borrowing a theme in Smith's book, to develop sufficient discipline in preserving it. This called for individual as well as collective discipline, meaning there should be a willingness among all citizens to adhere to the laws and rules enacted democratically by the majority, and that the majority should take into account the views and feelings of the minority. The minority, in turn, should have the discipline to abide by and respect the laws and rules enacted by the majority.

My philosophical presentation clearly did not meet the needs of my listeners. When I invited their inquiries, they peppered me with down-to-earth questions: "How should we get rid of old neighborhood association bosses?" "What should young workers do against mean employers?" "How can inexperienced youth make good decisions?" They also asked about youth in America: "How do young people get jobs?" "Do young people own cars?" "How do young men and women play together?" "Are many marriages arranged?" I did my best to answer these and other questions but I sensed my explanations were not very satisfactory. This was a troubled and apprehensive group which included former soldiers in Japan's now-demobilized Army.

Because of their considerable curiosity about the activities of young Americans and the relationship of the sexes, I took the opportunity to emphasize the importance of establishing more equality for girls and women in Japan if their country was to become a democracy. This enabled me to cite several articles in the new Constitution and two impending laws (not enacted by the Japanese Diet until late March 1947) mandating educational equality of girls with boys and of women with men. Certainly, it would take time to become accustomed to this concept, given Japan's culture, but all western democracies now treated girls and women far more equally than in the past. One step towards this goal would be for young men and women in Yamanashi Prefecture to begin meeting occasionally together rather than separately. My young, all-male audience responded with silence to this proposal.[2]

After answering additional questions about American and western democracies and the need for Japan to follow their example, I ended the meeting. My departure was similar to what I had experienced at other schools with scores of primary school students and many of Funatsu's youth waving or shouting farewells. It had been another memorable experience. The questions asked during the meeting underscored, however, the many social, working, and educational difficulties confronting Yamanashi's young men.

Resolving Two Religion and State Problems

November 1946 also required the resolution of two religion and state issues. I had received scant briefings on this subject and on the landmark SCAP directive of December 15, 1945, abolishing State Shintoism in Japan and establishing the principle of the separation of religion from the state.

The first case arose after several citizens, in signed and unsigned letters to the Yamanashi Military Government Team, complained that a village headman had failed to remove completely from the grounds of a primary school the remnants of a *hoanden* shrine. This type of shrine, placed at or near the entrance to every school in Japan, formerly contained the portrait of the Emperor in uniform. For decades, students had been taught to bow before the shrine upon arriving or leaving a schoolground. With the onset of the occupation, SCAP banned worship of the Emperor in the schools and ordered the Emperor's portrait removed from the shrine. This was done, although many *hoanden* shrines were not physically taken away until the Japanese government, on instructions from SCAP, ordered their removal from school premises by August 31, 1946. As noted, one school apparently had failed to abide by this order.3

As the school was not far from Kofu, I decided to make a personal investigation. Thus, on November 15, I motored with my interpreter to the school. As we drove onto the schoolground, it was easy to spot the remnants of the shrine. Our unannounced arrival, as at other schools, attracted immediately scores of curious students on the playground or who bounded out of their classrooms, shouting their greetings while the head teacher plowed through the youthful throng to meet us (the principal was absent). I explained I had come not to inspect the school but to determine why all of the shrine had not been removed according to General MacArthur's instruction (invoking the great general's name, I learned quickly, was an effective way to rivet the attention of a Japanese official on a problem).

Visibly flustered, the head teacher conceded the shrine should have been removed but attributed the delay to the village headman. The latter, he explained, because of the lack of funds from the prefectural government, had been unable to hire workmen to perform the task. When I asked why a few students and teachers could not volunteer their labor to remove the shrine's remnants, the head teacher said the school principal was loathe to trespass on the authority of the village headman. I then conferred briefly with my interpreter, who explained the nature of tradition-encrusted responsibility in a Japanese community. She opined that the head teacher appeared unusually conscientious and eager to tell the truth. Whereupon I thanked him for enlightening me about the nature of the problem and said I would pursue the matter in another way.4 As we left, I told my interpreter I desired to have a brief chat with the village headman, so through the prefectural Education Section, she conveyed my request to see him.

Early the next morning the village headman, a fairly elderly fellow who so identified himself, was waiting to see me. After several bows he launched immediately into a lengthy exposition of the reasons all of the *hoanden* shrine had not yet been removed from the schoolyard, although he did not cite the lack of funds to pay the workmen. His monologue became so convoluted that my excellent interpreter, after several attempts to elicit clarity, quietly informed me she could not fathom all of his explanations. She also indicated he appeared to be an old-fashioned bureaucrat who had not yet adjusted to SCAP's reform measures.

After his second attempt to inform me of the reasons for the delay in removing the shrine, I interrupted him and waved a paper that I said contained General MacArthur's instruction requiring the complete removal of all *hoanden* shrines from school grounds by August 31, 1946. Was that clear? The headman said it was, promised to take action immediately, bowed and departed. Near the end of the day, a member of the prefectural Education Section phoned to report that the shrine's remnants had been carted away.[5]

The second religion and state case in November arose when several parents in a village complained in letters to the Yamanashi Military Government Team that the principal of the local primary school recently violated SCAP's order abolishing State Shintoism by leading students to a local Shinto shrine where they engaged in a Shinto rite. Some of the letters alleged he was still a "militarist" and others claimed he was very unpopular in the village as well as in the school.

I discussed the allegations with Mr. Ito, the retired middle school principal on my staff whose knowledge of prefectural education matters, not surprisingly, was considerable. By chance, he was somewhat familiar with the accused's reputation, which he said was not very good. He suggested and I agreed that the allegations against the principal should be reviewed by the Yamanashi Teachers' Qualification Committee. As has been mentioned, the committee had been established many months earlier for the express purpose of screening principals, teachers, and other educators to determine their suitability to serve in Japan's postwar reformed educational system.

As a first step, I conferred with the committee's chairman, whom I had met barely a week earlier, and cited the nature of the accusations the team had received about the principal. Unpopularity, I cautioned, was not in itself sufficient reason to dismiss someone from the teaching profession. Nonetheless, taking students to a Shinto shrine to engage in Shinto rites during the school day sharply violated SCAP's directive of December 1945 and the new Constitution.

The committee's chairman submitted a report to me shortly. It stated that the accused primary school principal had once served as a Shinto priest, was previously known for his strong advocacy of State Shintoism, possessed a very authoritarian manner, and was unpopular among students and villagers. On more than one occasion since the occupation began, he had indeed taken students to a Shinto shrine where they participated in a Shinto rite. Accordingly, it was the committee's judgment he fell under SCAP's criteria of a "militarist" and "ultranationalist" and thus was subject to dismissal from the school system. I saw no reason to disagree. Before the committee officially ordered his removal, however, the principal, aware of the impending action against him, resigned from his post.[6]

6

Democracy's Pangs in the Classroom

Expansion of the CI&E Workload

From December 1946 through the end of March 31, 1947, which marked the end of the 1946–47 Japanese school year, my work load increased by leaps and bounds. There were more meetings with Mr. Yamaguchi, the prefectural education chief; school inspectors; the chairman of the Yamanashi Teachers' Qualification Committee; school principals; normal school and technical college presidents; teacher delegations; and representatives of two teachers' unions. I also made numerous inspections and visits to schools. In January 1947 there were planning sessions preparatory to inaugurating a limited prefectural school lunch program. There were lectures before newly organized youth, women, and Parent-Teacher Associations and before prefectural officials and citizens during the dedication of a citizens' public hall (CPH).

I also sought ways to speed up the repair of many school radios, an information medium on which SCAP's CI&E officials placed great store for teaching students and teachers about democracy and the New Education. I investigated complaints from private citizens about illegal fundraising by neighborhood associations to support local Shinto shrines and Buddhist temples; and I gathered additional data on the extent to which *romaji*, a romanized form of Japanese, was taught in the schools. This last project was for my friend Abe Halpern, the language anthropologist. Periodically, I issued press releases to clarify various facets of the New Education and to emphasize the importance of religious freedom. These releases were published in the three prefectural newspapers and broadcast over the local radio station.

As noted previously, I inherited a very capable Japanese staff and, with the arrival of more enlisted men in late December 1946 and January 1947, the team commander assigned variously two or three of the better-educated ones to my office. They performed a variety of tasks, such as making spot inspections, assembling data on a problem, or conducting investigations. They also assisted Miss Aramaki in organizing the numerous educational exhibits for students and adults in the team's library room. One talented sergeant drafted summaries of educational and religious activities which were included in the team's activity reports to the Kanto Military Government Region, IXth Corps headquarters in Sendai, and Eighth Army headquarters in Yokohama. He also oversaw the receipt and distribution of food for a school lunch program that began in February 1947.

Two Unusual Problems

Shortly after assuming my CI&E duties, I encountered two unusual problems. In December 1946, several students from a girls' middle school delivered to my office a long petition "signed in blood" (i.e., next to the signature of each student who had signed it was a small drop of blood). The petition asked for the reinstatement of one of the middle school's teachers, deemed an excellent one, who had been purged recently by the Yamanashi Teachers' Qualification Committee. Surely, the petition stated, there must have been a mistake as the teacher had not committed any "war crimes." Would military government reinstate him? I promised to look into the matter. It proved to be a difficult case.

The Teachers' Qualification Committee, as noted, had undergone earlier personnel changes and had been subject to public criticism for some of its decisions. Nonetheless, the committee's responsibility was clear: to screen thoroughly the records of all prefectural educators and weed out any remaining former militarists or ultranationalists in accordance with SCAP's purge criteria. I summoned the committee chairman to my office and asked him to review once more the teacher's record. Unfortunately for the young student complainants, the committee chairman advised me shortly that the teacher had once belonged, albeit briefly, to the ultranationalistic Imperial Rule Assistance Association, whose former members were barred automatically from public service. Thus the committee had no recourse but to adhere to its original decision.

A second unusual problem arose on a cold morning in January 1947. I arrived at my office to find the principal of the Kofu Girls' Middle School waiting to see me. He was in a highly emotional state. During the night the school had been destroyed completely by fire. (I had already been apprised of the fire by a Japanese employee in the BOQ who had been listening to his radio.) The principal was on his way to see Mr. Yamaguchi, the chief of the prefectural Education Section, to report on the catastrophe and to offer, as was customary by an official in Japan in the aftermath of a serious mishap, his resignation. He believed it was his duty, however, to offer his resignation first to the CI&E officer of the Yamanashi Military Government Team.

I spoke briefly with the principal, who explained that the fire's cause was unknown but appeared to be accidental. Thus all classes for the school's 1,600 girl students had been forcibly suspended until temporary classrooms could be found elsewhere, an enormous task. He was profoundly concerned lest his students not be able to complete their studies by March 31, the end of the 1946–47 school year. He could scarcely control his enormous grief.[1]

After completing our conversation I decided to consult privately with my interpreter and Mr. Ito, both former educators. They knew my visitor quite well, especially Mr. Ito, a retired middle school principal. They spoke very highly of his reputation as an educator and said his students and their parents also held him in high esteem. I asked them, given the excellent reputation of my visitor and the enormous educational and economic difficulties in Yamanashi Prefecture and else-where, why the prefectural Education Section should not retain his services. Admittedly, his retention would be contrary to a Japanese tradition requiring the resignation of the top official of a public or private institution following a major accident, tragedy, scandal, or the disclosure of a serious problem.

My two staff members agreed that his school—and education in Yamanashi—would be served best if he did not resign as principal. I then informed him it was his duty in wartorn Japan to remain as the head of the girls' middle school. I said I would convey my decision immediately to Mr. Yamaguchi. This would enable him to take the lead in finding temporary classroom space for his students and in planning for a new school. At this juncture, the principal's emotional distress over the fire and my refusal to accept his resignation was too much for him. He wept openly. Quickly recovering his composure, he thanked me profusely and, with several bows, took his leave. My interpreter then phoned the prefectural education chief to convey my decision that the principal's planned offer to resign should not be accepted. He concurred.

Very soon afterwards, the principal again came to my office to report that prefectural officials had found space for temporary classrooms in the barracks of a former Japanese Army regiment on the outskirts of Kofu. Several months elapsed, however, before construction of a new school began.

Explaining the New Education

The first step toward changing the Japanese educational structure to a 6–3–3–4 system would begin in April 1947, with the establishment of new lower secondary schools encompassing the seventh, eighth, and ninth grades. Because the impact of educational reform would be felt later by other secondary and higher institutions of learning, my major efforts from December 1946 through March 1947 were devoted toward assisting prefectural education officials and primary school principals and teachers to understand the nature and importance of these educational changes. These were spelled out in two new pieces of Japanese legislation, the School Education Law and the Fundamental Law of Education, which came into force on March 29 and 31, 1947, respectively.

The first law mandated compulsory education through the ninth grade. (As six years of schooling was already obligatory, its extension from the seventh through the ninth grade would be instituted incrementally beginning April 1, 1947.) The law also "recognized" coeducation, development of personality, a sense of individual responsibility, and other "democratic" objectives. It specifically required a 6–3–3–4 educational system and contained guidelines for the licensing of private, correspondence, vocational, religious, and other institutions of learning.[2]

Consequently, I conferred frequently with prefectural education officials and inspected or visited as many primary schools as time allowed, plus a few secondary schools. From the outset, it was evident that neither students' nor faculties of Yamanashi's educational institutions were enthusiastic about the 6–3–3 portion of the new education system. On April 1, 1947, as noted, the new lower secondary schools (also called upper primary schools) were established. Most were housed in existing primary schools already offering education through the eighth grade. No longer would sixth graders have to undergo an "examination hell" to enter a traditional middle school. As compulsory schooling was gradually extended, additional new lower and higher secondary classrooms and/or schools would have to be built. Students and faculties of the eleven middle schools, youth and technical schools, two regular normal schools and the one youth school normal school, were all apprehensive about the coming changes.

From the onset of my CI&E duties, a primary school inspection was a fairly stereotyped event. Upon my arrival, the principal or head teacher would rush out to greet me and my interpreter. Immediately, my jeep or the black De Soto sedan would be surrounded by scores and sometimes several hundreds of friendly boys and girls who happened to be on the playground or who left their classrooms to get a close look at the CI&E officer, all shouting "Hello!" "Hello!" Many others would peer at us from classroom windows. We would be escorted quickly into the teachers' room, usually furnished with a long table, many chairs, and several *hibachis* containing charcoal for heat. I would be seated, because of my gender and status, in the largest chair, whereas my interpreter would be offered a smaller one. The same custom dictated, when proffered tea, that my cup or mug should be larger than hers.

After an exchange of greetings with the principal or head teacher, or both, I would cite three reasons for my visit: to determine if the school was complying with General MacArthur's educational and religious directives, to examine the school's facilities, and to discuss briefly with the faculty the salient points of the New Education and Constitution. There was little need to dwell on the first reason. School authorities had quickly complied with General MacArthur's directives requiring the elimination of all militaristic or ultranationalistic practices and teachings. Violations were usually technical or due to inadvertence.

I would then walk through the school, noting its physical condition, the extent of overcrowding, the condition of the library, if one existed, and whether the school's radio and public address system functioned. I relied on my interpreter to make a spot check of textbooks to determine if they had been properly censored and were all authorized. I would pause in a few classrooms to observe teachers instructing their students—usually by rote. If perchance I encountered a teacher who was teaching the "American way" (i.e., asking individual students to reply to his or her questions), I would extend a warm compliment. For the overwhelming majority of the primary school teachers, it was very difficult to abandon the traditional pedagogical system.

Next, I would invite all of the teachers to assemble in a fourth-, fifth-, or sixth-grade classroom to demonstrate teaching without the rote technique. Most American educators believed the rote system smothered creative thinking, but it should be noted that the authors of the *Report of the United States Education Mission to Japan* (March 1946) were ambivalent on the subject:

Japanese teachers need no one to tell them how to conduct memory exercises or to develop skill of hand. They are masters of this art. It is not proper to detract from the value of this kind of teaching; it is bad only when it shuts out the development of curiosity and originality in the attack on problems of judgment in dealing with social and moral questions.[3]

Assuming the role of teacher, I would ask the students to be quiet and, rather than answering a question in unison, to raise their hands if they knew the answers to my questions. I would then call on them individually to reply. First I would quiz them on their knowledge of their prefecture and country: What is the capital of Yamanashi Prefecture? What town is the headquarters of your *Gun* or district? What is the population of Yamanashi? I would test their knowledge of the new Constitution: What is the role of the Emperor? (Answer: He is now the symbol of the nation.)

What are the three main branches of your new national government? (Answer: Executive, legislative, and judicial.) What is the role of public officials? (Answer: They are the servants of the people.) How does the new Constitution treat men and women? (Answer: They are now equal.)

The boys and girls invariably responded with unbridled enthusiasm, especially the boys, with my presence inspiring many of them to raise the decibel level of their normal speaking voices as they competed for attention. Some would shout "Here! Here!" or "I know! I know!" The teaching demonstration for many was theater, a new form of entertainment. Meanwhile, the assembled teachers watched carefully, their attention riveted alternately on the students and my interpreter, who rapidly and expertly translated my questions into Japanese and the student's replies into English. Upon completing the question and answer session, lasting fifteen or twenty minutes, I would ask the students whether they preferred the old way or the new way of instruction. Happily, nearly all would chorus that the new way was best, although an occasional upstart would shout a preference for the old way and would have to be diplomatically squelched.

In some primary schools, teachers were experimenting with a recommended group-discussion method, whereby small numbers of students would gather around a table to work jointly on a lesson such as arithmetic or grammar or to engage in an art project. A severe shortage of small tables in most schools precluded breaking up a class of 40, 50, or more students into small groups. The concept was not always fully comprehended: In one instance, group discussion was combined with the traditional practice of vocal recitation. A class had been divided into ten groups of five students each. Each group was reading loudly from different pages of a grammar book, thus adding to the din of rote recitation in nearby classrooms.

Questions and Answers

Upon completing my classroom inspection and teaching demonstration, we would assemble in the teachers' room to discuss the New Education. I would begin by assuring my listeners that teaching students in a more democratic way, with practice, should not prove too difficult and would inspire students to think for themselves. As the meeting continued and the tea flowed, numerous teachers would begin to express their vexation with the precepts of the New Education as set forth in SCAPS's directive of October 1945, in the report by American educators of March 1946, in the two major education laws enacted by the Japanese Diet at the end of March 1947, and in their new, hastily written teachers' manuals.

Especially baffling was how to teach students to think "independently" and "develop their personalities" (translated in Japanese as "development of the inner self"). Teaching in a "quieter" and more "democratic" way left many questions unanswered. For example, when teaching the quieter way, should teachers record which students answered correctly or incorrectly? Should only students who raised their hands be asked to reply? With forty to forty-five or more students in some classrooms, how could each student have an opportunity to recite? In preparing grades, how much weight should be given to classroom recitation? My answers to these and other queries, I feared, were not fully satisfactory or convincing to teachers long accustomed to detailed instructions on what, when, and how to teach their subjects.

Because the new school year beginning in April 1947 would extend coeducation in classrooms through the sixth grade, most teachers (and parents) expressed deep concern about the absence of a morals course to replace the one SCAP had banned because of its "undemocratic" content. A morals course was essential, they believed, to reduce student misbehavior on and off the schoolground, a phenomenon aggravated by harsh postwar economic conditions. Prefectural newspapers often addressed the subject. For numerous teachers, a possible solution was to devise a course on religion which could be taught variously as "history," "literature," or "classics," giving equal time to the moral precepts inherent in Confucianism, Buddhism, and Christianity to avoid proselytizing.

I had no alternative, of course, but to discourage the teaching of a religious course. It would have conflicted not only with SCAP's order of December 1946 abolishing State Shintoism, and with other directives mandating the separation of religion and the state, but also with the new Japanese education legislation and the new Constitution, in which Article 20 specifically enjoined the state and its organs "to refrain from religious education or any other religious activity." Unfortunately, the rise of "bad behavior," especially among boys, placed the New Education somewhat on the defensive. Consequently, I had to stress constantly that educational reform did not countenance immoral or bad behavior by youngsters, and that teachers still had to enforce discipline in their classrooms. Failing that, some students would have to be punished, albeit not as brutally as some principals or teachers had been wont to do in the past.

Women teachers were particularly curious to know what "equal education" portended in newly enacted Japanese legislation and the new Constitution. A frequent question was: "If girl students take the same courses as boys, how will they ever learn the domestic arts of cooking, sewing, caring for children, and flower arrangement?" My standard reply was that whereas a course or two in domestic arts could be retained in the curriculum, girls in Japan, as in America, learned a great deal about these matters at home. Further, well-educated girls would have no difficulty in reading articles or books on the domestic subjects. I sensed this answer was not very convincing. Men teachers rarely asked about equal education, their silence perhaps indicating their considerable lack of enthusiasm for the SCAP-imposed reform.

Dear Sir, I wish you would accept this for a memory of your inspection. Yours faithfully Fumio Okumura (principal of Chiasato National School) 1947-3-14

Eighth-grade students and teachers in a small school in Yamanashi Prefecture, 1947. Front row, center, the author, interpreter Enomoto Aiko, and the school's principal.

Award-winning middle school girls with their teachers after a student art exhibit at Yamanashi Military Government Team headquarters, 1947. Yamaguchi Konosuke, education chief of Yamanashi Prefecture, is in back row, second from left. To right of author are educational exhibits director Miss Aramaki and interpreter Enomoto Aiko.

Primary and middle school students line up for an exhibit of archaeological discoveries in Yamanashi Prefecture assembled by local amateurs and shown in the library of Yamanashi Military Government Team headquarters, Kofu, 1947.

Donald B. McMullen, Ph.D., noted American parasitologist, at an exhibit on schistosomiasis at team headquarters, Kofu, 1947.

Students make notes on how to prepare meals using American foods, at an exhibit at team headquarters, Kofu, 1947.

An adult education conference in Yamanashi Prefecture, 1947.

Japanese educators and other leaders at an adult education conference, Yamanashi Prefecture, 1947.

Eleanor Lee, Women's Affairs officer of the Kanto Military Government Region, addressing an audience of Japanese women in Yamanashi Prefecture, 1947, to explain women's new educational, political, and legal rights. Interpreter is Enomoto Aiko.

Paul Patrick Judge, a civilian information officer assigned full time to the Yamanashi Military Government Team, with two visiting schoolgirls at team headquarters in Kofu, 1948.

To the greatest benefactor of Education in Yamanashi prefecture Mr. Van Steaveren with best wishes Sukefumi Ito 2nd august 1948

Ito Sukefumi, retired principal of a middle school, who served as consultant to the CI&E office of the Yamanashi Military Government Team from 1946 through 1948.

At a primary school in Yamanashi Prefecture, 1947, a boy and two girls read from their new textbooks.

The author with his interpreter and education adviser, Enomoto Aiko, meeting in 1947 with the principal and the head teacher of Yamanashi Primary School, one of the best in the prefecture.

A primary school in Yamanashi Prefecture, 1947.

A seventh-grade girl with her baby brother on her back attends school while her mother works in a field, 1947. Occasionally, girls in primary school also took turns carrying a teacher's baby on their backs during the school day.

Three young girls in Yamanashi's school for the handicapped learn the art of silk weaving, 1947.

During these question-and-answer periods I would be asked how this and that was done in America, especially how American schools functioned. I would explain briefly how America's educational system had evolved and the manner in which towns, counties, cities, and states exercised authority over their schools. I would cite, as an example, how schools in Polk County, Oregon, where I grew up, possessed their own school boards, including the one I had attended where my father was a school-board member. The board hired or dismissed principals and teachers, set their salaries, calculated school operating costs, and dealt with related matters. At least once a year, the county superintendent of schools inspected each school to assure that the minimum education standards set by the state of Oregon were met, to determine whether school facilities were adequate, and to make recommendations to improve school operations. He would meet with each school's faculty and talk to its students in the school auditorium, usually stressing the importance of education. The U.S. Government in Washington, D.C., had no significant role in the educational process, there being no Department of Education (this was in the 1946–48 period). In short, control over education was highly decentralized in America. This was also the objective of the New Education, which would lead to the creation, beginning in 1948, of local school boards in Japan, which in turn would work closely with newly created Parent-Teacher Associations. Again, I sensed that my listeners did not look forward to this revolutionary change and doubted its feasibility in Japan.

Frequently, I was asked to explain America's "pioneering spirit" and "the secret of American democracy." The two questions enabled me to expound briefly on America's "creative spirit" as demonstrated by the development of the cotton gin by Eli Whitney (c. 1793), the electric telegraph by Samuel Morse (c. 1837), the grain reaper by Cyrus H. McCormick (c. 1834), the telephone by Alexander Graham Bell (c. 1876), the phonograph and electric light bulb by Thomas A. Edison in 1877 and 1879 (plus his hundreds of other inventions), as well as the first flight of an airplane by the Wright brothers in 1903, and first use of the assembly line for auto production by Henry Ford in 1914. Although most of these famous inventors, I would explain, had scant formal education, they all possessed imagination and inventiveness, which flourished in American democracy. On one occasion, I addressed this subject in a short article for a local newspaper, wherein I further defined the pioneering spirit as meaning: "What was good enough for my father and grandfather is not good enough for me." In brief, each new generation of Americans strove to build on past science and technology to improve living standards, and this accounted for America's wealth and advancement in most fields of learning.

The foregoing explanation appeared especially apt when I was told that traditional Japanese social restraint would normally inhibit a small lower-class farmer from purchasing a new, advanced rice-threshing machine until after the local wealthy land owner had purchased one. Otherwise there would be taunts: Who does farmer Suzuki think he is—being the first to show off his new threshing machine!

The queries of some very young teachers revealed, not surprisingly, a pervasive misperception about the living standard of Americans, given the conspicuous opulence of military and civilian occupationaires and the photos and advertisements in American magazines. "Does everyone own a jeep or a car?" "Do families go out to dinner every night?" "Do most Americans travel abroad each year?" "Do all housewives have maids?" I tried to portray an America of more modest means, explaining that most citizens lived more spartan lives than did occupationaires in Japan.

One young woman teacher in a very remote school was curious about a strange American trait: "Do most office workers like to rise early and sing?" When I asked her what prompted the question she said she enjoyed listening every morning to the American Armed Forces radio station WVTR in Tokyo which featured, besides news, sports, and weather reports, frequent group singing, which she enjoyed. She assumed these workers for General MacArthur arose early each day and stopped by the radio station to sing several songs before proceeding to their offices. I shattered the young lady's innocence by explaining that the singers were not employed by General MacArthur but were members of a popular American chorale called "Fred Waring and his Pennsylvanians," and that these were instances of the group's recordings of their tunes. She appeared astounded to learn that Japanese radio broadcasting included many recorded programs.

Occasionally a teacher inquired about the famous educator John Dewey, but it was rare to meet a principal or teacher who was conversant with Dewey's essays and books. "Knowledge about this American pragmatist," I wrote to a friend, "is extremely limited in this prefecture, and Professor Dewey's writings are perhaps best known among Japanese educators in large urban areas." (Feb. 18, 1947)

Throughout January 1947—as Japan's major labor unions, including the national Japan Teacher's Union, were threatening to call a nationwide strike on February 1 if salaries and benefits were not increased substantially—many Yamanashi teachers solicited my advice on whether it was proper for "educators" to unionize like "common workers." Because SCAP encouraged the growth of unions and recognized their right to bargain collectively with employers, I could only urge that teachers and principals should decide for themselves whether to become members (as will be noted later, General MacArthur prohibited the strike).4

School Radios

Because SCAP's CI&E officials required the Japan Broadcasting Corporation to sponsor special radio programs for students and teachers to explain the precepts of the New Education, I took pains during school inspections and visits to inquire if the programs were worthwhile. The answers were always affirmative, but close questioning indicated that listening habits were quite erratic. One reason for this was the large number of nonfunctioning radios in the schools. A survey in January 1947 disclosed that 161 schools, mostly primary but also some secondary, had radios that lacked vacuum tubes and other essential parts despite the existence of a special radio repair service established by the Ministry of Education in all prefectures. Some schools were unaware of this service. Consequently, I instructed the local newspapers and the radio station to publicize how nonfunctioning radios could be fixed quickly.5

There were difficulties in the use of school radios. Oftentimes, the overburdened local electric generators produced such low voltage that special education or other programs were virtually inaudible.6 In badly crowded schools, not all students in selected classes could crowd into the largest classroom to listen to a special broadcast. It was also apparent that the majority of teachers failed to listen even to broadcasts aimed at them. Scheduled for 3:30 to 4:00 P.M. on Mondays, Wednesdays, and Fridays, the radio lesson was broadcast at a time when many teachers were either still teaching, working on student records, or had to leave their schools early, often to scrounge for food items for themselves or their families. The listening problem was partially resolved by having the principal or head teacher appoint two faculty members to listen to the radio lesson. The appointed listeners would then inform their colleagues the next day what they had heard.

Finally, education broadcasts to students and teachers alike were not as effective as SCAP officials were wont to assume because the well-educated announcers in Tokyo, male and female, often used words and phrases their listeners in rural Japan did not fully understand. This was especially true for many young women teachers who suffered from highly abbreviated normal school education during World War II, or who had not gone beyond middle school and held only provisional teaching certificates.

Departure from a School

As noted earlier, at the request of the Yamanashi Military Government's medical officer, I always ended school inspections by visiting the coeducational outdoor lavatories, (*benjos*). Their conditions were often deplorable. I could praise them only for the absence of graffiti on the walls. The frequency of removal of their waste (called "night soil") for fertilizer was often subject to the whims of one or two nearby farmers, who usually had an agreement with a school on emptying the lavatories. I quickly learned that the task of keeping them clean devolved upon girl students and the youngest women teachers. Invoking the provisions and spirit of new Japanese education legislation and the new Constitution, I issued two dictums on school *benjos*. First, both sexes should be assigned the duty of keeping them clean, and second, the prefectural school inspectors should meet with the team's medical officer, who would explain to them the importance, from the standpoint of the health of all students and faculty, of keeping the *benjos* as sanitary as possible.[7]

Upon completing a school inspection, I would meet briefly with the principal or head teacher to summarize what I had observed. (Principals, who held an honored position in their communities, were often absent attending funerals, civic events, and meetings.) With rare exceptions, I could assure them I had seen no violations of a SCAP directive. If the classrooms, schoolyard, and lavatories were unusually clean and tidy, or if some faculty members were employing successfully a more democratic or innovative method of teaching, I would compliment them on their leadership. In turn, I would ask them to comment on SCAP directives or any facet of the New Education. Unusual was the principal or head teacher who would concede he did not grasp all of the facets of educational reform, but some politely asserted they were required to institute too many reforms too rapidly. Privately, I agreed.

I would then walk to my jeep or sedan already surrounded by scores and sometimes several hundred boys and girls who desired a close look at a military government officer. I would banter with them and ask: "What is your favorite subject?" "Do you all study hard?" and "What is your favorite sport?" The last question invariable drew the loudest response. Girls liked volleyball best; boys, baseball. To my inquiry, "Can you name an American baseball player?", all would chorus "Babe Ruth!" The great Babe left a remarkable, lasting impression on the Japanese public during his seventeen-game tour of the country with a group of other baseball luminaries late in 1934.[8]

Sometimes a bold boy student would touch me (a most heady experience!). Then amidst the bows and farewells of the principal or head teacher, numerous other faculty members, and students, I would take my leave, often elated by my reception. Upon reaching my office, sobriety was always restored quickly as I prepared a briefing for the team commander, worked on near-due reports, or learned that another Army chaplain was en route, for whom I would have to serve as team host during his brief visit.

Some General Observations

By March 31, 1947, the end of the 1946–47 school year, I had inspected or visited thirty-five to forty schools, mostly primary but also a few middle, youth and technical schools, the three prefectural normal schools, and the school for the handicapped. Except for the middle schools, nearly all were quite rudimentary in structure. Some primary schools had two floors. A solitary light bulb hung from the ceiling of most classrooms to provide additional illumination on dark winter days, albeit some were burned out and replacements were not easily obtained.

Classrooms during the late autumn and winter months of the 1946–47 school year were unusually cold because of many cracked, broken, or missing window panes, not owing to wanton vandalism, as I had first surmised, but because of theft by otherwise responsible adults. When wartime needs created a scarcity of commercial glass, desperate family members, or owners of small businesses or their employees, would steal in the dead of night a pane or two of glass for the home or shop. In addition, a severe shortage of lumber and other construction materials and the lack of funds had made it impossible to construct additional classrooms or new schools.

In addition, most schools were severely overcrowded, a situation exacerbated by the repatriation to Japan of slightly more than six-and-a-half million military and civilian citizens, many with children, who had served or worked in China, Taiwan, Korea, Southeast Asia, and the Pacific islands prior to or during World War II. Thus "small" primary schools in remote areas might enroll 400 to 500 students; those in towns might enroll 1,000 or more. Rare was the teacher with only 30 or 35 pupils in his or her class; most had 40, 45, 50, and up to 70. One had 120, a record. Some schools had double shifts, with separate groups of students taught in the morning and in the afternoon. Nonetheless, student absences, except for reasons of health or work on a small farm were rare, so ingrained was Japanese parents' respect for education.9

Despite the overcrowded classrooms, all schools appeared to possess the bare essentials: desks, chairs, blackboards, new teachers' manuals and/or revised textbooks—including two censored ones—and a few maps, although those showing Japan's former Greater East Asia Co-Prosperity Sphere could not be displayed. Many schools, however, sorely lacked for paper, notebooks, and occasionally chalk, although there appeared to be sufficient paper for the student art that brightened many a classroom wall. Art training began in the first grade, and it was obvious that Japanese students possessed a stronger artistic bent than did their counterparts in America. In black and white and in a variety of colors, mostly in crayon but occasionally in oils, the youngsters sketched their homes, train stations, post offices, oxen and ox-carts, portraits, fields, and mountains, the last featuring frequently the incomparable Mt. Fuji, which stood majestically astride the boundary of Yamanashi and Shizuoka Prefectures.

Given the immediate postwar circumstances in nearly all educational institutions, it was understandable if some classroom instruction periods lasted only twenty-five to thirty minutes instead of the requisite forty-five to fifty minutes. Another reason for shortened instruction periods in some schools arose from a misinterpretation of the New Education, whereby teachers absented themselves in a classroom to enable their students to "develop their inner selves." The learning period in very rural areas was also shortened to celebrate numerous local holidays in addition to the twelve official national ones. Finally, some schools took a seven- or ten-day holiday period to enable students to assist their parents during the peak planting period in the spring and the harvesting period in late autumn. As no SCAP directive presently dealt with the "holiday problem," I counseled only that holidays should be kept to a minimum.[10] To escape from their many tribulations in this early postwar period, especially during the cold winter days, it was not surprising that many teachers were inclined to seek refuge for longer periods than usual in the teachers' room. There, several *hibachis* dispensed heat from charcoal, and kettles on small electric plates boiled water to make green tea, which was consumed in enormous quantities. In this room I encountered periodically an interesting fixture of Japanese education: the school janitor, who appeared to spend an excessive amount of time arranging and rearranging teacups, and making and pouring tea for the school principal and faculty. My interest in him was piqued when I learned, as already noted, that the cleaning of a school and its toilet was the duty of students, mostly girls, who were assisted and supervised by the youngest women teachers. In America, cleaning tasks were left entirely to the school janitor (today called "custodians"). Upon receiving ambiguous answers at schools about the duties of this important school employee, who held a position of some esteem, I conveyed my observations in a letter to a friend:

It appears that a school janitor's duties are four: first, taking care of school supplies (of which are very few at present); second, unlocking and locking daily the school doors—although there are ample missing window panes and even window frames through which an intruder could easily gain access; third, ringing the school bell or beating the school drum to signal the beginning or end of classes; and fourth, preparing and serving tea to the principal and faculty. My strong suspicion is that the last is his most important duty, albeit no principal or teacher will admit to this. I shall continue my research into the matter. (Jan. 12, 1947)

In accordance with my CI&E responsibilities to persuade local educators and citizens that the historic Confucian precepts relegating females to an inferior status in society was "undemocratic" (although I never mentioned Confucianism), I urged principals and faculties, as noted earlier, to assign the daily task of cleaning classrooms and toilets equally between girls and boys, and women and men. Women teachers invariably murmured approval, men teachers remained silent, and principals responded with several "Ah so's." Although my views on this subject were well known, subsequent school inspections and visits indicated that this particular reform continued to be honored as much in the breach as in its observance, undoubtedly because SCAP had never issued a directive on the subject. Upon the advice of my interpreter, I refrained from insisting on extending the equality doctrine to boy students for sharing with the girls the task of carrying a family baby in school.

Amidst the considerable postwar disarray and turbulence in most of Yamanashi's primary schools and the uncertainty of most teachers over how to apply the precepts of the New Education, there existed one very bright educational light. This was the Fuzoku Primary School attached to the prefectural men's normal school. It was headed by a fairly young and imaginative head teacher and a small faculty which appeared to comprehend better than most the objectives of the New Education and how to apply them. In early February 1947, having noted "how this school had displayed surprisingly advanced teaching techniques," I encouraged the head teacher "to take the lead in helping prefectural teachers to improve their performance by holding teaching demonstrations."[11]

Accordingly, with the assistance of some members of the men's and women's normal school faculties and the prefectural Education Section, he and his faculty sponsored the first "clinic" on March 4. Approximately 500 teachers were present. The morning session was devoted to demonstrating progressive instructional techniques in the classrooms for the visiting teachers. Lectures and discussions on teaching problems were held in the afternoon.[12]

So favorable was the response of all attendees that the head teacher and his faculty planned immediately to hold additional clinics, with the next one scheduled for May 1947.

7

Secondary, Normal, and Medical Schools

As has been noted, from November 1946 through March 1947, the end of the 1946–47 school year, I concentrated on inspecting and visiting primary schools because they bore the immediate brunt of the New Education. Nonetheless, I worked into my schedule inspections or brief visits to six middle schools (three for boys, three for girls), a few youth schools, three normal schools, and a medical school.

Middle Schools

Popularly called high schools by Americans, the grade structure of middle schools differed from that of their counterparts in the United States. Yamanashi's five boys' middle schools provided for five years of study beyond the sixth grade, whereas the six girls' middle schools (including the one destroyed by fire in January 1947) provided only four years of study beyond the sixth year. The total boy and girl enrollment of the eleven middle schools was roughly equal. Each had at least 1,100 or more students, the Kofu boys' school being the largest with 1,800. Altogether they contained some 15 percent of primary school graduates, about the national average. Officially, entrance was based upon passing a rigorous examination, but I learned from various sources that the offspring of parents who enjoyed fairly high social, political, or economic status were rarely excluded. Although students paid a tuition fee, the bulk of funding came from the prefectural and national treasuries.

The middle schools were the sole preparatory educational route for students desiring to attend a reputable college or university. Compared with most primary schools, they were of sturdier construction and possessed fewer cracked or missing window panes, thus assuring more warmth for study. Desks and chairs of students were of better quality and the offices of principals and teachers were more spacious and better furnished. All had auditoriums, gymnasiums, small laboratories, and libraries, although the last were usually under lock and key. Lavatories or *benjos* were well constructed and better maintained. The girls' middle schools were especially attractive, with classroom walls displaying many colorful art and handicraft items and with schoolgrounds well kept. Boys' middle schools had a more spartan look. Classroom walls were barren except for some artworks and maps, and the schoolgrounds showed evidence of harder use for baseball, soccer, and other athletic activities.

Student attire further attested to the special status of these schools. Boys wore a dark uniform with matching cap, and girls dressed in a white middy, black middy scarf, and dark skirt. Their footgear was akin to American tennis shoes, but sandals and *getas* were also worn. Principals and men and women teachers also appeared better dressed than their primary school counterparts, with many men teachers favoring a suit while others wore jackets and trousers. With few exceptions, women teachers favored western-style dress.

Both the curricula and the status of men and women teachers reflected a long tradition. Boys' middle schools were bastions of masculinity. In addition to longer study of the Japanese language, their courses emphasized mathematics, chemistry, physics, and other sciences. They had no women instructors. Girls' middle schools invariably had a male principal and a predominately male faculty. A sisterhood of teachers taught language and the more classical subjects of art, sewing, flower arrangement, childcare, and cooking. All schools possessed teachers of English, several of whom demonstrated an unusual facility for the language, despite their use of some archaic or "dictionary" words and phrases. The middle schools also offered brief courses in *romaji*, the romanized version of Japanese, but unlike a few primary school teachers, they did not confuse *romaji* with English. Some students managed to read, write, and speak English remarkably well. On several occasions, a bold English-speaking middle school boy managed to obtain an audience with me, ostensibly to discuss some "important" student problems but whose main purpose, I would conclude, was to obtain a quick peek at my office and impress me with his mastery of English. Reportedly, these students achieved some notoriety among their friends for having ingeniously talked their way past the Yamanashi Military Government Team's visitor-screening procedure.

Despite their more affluent appearance, middle school students and their families were not exempt from the severe postwar economic distress. Absenteeism among those who resided in Kofu or other towns was well above normal because of the need periodically to join a family member to forage for food in the countryside, buying directly from farmers. A survey by one boys' middle school near the end of 1946 disclosed the following: only 40 percent believed they could afford to attend school full time, 40 percent every other day, 13 percent only a half day, and 7 percent wished to discontinue schooling altogether (author's notes, Nov. 21, 1946). Principals conceded that absenteeism, primarily for economic reasons, remained a serious problem in early 1947.

An inspection or visit to a middle school did not create nearly the excitement I had experienced at primary schools. Being older and more restrained, students did not rush out by the scores to greet me and my interpreter but on the playground would crowd around my jeep or sedan not only to say hello but to try out a few phrases in English: "How are you?" or "Did you have a good trip?" The principal, assistant principal, or head teacher would escort me to his office where, between the usual cups of tea, we would have a preliminary discussion. I would then begin my stroll through the school. The noise level in middle schools was far less than in primary schools, as teachers did not appear to rely as heavily on teaching by rote.

In meeting with some or all faculty members, it was evident they were better educated than their primary school counterparts and comprehended more readily the significance of the New Education as outlined in pending Japanese education legislation and the new Constitution. They could not conceal their concern—sometimes their great distress—over the impending educational changes that promised to emasculate their beloved institutions, especially upon the creation of new lower secondary schools for the seventh, eighth, and ninth grades beginning April 1, 1947.

As Mr. Ito, the former teacher and middle school principal on my staff, had informed me frequently, the change would be heartwringing to both students and faculties, so great was their loyalty to their schools. The students realized they belonged to a social and educational elite. Boys especially knew they were marked to become, after higher education, future leaders in education, government, business, science, and other professions. Girls, too, knew they could obtain additional quality education and thus be assured of a marriage to a husband of some professional standing and, to the extent Japanese culture allowed, become educators and leaders in their communities.

On the subject of coeducation, secondary school faculty members expressed as much concern as primary school teachers about its "moral" implications. As noted earlier, the 1946 *Report of the United States Education Mission to Japan* had recommended coeducation for primary schools and had urged its adoption in the new lower and upper secondary schools as rapidly as finances warranted. Article 5 of the Fundamental Law of Education (March 1947) stated in part: "Coeducation . . . shall be recognized." With the concurrence of SCAP education officials, the Ministry of Education planned to introduce coeducation only one grade at a time beyond grade six, beginning with the 1947–48 school year.

Few male teachers wished to discuss the subject, but most women teachers, while receptive to the idea in theory, were in no rush to put it in effect. Again, as in the primary schools, most women teachers appeared reluctant to reduce the number of courses in the domestic arts. A few were emboldened to inquire if, through coeducation and equality of education, women might become school principals. One woman teacher in a middle school where the principal seemed more feared than admired asked: "Why doesn't General MacArthur try principals as war criminals?" One girl student, clearly upset by the eventual breakup of her middle school asked: "Why can't girls obtain an equal education in their own schools?" It was a very good question, as I knew that numerous private girls' and boys' schools in the United States provided high quality education. Repeatedly, I was asked how coeducation worked in America. I explained, based on my own coeducation experiences in grade school, high school, college, and university.

Nevertheless, it was the responsibility of a military government CI&E officer to convince his middle school listeners of the importance of equal education in the public schools and how this goal could be obtained best through coeducation during twelve years of primary and secondary education. This would ensure that girls gained equal access to the study of the more difficult courses in mathematics, physics, chemistry, and other subjects, thus preparing them to assume a greater leadership role in their country.

To underscore the importance of women's leadership, I would cite the achievements of several outstanding American women of the past, such as Clara Barton, who founded the American Red Cross; Susan B. Anthony, a founding member and president of the National Woman Suffrage Association; and Frances Elizabeth Willard, also a noted suffragette and founder and president of the Woman's Christian Temperance Union. Unfortunately, their names were familiar only to very few middle school women teachers and not at all to girl students. There was one past French woman scientist, however, whose name most teachers and students recognized. This was Marie Curie of France, who, with her husband Pierre, received in 1903 the Nobel Prize in physics and in her own right won a second Nobel Prize in 1911 in chemistry. Madame Curie was my best example in the ensuing months of a woman's potential for developing her ability when given educational opportunity.

Vocational and Youth Schools

Distinguishing between Yamanashi's "vocational" and "youth" schools was often confusing. Nationally, there were six types of vocational schools; namely, technical, agricultural, fisheries, commercial, navigation, and practical. They were divided into Class A and Class B. Class A admitted boys and girls who had completed the compulsory six-year primary school, and Class B, those who had completed higher primary school (i.e., the eighth grade). Middle school graduates also could attend.[1]

Youth schools, however, were also vocational schools. Before World War II there were about 233 youth schools in Yamanashi Prefecture, but at present there were only about 47.[2] Like their counterparts in the vocational schools, students in the youth schools wanted an education beyond the primary school level. To the best of my knowledge, no middle school graduates attended youth schools.

I visited only a few vocational and youth schools. The former had better facilities and equipment than did the latter. I spent little time with either as their courses of study were scheduled to be phased into the new lower and higher secondary schools, some of which would provide (one hoped) better quality full-time and part-time vocational education for students seeking it. The "phasing out" would begin on April 1, 1947, upon the establishment of new lower secondary schools for the seventh, eighth, and ninth grades, with the seventh grade compulsory.

The youth schools I visited were housed in small, rudimentary structures and appeared to possess few books, no laboratories, and little in the way of workshop equipment. None seemed to have more than fifteen or eighteen students. Their teachers were graduates of Yamanashi's youth school normal school, an institution separate from the regular men's and women's normal schools. Their desire to be recognized as "educators" was manifested on their personal calling cards, on which they were wont to refer to themselves as a "Professor of Business," "Professor of Engineering," "Dean of Students," and "President" of their respective schools. Both the students and their teachers expressed considerable apprehension about the new 6–3–3–4 school structure. The students feared it might jeopardize their opportunities to continue their part-time vocational training, and their teachers saw the new and higher standards proposed for secondary faculties as a threat to their livelihood. It was difficult to convince the small delegations of youth school students or their teachers, who came to my office to air their deep concerns, that their educational opportunities under the New Education would be enhanced rather than diminished.

The Three Normal Schools

As mentioned earlier, Yamanashi Prefecture had two regular normal schools plus a youth school normal school. The regular men's normal school, initially located in Kofu, had been destroyed by the single B-29 bombing raid in July 1945, and was housed in a former Japanese Army barracks outside of Kofu until June 1947, when it found better accommodations in the city in a hastily built structure with fourteen classrooms. It offered a two-year preparatory course for graduates of "higher" primary schools (i.e., students who had completed the eighth grade), followed by a three-year regular course of study. The regular women's normal school in the village of Kanoiwa, not far from Kofu, had escaped destruction during the bombing. Its graduation requirements were similar to those of men's schools, which is to say the students of these two institutions underwent a total of thirteen years of schooling. With respect to facilities, the men's normal school possessed a library of about 3,000 volumes, a larger collection having been destroyed in the bombing. The women's normal school had a much larger library. Neither institution possessed much laboratory equipment.

Every year a fair number of graduates of Yamanashi's eleven middle schools enrolled for normal school study, but boy and girl requirements were different. Graduates of boys' middle schools (grades five through eleven) could complete their studies in only two years, whereas graduates of girls' middle schools (grades seven through ten) needed three years.

There were similarities and differences in the curricula of the two schools. Both provided for additional instruction in the Japanese language, literature, basic science (including mathematics), educational psychology, philosophy, teaching methods, and new course on American education. Women's textbooks were less detailed than those for men, however, and there were special textbooks and manuals on domestic-art subjects such as childcare, clothing, housekeeping, cooking, sanitation, and flower arrangement. Both sexes engaged in practice teaching at either the Fuzoku Primary School, attached to the men's normal school, or at other designated schools. Again there was a disparity in practice-teaching requirements for men and women: men had twelve weeks of practice teaching and women had only ten.

The New Education envisaged the establishment of four-year teachers' colleges (a term preferred by SCAP education officials to "normal schools"). Unfortunately, at a time when many more qualified teachers were needed in Yamanashi's—and in all of Japan's—burgeoning schools, enrollment in these two institutions was dropping. I asked Mr. Ito, my assistant, to list, if possible, the causes for this decline. I summarized his findings in the teams' report for March 1947:

> The major reason for reduced enrollment in the normal schools in Yamanashi arises from the lengthening (beginning April 1, 1947) of the preparatory course from two to three years. Thus eighty boys and forty girls entering the two schools will have to devote an extra year to study. This will create a "graduation gap" of 120 students for the normal schools which will not be filled easily. In addition, because examinations for entry into universities and the normal schools were held almost concurrently early in 1947, fewer middle school students took the examination for the latter. Furthermore, the formation of and participation by many teachers in teachers' union had diminished much of the dignity previously accorded the educational profession, thus discouraging some students to apply for enrollment in a normal school.[3]

Finally, a few students cited the uncertainty and anxiety created by the volatile changes in the Japan's educational system. Low salaries were also mentioned, but the prefectural Education Section, when queried on this matter, provided statistics showing that the income of Yamanashi's teachers was higher than that of ordinary business and office employees. Thus did the "teacher training" problem in Yamanashi Prefecture's two regular normal schools underscore the great difficulty in reconstructing and democratizing higher education, certainly in the near future.

Concurrently, there remained the problem of Yamanashi's youth school normal school, whose graduates taught in the prefecture's small youth schools. As this institution was slated to be phased into new four-year colleges and universities, some of which would offer more standardized vocational training, I visited it once. Like the regular men's normal school, its prewar building had also been destroyed during the bombing of Kofu on July 6, 1945, and its temporary building was virtually bereft of a suitable library and laboratory and possessed very little workshop equipment. Nonetheless, it would continue functioning for at least two more years. To prepare for a transition to the New Education, the school conducted special classes for faculty members from January 13 to March 20, 1947, to study and discuss the problems associated with the future teaching of vocational courses, both full time and part time.

Despite the deep concerns of both faculty members and students in all three of Yamanashi's normal schools, I did my best to sustain their morale. In late March 1947, as the 1946–47 school year neared its end, I delivered the commencement address to 155 graduates of these institutions, of whom 42 were from the youth school normal school. My discourse was on "Education in a Free Society," wherein I tried to persuade my listeners of the merits of the 6–3–3–4 educational structure and to assure them that the transition to a more democratic educational philosophy and teaching methods would probably be more rapid than they believed possible. I further emphasized that teachers were at the forefront of creating a more democratic Japan.[6]

Privately, I had my reservations as to whether educational democracy could be achieved over the next few years, given Yamanashi's—and the nation's—wartorn economy, overcrowded schools, the paucity of good textbooks, instructional manuals, and equipment. Conveying my thoughts on this subject to one of my former American professors in the same month, I questioned if present normal school teachers and students could adapt readily to the precepts of democracy without having experienced them in daily living. "I am presently disposed to believe," I wrote, "that democracy in the schools will be largely a carbon copy of what we give them." Further, the bonds of class consciousness, the deep respect for social and financial status, and the reluctance to assume individual responsibility in this Confucian society "are by no means fully broken in Yamanashi Prefecture." (March 23, 1947)

Closing of the Medical School

No problem in the area of higher education in Yamanashi Prefecture evoked more concern and emotion than whether it could retain its medical school. It was a matter that united all prefectural government officials, members of the prefectural assembly, health care professionals, and most of the public. The issue underscored the occupation's problem of trying to replace a highly elitist system of higher education in Japan, where only the graduates of Tokyo University and a few other schools dominated Japan's government and business community with a more egalitarian system of higher education permitting each prefecture to possess eventually a national and fairly prestigious university.[7]

After the original medical school in Kofu had been destroyed by the July 1945 bombing, an effort had been made to continue its functions in temporary quarters. By American or other western standards, the school was a woefully inadequate institution with few laboratory and other facilities. The Yamanashi Military Government Team's medical officer despaired over its future, and was skeptical that the prefecture's economic resources could ever sustain a good combined medical school, hospital, and research center.

On no single issue did Mr. Yamaguchi, the prefectural education chief, try harder to obtain the backing of the medical officer and me than for the continued operation of the medical school. Supporting his fervent appeal was Yamanashi's new governor, Yoshie Katsuyasu (who was appointed by the Home Ministry in February 1947, replacing Governor Saito Noboru) and the prefectural assembly which, by March 1947 had appropriated a total of 14 million yen to renovate the present medical structure and for additional facilities.[8] In truth, the decision rested not with the two members of the Yamanashi Military Government Team—even though we regarded the financial outlay unwise given Yamanashi's other crushing educational needs—but with medical authorities in the Japanese Home Ministry and SCAP headquarters in Tokyo. The prefectural government hoped that the appropriation would impress the higher authorities in Tokyo.

The upshot of final discussions in May between two SCAP and prefectural officials in Kofu was a decision by the American medical specialists not to reverse a March 29 finding by the Japanese Home Ministry that plans for a medical school in Yamanashi Prefecture should be dropped. It was a bitter pill for Governor Yoshie, Mr. Yamaguchi, and others to swallow. It was also very difficult for me.

Privately, I agreed with the argument put forth passionately by the governor when he spoke for all of his colleagues. Unless steps were taken now in Yamanashi Prefecture, he said, to establish a prestigious medical school, Japan's largest cities, such as Tokyo, Osaka, Kyoto, and Kobe would receive as in the past the lion's share of national funds to support medical institutions. Unfortunately, Yamanashi's present economic base was too small to help build and sustain such an institution. "Fourteen million *yen*", I noted "is a tremendous amount of money for a not-very-prosperous prefecture in the face of so many other compelling needs" (May 7, 1947). These needs included new lower secondary and other schools, a more modern and better-equipped prefectural hospital, health clinics, and upgraded training of physicians, nurses, and other health personnel.

Finally, it also appeared more prudent for the prefectural government to invest its limited financial resources into establishing a four-year Yamanashi National University. This was the goal as envisioned by SCAP education authorities. This project alone would tax Yamanashi's revenues to the utmost in the immediate future, but would constitute a significant step towards elevating prefectural education standards.

In fact, in May 1949, only two years later, a Yamanashi National University was established, although it was subsequently renamed the Yamanashi *Gakuin* University.

8

Yamanashi Teachers' Unions

Early Teacher Unionism

When I arrived in Japan in late September 1946, there were already many news stories about the activities of new postwar labor unions. The fact that Japan's teachers were also unionizing was mentioned several times during my initial briefings in Yokohama for the CI&E duties with the Yamanashi Military Government Team. Upon joining the team at the beginning of November 1946, however, I discovered that its reports had given scant coverage to prefectural teacher unionism until October 1946, when it noted that a sizable union was already extant. Shortly, I learned that the first union activity in Yamanashi occurred on February 26, 1946, when about 1,000 teachers assembled in front of the prefectural government building in Kofu to request substantially increased salaries. The demonstrators included not only teachers in primary schools but also a small number in the normal, middle, and youth schools.[1]

The rise of the organization followed the formation, primarily by a few Communist leaders, of the radical All-Japan Teachers' Union (hereafter, Japan Teachers' Union) in Tokyo on December 1, 1945. A more-moderate Japan Educators' Union was founded in Tokyo a day later by the then well-known Christian reformer Kagawa Toyohiko. The Educators' Union drew its initial membership mostly from teachers in middle schools, colleges, and universities. By November 1946, the radical union claimed to have 200,000 members in twenty-nine districts throughout Japan. The moderate union listed 130,000 members in thirty-one districts. Together, these constituted about 64 percent of all of Japan's educators from primary school through university.[2]

In Yamanashi Prefecture, a team report of October 1946 noted that the Kofu branch of the Yamanashi Teachers' Union held a meeting that month "to register opposition to the new salary scale established by the Ministry of Education." In addition, the teachers voted "to oppose the distinction in salaries between teachers in national schools and local schools." They further demanded "cash salaries and exemption from the income tax."[3]

It is essential to note that trade unionism in postwar Japan received its major impetus from SCAP's Political, Civil and Religious directive of October 4, 1945 (hereafter cited as Civil Liberties directive). It freed from prison about 3,000 of Japan's prewar and wartime political dissidents, many of whom held strong unionist and other liberal and leftist political points of view.[4] Among those released were several hundred Communists (one source places their number as high as 800). Many of those released had engaged in union activities in Japan prior to World War II, and they immediately took advantage, with SCAP's blessing, of their new democratic freedoms to organize workers to attain both economic and political goals.[5]

SCAP encouraged the growth of democratic unions, and officials of its labor and other divisions promptly assisted the Japanese government in writing new union legislation. In March 1946 there came into force the Trade Union Law and a supporting ordinance which guaranteed the right of workers inside and outside of government, except police, firemen, and penal employees, to organize. Effective October 1946, the government passed the Labor Relations Adjustment Law, which established a comprehensive method for settling labor disputes by conciliation, mediation, and arbitration.[6] Article 28 of the new Constitution guaranteed "the right of workers to organize and bargain collectively." The first twenty-four months of the occupation witnessed the enactment of at least fourteen laws or ordinances favorable to unionists.[7]

Although the Yamanashi Teachers' Union in early 1946 consisted of both primary and secondary school teachers, most of its members taught in primary schools. (This was also true of the Japan Teachers' Union headquartered in Tokyo.) Both educational and social differences, plus the radical leadership of the prefectural union, rather quickly impelled teachers in Yamanashi's middle schools, the men's and women's normal schools, the youth normal school, and a technical college to establish either separate "departments" loosely aligned with the large union, or their own small unions, all associated with the more moderate Japan Educators' Union.

The sudden creation of teachers' unions nationally and at the prefectural level followed the loss in influence of the Great Japan Education Association (the "Great" was dropped in early 1946), previously the main national professional education organization, which had been subverted during the war by the Ministry of Education into a propaganda organization for the militarists (see note 10, chap. 3). Presently, its officers were headed by elderly educationists who had escaped SCAP's personnel purges, and whose traditional education and experience constrained them from assuming a leadership role in the reformation of Japan's educational system.[8]

Given the rapid growth of postwar trade unions throughout Japan, it was not easy for a CI&E or a labor officer on a prefectural military government team to keep abreast of the union movement among teachers. Just fourteen months into the occupation, it seemed that employees of every possible organization had joined a union. In early January 1947, for example, the team's labor officer, in a report on labor strikes, lockouts, and other labor disputes involving 15,347 workers in Yamanashi Prefecture, listed no less than nineteen separate unions representing public works, the national railway, meteorology, postal savings, electrical power, farming, and teaching. In addition, five new unions were "registered" only days after the new year began. Even SCAP labor and CI&E officials were unable to keep fully abreast of the union movement, as evidenced by their inadequate reporting in "guidance papers" for military government teams, sent through Eighth Army headquarters, and by their inadequate replies to team headquarters during phone calls.[9]

Teachers as Reluctant Unionists

From the onset of my inspections and visits to primary and secondary schools in Yamanashi Prefecture, teachers had reluctantly joined unions, traditionally regarded as suitable only for "common laborers." Nevertheless, despite their concern that it detracted from the dignity of the teaching profession nearly all of Yamanashi's educators would shortly be unionists. There were at least four transcendent reasons: union leaders were at the forefront of the drive to secure better salaries and benefits in the nation's inflation-wracked economy; the Great Japan Education Association and its prefectural affiliates had been discredited; and teachers apparently believed not only that unionization was necessary to transform Japan into a democracy but also, and most important that SCAP wanted all educators to join a union. For most teachers, accustomed to imperial edicts, how else could SCAP's prolabor policies and extensive publicity about forming and operating unions be interpreted?

During the November 1946–March 1947 period, most primary school teachers, men as well as very young women, seemed vague about their union membership. When asked, many did not know the full name of their union and its purposes, other than its promise to fight for better salaries, benefits and working conditions. With respect to union dues, most appeared to rely completely on the local union leaders to handle their payments prudently. In addition, many continued to pay dues to the Yamanashi affiliate of the Japan Education Association, never inquiring whether it provided any useful information or services.

Because the leaders of the Yamanashi Teachers' Union (at least two were avowed Communists) vigorously publicized the economic hardship of teachers, I received more direct information and letters from its union members than I did from those who belonged to the smaller, more moderate Educators' Union. At the end of November 1946, a month after assuming my CI&E duties, I described in a team report a few of the main issues in the struggle of the primary school teachers:

> The Yamanashi Teachers' Union, which is affiliated with the Japan Teachers' Union, is demanding a minimum monthly salary of 600 *yen* and the removal of salary differences because of sex and geographical locations. There has been no strike thus far.
>
> The average monthly salary of teachers in Yamanashi is a little less than 600 *yen*. The average salary of prefectural government officials is about 550 *yen* and that of policemen about 500 *yen*. Although the national government plans to appoint a committee to study the salaries of all public employees, immediate action appears necessary if the rising dissatisfaction of public employees is to be resolved.[10]

Although there was much strike talk in the air, not merely among teachers and other government employees and trade unionists in Yamanashi, but also nationally, to obtain higher salaries because of the deteriorating economic situation throughout Japan, there were also other teacher issues in this predominately rural prefecture. One especially controversial issue was a demand by leaders of the Yamanashi Teachers' Union, in conformance with a decision by the union's headquarters in Tokyo, that the prefectural education authorities abolish traditional gender-based differences in salaries. All women teachers and especially Yamanashi's westernized women (including several employed by the Yamanashi Military Government Team) strongly supported the proposal, but male teachers and prefectural education officials, with few exceptions, were unenthusiastic.[11]

Another demand by union leaders stirred even more controversy. Their proposal to eliminate salary changes based on school locations was strongly opposed by teachers living in the prefecture's cold mountain regions who customarily received a small, extra allowance to purchase additional charcoal for heating in *hibachis*. On this issue, the vast majority of teachers of both sexes agreed. In fact, opposition to this proposed "reform" was sufficient to force union leaders to drop it, demonstrating the propensity of a small clique of officials to make a decision without troubling to obtain the views of members.[12]

The inordinate activism of a few union officials and teachers to secure better salaries and other perquisites alarmed many Japanese parents whose children were in primary or middle schools. It led to an unusual meeting between the leaders of several newly formed PTAS in Kofu and the Yamanashi Teachers' Union to discuss the practice of some teachers conducting street campaigns during school hours to gain public support for their economic grievances. The parents extracted a promise from the union officials to prohibit teacher demonstrations during school hours. The officials, in turn, obtained the backing of PTA members to support the economic demands of teachers.[13]

In partial fulfillment of the latter promise, several of Kofu's new PTAS sent letters in December 1946 to other recently formed associations outside of the city urging them to support better salaries and benefits for teachers. At the same time, the new PTA of a girls' middle school asked every household with a pupil to contribute "200 *yen* for a special fund to construct homes for four teachers . . . and 20 *yen* per student to supplement the salaries of the teachers in the middle school".[14]

Still another troubling issue among primary and secondary teachers who had joined the Yamanashi Teachers' Union was the radical makeup of the union's leaders. Only a few teachers broached the subject gingerly during my initial inspections or visits to schools in late 1946 and the early weeks of 1947. The questioners were aware of the domination by admitted Communists of the national Japan Teachers' Union in Tokyo and also of the presence of several known or suspected Communists at the helm of the union in Yamanashi Prefecture.

Yamanashi's Governor Saito Noboru had expressed his apprehension over the undue influence of the Japan Communist party within the union when he met on December 11 with the three top union leaders. Although the latter conceded that one (soon there were two) of three delegates to the national union headquarters in Tokyo were Communists, they nonetheless considered the governor's concern "unfortunate." The prefectural union, they explained, did not expect fulfillment of all of its demands but desired merely "intelligent and specific answers" by local authorities to the teachers' many economic problems. A second major concern of the governor—and of the prefectural Education Section—was that the unionists supported only the education positions of the national union in Tokyo rather than those of the Ministry of Education.[15]

The strong Communist element, not only in the Japan Teachers' Union nationally and locally but apparently in most trade unions throughout Japan, was highly disturbing to Yamanashi's officials and citizens as well as to all members of the Yamanashi Military Government Team. My uniformed colleagues were greatly perplexed over General MacArthur's tolerance of the "Reds," who appeared to be leading the weak postwar Japanese government towards a political and economic abyss.

To the few teachers and principals who continued to ask me warily about the Communists, my response was that MacArthur's directives had placed no restrictions on Communists. This did not mean, however, that SCAP necessarily approved of all of their views or tactics. I urged my questioners to learn to express their opinions during union meetings, pointing out that they need not simply "approve" all of the proposals laid before them by fast-talking and self-appointed leaders. Most important, they had the right to vote radical Socialists or Communists out of their leadership positions. It was not easy to persuade Yamanashi's rank-and-file educators to be more assertive during union meetings after their years of following unquestioningly instructions from higher authorities.

Teachers and the National Labor Offensive

The struggle of the Yamanashi Teachers' Union near the end of 1946 and January 1947 increasingly merged, meanwhile, with the nationwide labor offensive orchestrated by leaders of the larger national government, manufacturing, transportation, mining, communications, and other labor organizations. Since the onset of the occupation, unionism had enjoyed phenomenal growth with more than 16,000 unions claiming a membership of nearly 4,300,000 by the end of November 1946.[16] On December 17, half a million unionists in Tokyo plus thousands more in other cities and towns in Japan marched through the streets, shouting their economic demands. Rallies featured fiery speeches by labor and political leaders, the vast majority of whom were of the Socialist and Communist parties. They threatened a national strike on February 1, 1947, unless the Tokyo government, headed by Prime Minister Yoshida Shigeru since May 1946, met their many economic objectives.[17]

In Kofu, about 4,000 demonstrators gathered at the city's railway station and rallied under the banner of the Yamanashi Public Workers Union, comprised of about nineteen smaller railway, communications, postal savings, tobacco control, and other unions. Nongovernment unionists, such as those engaged in the electrical and farming professions, were also present, as were prefectural leaders of the Socialist and Communist parties. From the railway station they walked a short distance, waving flags and shouting slogans in unison, until they reached the Yamanashi Prefecture government headquarters, directly across the street from the headquarters of the Yamanashi Military Government Team. There they listened to impassioned speeches by Socialist and Communist orators who demanded quick action on salary and other grievances and the overthrow of the Yoshida government.[18]

Although we Americans did not anticipate violence, the team commander nonetheless had directed us to cancel all field trips for the day and to remain at our desks and out of sight. Several dozen extra Japanese police surrounded our headquarters building, the BOQ, the enlisted men's quarters, and the motor pool.

On the plus side, the labor offensive provided a temporary catalyst to Japanese government decision-making on education issues. On December 19, the Ministries of Education and Finance agreed to provide a minimum salary of 600 *yen* for all of Japan's public school teachers, but only for the month of December. This was followed by a second tentative decision to give all teachers a year-end bonus equal to about two month's salaries. The two ministries rejected numerous other teachers' demands on the grounds that it would be unfair to give preferential benefits solely to teachers and not to other government employees.[19]

The limited salary concessions failed to mollify the leaders of the national Japan Teachers' Union as well as the leaders of other government and nongovernment unions. Consequently, they decided to display their dissatisfaction by joining other unions again for a nationwide labor offensive on January 15, 1947, in Japan's towns and cities, preparatory to a national labor shutdown on February 1.

The national labor offensive was held as planned. In Kofu, the chief sponsor was again the Yamanashi Government Public Workers Union, which included members of the Yamanashi Teachers' Union and numerous nongovernment unions. Socialist and Communist leaders again were at the forefront of the demonstration.

It was a reprise of December 17. The participants, estimated at 4,500 or somewhat more than in the previous month, assembled at the city's railway station, then marched, waved flags, and shouted slogans until they reached the headquarters of the prefectural government building. They gave Governor Saito Noboru a message highlighting the unionists' demands, elaborated in fiery oratory, for minimum wages, cash payments with fewer exceptions for special allowances, more income tax exemptions for higher salaries, an end to "unreasonable" dismissal of workers, and replacement of the Yoshida government—largely the same agenda as in the previous month. In the absence of concessions, the speakers vowed to join the national labor shutdown planned by leaders of major unions in Tokyo on February 1.[20]

Once more the commander of the Yamanashi Military Government Team ordered all of us Americans to remain at our desks throughout the day, and extra police again surrounded our headquarters building, the BOQ, enlisted men's quarters, and the motor pool. This time, the larger rally and the greater zeal of its participants created uneasiness among all team members. Not until now had we reason to wonder if the rising discontent of the demonstrators might get out of hand and spark physical attacks on Americans stationed in rural parts of Japan. Our uniformed officers became outspokenly critical of General MacArthur and his alleged "pink" labor advisers for tolerating a snowballing national strike in which, the newspapers reported, nearly six million unionists would participate.

Several days before the January 15 rally, a few prefectural government officials had expressed their apprehensions to team officers and the commander about the increasing militancy of the union movement. They included Mr. Yamaguchi, the education chief. During a meeting in my office, he openly decried the manner he believed the Communist leaders within the Tokyo-based central committee of the Japan Teachers' Union were exploiting the vast majority of the members of the Yamanashi Teachers' Union. I agreed with him but could only explain that the labor turbulence was a temporary "growing pain" as Japan moved towards democracy. Privately, we were greatly concerned lest there be a breakdown of law and order.

Many if not most teachers in primary and secondary schools were likewise deeply troubled about joining a possible national labor walkout on February 1. This was manifested by visits of small groups of teachers to my office and in letters to the Yamanashi Military Government Team. Numerous parents also wrote to the team, stressing the need to keep the schools open. I summarized some of these concerns in a team report:

> As the threat of a general labor strike on February 1 draws near, many teachers question the advisability of joining the walkout. The faculty of one girls' middle school has already declared it will continue teaching. A small independent union of primary school teachers in two *Guns* has likewise gone on record as opposing the strike. Several parents' organizations are also strongly opposed to having teachers leave their schools.
> It appears that most prefectural teachers, however, will reluctantly join a walkout for a few days but earnestly hope it can be avoided. A major problem is the prefectural union's small active leadership which relies completely on orders from Tokyo on what course of action to take.[21]

Since December 1946, during inspections of schools, visits to my office, and in letters, primary school teachers especially also complained more frequently and openly about the many "orders" from their union leaders to hold quick meetings, sometimes during the school day, to "discuss" and "approve" immediately various union proposals drafted by officials of their national union in Tokyo. Despite my counsel not to merely rubber-stamp every proposal placed before them, very few seemed willing to resist their union officials. In fact, none appeared willing to express their discontent to the point of resigning from the union, so long as it was championing higher salaries, allowances, and other benefits in the face of a worsening economic situation.

First CI&E and Labor Education Conference

Meanwhile, in SCAP headquarters in Tokyo, labor division officials who had been encouraging the formation of unions throughout Japan since the onset of the occupation, became sufficiently alarmed about the marching, sloganeering, and flag-waving of million of unionists, the fiery speech-making of their predominately Socialist and Communist leaders, and the threat of a national walkout on February 1, to step up their "labor education" efforts. This included, on very short notice, some special "Information Conferences" on labor-management relations for all military government labor and CI&E officers on Japan's forty-five military government teams. A few SCAP/CI&E officials, I soon learned, were not pleased to have CI&E officers in the field take on an additional workload. Nonetheless, the conferences were held.

For northern Japan, conferees assembled at IXth Corps headquarters in Sendai during January 21–22, 1947. In attendance were numerous IXth Corps officials, the labor and CI&E officers from fifteen prefectures (including the Hokkaido district), the Kanto and Tohoku Military Government Regions, three members of SCAP's Labor Division and two from SCAP's CI&E section. The Yamanashi Military Government Team was represented by Captain John Kopke, who was the team's labor officer, and myself. Upon our arrival in Sendai, just before the conference began, informal discussion with our counterparts indicated considerable anxiety about the growing labor turbulence. All with whom we talked deplored General MacArthur's failure to halt the unrest, and some believed there was danger if he did not.[22]

The conference's first major speaker was Theodore Cohen, chief of SCAP's Labor Division. To our surprise, he did not focus on current labor developments and the threatened national walkout by millions of Japan's unionists on February 1. Nor did he even mention the radical Socialists and Communists, who were at the forefront of the rising labor unrest. Instead, he recommended stepping up existing labor information, education, and training programs in Japan's union movement, and teaching union leaders how to negotiate with management whether it was the Japanese national or prefectural governments, businesses, or industries. Labor grievances should be settled as in America by collective bargaining. His discourse conveyed no unusual alarm about the impending crisis.

After SCAP's labor chief completed his address, audience questions focused not on how to teach union leaders to negotiate with management, but whether General MacArthur planned to curb the increasingly frenzied labor demonstrations and would permit a national walkout on February 1. The uniformed officers (there were still not many civilians on military government teams) were polite but very sharp: Didn't SCAP headquarters foresee the possibility of mounting labor unrest as a threat to American lives, especially in outlying prefectures? Would not a national strike bring total ruin to war-ravaged Japan? What was SCAP's policy towards the predominance of Socialists and Communists at the head of the largest unions? Was there not a danger of a complete Communist takeover of labor in Japan? Some attendees spoke with considerable emotion.

SCAP's labor chief appeared taken aback by the passion with which some questions were put to him. He tried to assure his audience that their worst fears were unfounded and that matters would not be allowed to get out of hand. (Unbeknown to everyone, Maj. Gen. William F. Marquat, the chief of SCAP's Economic and Scientific Section, planned to warn union leaders the next day not to proceed with a nationwide labor shutdown on February 1.) The number of *bona fide* Communists heading major labor unions in Japan were comparatively few, Cohen declared—contrary to what we had read—and the Communist party was legal. Thus neither SCAP nor military government officials should openly condemn the Communists, albeit their tactics left much to be desired. Workers and citizens, he was confident, would soon learn that Communism was incompatible with "freedom" and "democracy" as defined in the new Constitution. An outlawed Communist party would go underground, creating far more difficulties for SCAP and military government teams than if it operated openly as at present. In any event, there were not sufficient interpreters and other occupationaires to monitor with much accuracy the activities of the party and its many members.

Although Captain Kopke agreed with a number of us that SCAP did not possess the personnel resources to keep track of an underground "Red network" in Japan, many of the attendees in Sendai were unpersuaded by this argument. More to the point, SCAP's first speaker reinforced the pervasive opinion of the majority of uniformed officers in Japan at this time (including, as noted earlier, most of my colleagues in Yamanashi Prefecture); namely, that SCAP's Labor Division was "soft" on Communism. After his talk, the SCAP labor chief quickly disappeared from view, having returned immediately to Tokyo to deal with the accelerating nationwide labor unrest.

Other SCAP officials the same day and the next outlined for us in more detail how to step up a labor-management relations and information offensive in our respective prefectures.[23]

The lectures were based on prepared papers, all of which also avoided—amazingly—citing specifically the dominant role of radical Socialists and Communists in Japan's labor movement. They were followed by lengthy question-and-answer periods, none quite as heated, however, as those that had followed the opening presentation. Each attendee received copies of the papers, the contents of which tended to be quite redundant. The upshot of the lectures and discussions was a promise by SCAP labor officials to send quickly to all military government teams in Japan a series of short "talking papers" on such subjects as a history of trade unionism in the United States, and how "democratic" unions should negotiate with management, whether government or private.

The officials also promised to send many more Japanese-language "guidance papers" to prefectural and local union leaders and their members on labor-management issues and on how to arrange for labor-management conferences at the prefectural level. We attendees had an opportunity to converse frankly with the SCAP labor specialists during coffee breaks, luncheons, and one cocktail hour, during which all conceded that dealing with Communist and radical Socialist union leaders was a difficult problem. I found Richard Deverall, chief of the Education Branch of the Labor Division (with whom I met some weeks later in Tokyo) to be the most outspoken critic of the inordinate influence of Communists in the Japanese labor movement.

Compared with other labor and management and education conferences that I attended in subsequent months, the one in Sendai in January 1947 was not very successful. All of the prefectural military government team labor officers and most of the CI&E officers within IXth Corps were still in uniform. World War II had been over for sixteen months, but Pearl Harbor and the Bataan Death March remained fresh in their minds. As veterans of the Pacific campaigns, some appeared reluctant to "reeducate" the Japanese for anything, particularly how to organize and operate labor unions. In fact, most were quite conservative politically and disliked unions in the United

States, let alone in Japan, where radical Socialists and Communists dominated the leadership of most. The revelation during the conference that one of SCAP's labor officials had worked for John L. Lewis, the "radical" founder of the Congress of Industrial Organizations (1935), did not enhance the popularity of SCAP's labor proponents among the conference attendees in Sendai.

MacArthur Bans a National Labor Strike

By the time Captain Kopke and I returned to the Yamanashi Military Government Team, only a week remained before the February 1 national labor strike was scheduled to begin. All of my colleagues, including the usually reticent team commander, remained perplexed and angry over General MacArthur's failure to crack down on the unions. Stories about the impending strike dominated both the English and Japanese-language newspapers and radio broadcasts.

Yamanashi prefectural officials continued to visit team offices to warn of the dire effects of a labor stoppage on food supplies, health care, transportation, communications, education and other essential activities. Mr. Yamaguchi, the prefectural education chief, again conferred with me about the adverse consequences a strike would have on the schools, and several more teacher representatives also arrived to seek counsel on what they should do, despite the fact the Yamanashi Teachers' Union was already committed to joining the walkout. I felt most uncomfortable talking to my visitors. I "guessed" in my responses that perhaps MacArthur would not allow a strike, or at least not a prolonged one. Some letters from citizens urged the team commander to forbid the strike in Yamanashi, and a prefectural government report warned that Yamanashi was a "deficit *ken*" and very dependent on outside imports for its existence.[24]

In Tokyo, the closing days of January 1947 witnessed a closer but uneasy alliance not only between the leaders of the national radical and more moderate teachers' unions but also among unions of other public and private employees. The teachers' unions joined a loose coalition of other trade unions—the "Joint Struggle Committee of National Labor Unions." At its head was Yashiro Ii, a noted Communist and a leader in organizing railway workers. Claiming to represent all of nearly six million trade unionists, the Joint Struggle Committee set forth various demands with respect to salaries, benefits, working conditions, and related matters. They insisted that the Yoshida government resign. Union enmity against Yoshida was high because of his periodic statements that the nation's near-empty financial offers made it impossible to relieve significantly the economic distress of workers. In an address on New Year's Day 1947, he had further infuriated the pro-strike union leaders by branding them as "outlaws."[25]

The strike was not to be. From mid-January 1947, the Labor Division's strong pro-labor officials were counseling General MacArthur to prohibit a national strike.[26] Lieutenant General Robert L. Eichelberger, the Eighth Army commander in Yokohama who controlled all American and Allied forces in Japan, including the forty-five prefectural and eight regional military government teams, adamantly opposed the threatened walkout. In fact, team members in Yamanashi had learned from visiting Eighth Army officers that Eichelberger earlier had urged the Supreme Commander to curb the Communist and other radical labor leaders and to dismiss some of SCAP's Labor Division members who appeared far too solicitous towards them. Eichelberger feared that a highly emotional national labor strike would pose considerable danger to American personnel, and we few Americans in Yamanashi certainly felt vulnerable. It seemed, however, evident that officials in SCAP headquarters did not share the concern of many military government personnel in outlying prefectures.

As revealed later, however, General MacArthur had actually made up his mind by late January to ban the strike. Through Major General William F. Marquat, MacArthur warned top union leaders not to proceed on February 1. But he issued no direct order until the afternoon of January 31, not many hours before the strike was scheduled to begin. He then issued a statement for the press and radio. It was probably his most famous pronouncement during the occupation:

Under the authority vested in me as Supreme Commander for the Allied Powers, I have informed the labor leaders, whose unions had federated for the purpose of conducting a general strike, that I will not permit the use of so deadly a social weapon in the present impoverished and emaciated condition of Japan, and have accordingly directed them to desist from the furtherance of such action.

It is with greatest reluctance that I have deemed it necessary to intervene to this extent in the issues now pending. I have done so only to forestall the fatal impact upon an already threatened public welfare. Japanese society today operates under the limitations of war, defeat, and Allied occupation. Its cities are laid in waste, its industries almost at a standstill, and the great masses of the people are on little more than a starvation diet.

A general strike, crippling transportation and communications, would prevent the movement of food to feed the people and coal to sustain essential utilities, and would stop such industry as is still functioning. The paralysis which inevitably would result might reduce large masses of the Japanese people to the point of actual starvation, and would produce dreadful consequences upon every Japanese home regardless of social strata or direct interest in the basic issue. Even now, to prevent starvation in Japan, the people of the United States are releasing to them quantities of their own scarce food resources.

The persons involved in the threatened strike are but a small minority of the Japanese people. Yet this minority might well plunge the great masses into a disaster not unlike that produced in the immediate past by the minority which led Japan into the destruction of war. This in turn would impose upon the Allied Powers the unhappy decision of whether to leave the Japanese people to the fate thus recklessly imposed by a minority, or to cover the consequences by pouring into Japan, at the expense of their own meager resources, infinitely greater quantities of food and other supplies to sustain life than otherwise required. In the circumstances, I could hardly request the Allied peoples to assume this additional burden.

While I have taken this measure as one of dire emergency, I do not intend otherwise to restrict the freedom of action heretofore given labor in the achievement of legitimate objectives. Nor do I intend in any way to compromise or influence the basic social issues involved. These are matters of evolution which time and circumstances may well orient without disaster as Japan gradually emerges from its present distress.[27]

General MacArthur's statement was broadcast immediately. All members of the Yamanashi Military Government Team were at their desks when the news broke. Mr. Yamaguchi came immediately to my office to deliver the thanks of his staff and the majority of the teachers, who he well knew were most reluctant to join a national walkout. Nonetheless, by early evening, radio broadcasts reported some unions were considering defying MacArthur and might strike anyway, which suddenly raised tensions again. Shortly after the dinner hour, a representative of the Yamanashi Teachers' Union came to the BOQ to inform me that, in the event of an illegal strike, his union would refuse to participate. I thanked him for this assurance. As it turned out, the firebrand Communist Yoshiri Ii, who headed the Joint Struggle Committee in Tokyo, decided with his colleagues later that evening to abide by General MacArthur's dictum.

Upon reading the text of MacArthur's statement in the newspapers the next day, all team members noted the same omissions that had characterized the prepared papers of SCAP Labor Division officials during the January Labor Education–CI&E conference in Sendai. This was the reluctance of General MacArthur to identify politically the "small minority" who threatened to "plunge the great masses into disaster." There was no mention of Communists, Socialists, or radical Socialists. Team members were more convinced than ever that the Supreme Commander and his top labor and other officials were far too "soft" on "Reds" and labor unions.

Despite the decision of the Yamanashi Teachers' Union not to defy SCAP's ban on a February 1 nationwide walkout, its leadership paid a price for its propensity to walk always in lockstep with the largely Communist-led Japan Teachers' Union headquarters in Tokyo. The few members of the Yamanashi middle school "department" of the union withdrew completely from it and officially joined the more moderate National Federation of Teachers' Unions, composed primarily of secondary, college, and university teachers. A second aftermath of SCAP's strike ban was a decision by the Yamanashi Teachers' Union to oust its two acknowledged Communist representatives to the Japan Teachers' Union headquarters in Tokyo and replace them with non-Communists.[28] Whether my frequent urgings upon teachers to discuss rather than merely "rubber-stamp" union proposals placed before them had anything to do with their action I do not know. Perhaps more important, according to Japanese employees of the team, was that Japan's Communists had "lost face" when SCAP dramatically halted the planned February 1 national labor walkout.

A New Assignment: Labor Education

I did not look forward to being designated the Yamanashi Military Government Team's "labor education officer" in addition to my manifold CI&E duties. Still this is what higher authorities wanted all military government CI&E officers to be, based on the seemingly logical premise that inasmuch as they were already in the information business, distributing SCAP-provided data on and talking about democratic unionism would not pose much of an additional burden. In my case, the team commander was also fully aware that during World War II, I had spent some time with the National Labor Relations Board in Chicago monitoring with others the elections of union officers, or on labor proposals in the steel, meat packing, and other industries to assure they were free and unfettered, and assisting in compiling reports on them, noting any violations in election procedures. This was an additional reason, he opined, why I should be able to handle the labor education assignment.

Because of my already heavy CI&E workload, I made an informal agreement with Captain Kopke, the team's congenial labor officer, to concentrate initially, at least, on providing the local newspapers and the radio station with more materials about the need for democratic unions generally and on how to engage in collective bargaining with management in particular. I would give only an occasional speech. Fortunately, SCAP's Labor Division very promptly had sent to all military government teams additional materials for an expanded labor information and education program.

I delivered my first labor education talk before a conclave of unionists—I failed to record the name of the group—on February 12. Generally, my address was not fundamentally different from the ones I had given frequently to the teachers; namely, the need for worker participation in drafting resolutions, salary, benefits and other demands rather than relying entirely on what a handful of union leaders wanted the rank and file to ratify without debate. I also tried to make clearer the distinctions between arbitration, mediation, and conciliation in settling disputes with management, whether government, business, or industry. There were only a few questions. Most attendees deferred to their "leaders," who inquired politely how labor unions functioned or "bargained" with management in America. It was a far cry from the boisterous meetings for which unionists were noted in the United States.

I agreed, of course, with the objectives of the SCAP Labor Division members to make Japan's predominately Socialist and Communist union leaders more responsive to their members, but it was obvious this would take quite a while. I was sufficiently familiar by now with the Yamanashi Teachers' Union and trade unionism generally in Japan to explain in a letter to a friend:

Here in Yamanashi Prefecture, workers go in a big way for marches, flag-waving, slogans, and listening to orators. When they have to engage in collective bargaining with employers, however, they are lost. So SCAP is distributing much literature on trade unionism so workers will be more knowledgeable about how to settle disputes with employers. This labor education effort is also for the purpose of combatting Communism.

Although Socialists and Communists dominate the leadership of the major national trade unions in Tokyo, in this prefecture, it is not always clear who is a "Communist." Many citizens, according to their letters, are inclined to label as a "Communist" anyone who displays unusual initiative or appears aggressive. (Feb. 10, 1947)

Some of these letters from citizens, I further noted, also inquired politely why General MacArthur, whom so many citizens admired, tolerated Communists in labor unions and the Japan Communist party.

In labor affairs throughout February and March 1947, I concentrated mostly on monitoring the development of unionism among Yamanashi's teachers. Four distinct unions had emerged, although the largest by far was still the Yamanashi Teachers' Union, now composed exclusively of primary school teachers. After extensive negotiations with prefectural education and other authorities, it finally reached an agreement with the prefectural government on the details of three vital issues: the right to engage in collective bargaining, establishment of a consultative group, and the right to strike, although no one expected the teachers to exercise the last option in the foreseeable future.[29]

As part of the team's special labor information and education activities, I included numerous SCAP-prepared Japanese-language booklets on democratic trade unionism in a display of Japanese and English language materials on various subjects in the team's library reading-room, which was open to the public. A small but steady number of visitors henceforth could be seen perusing these materials.[30]

Beginning in May 1947, the time devoted to labor education would greatly increase.

9
Teaching Democracy
to Japan's Adults

Basic Objectives

SCAP's educational reform programs were not limited to primary and secondary schools and institutions of higher learning. They were also aimed at Japan's adults. Although there was no SCAP directive for adults comparable to "The Administration of the Educational System in Japan" of October 22, 1945, SCAP's Education Division did establish an Adult Education Branch, which began devising democratic goals for Japan's adults. The influential *Report of the United States Education Mission to Japan* of March 1946 gave further impetus to an adult education program:

A broad program of adult education is essential to any society that looks toward the highest development of its human resources. Stunned and scared by a disastrous war caused by military domination of the masses, the Japanese are now turning toward a new battle, with peace and world cooperation as its objectives.[1]

To redirect the intellectual and spiritual resources of Japan, the report continued, required the use of every available means to effect a wide distribution of information and ideas related to human welfare. It further recommended that

the present adult education service of the Ministry of Education be revitalized, democratized, and given the prestige of an independent department. The staff should be highly qualified in leadership and social experience. Educators should be drawn also from Japan's institutions of higher learning. It might be helpful to set up a board advisory to it, composed of men and women representing education, labor, industry, the press, and youth, together with committees of like character and function on the prefectural level.[2]

Guidelines were disseminated through various SCAP documents during the ensuing year. On February 27, 1947, SCAP's Adult Education Branch issued a nine-point statement of objectives. The goal of occupation authorities, according to this paper, should be (1) to redirect the adult population from militarism and ultranationalism towards peace and world cooperation; (2) to provide improved or new educational opportunities through evening classes in local schools, correspondence courses, university extension courses, libraries, local institutions such as citizens' public halls, and private associations; (3) to provide opportunities for technical and vocational training; (4) to stimulate adult interest in government and world affairs through radio, films, and the press; (5) to encourage formation of discussion groups fostering independent thinking and understanding of and regard for others; (6) to encourage constructive use of leisure time; (7) to encourage joint male and female participation in adult education activities; (8) to assist governmental education offices to serve as advisory agencies, but to limit their control of adult education; and (9) eventually to free adult groups from all government control and subsidies. The nine objectives should be achieved, the paper added, by encouraging the formation of youth and women's groups and Parent-Teacher Associations (PTAs), by holding art and music festivals, and by using radios, movies, and the press.[3]

Yamanashi's Youth Associations

A number of adult education programs in Yamanashi were well under way by the time the aforementioned SCAP statement was issued. As it did not cite which programs deserved the highest priority, military government CI&E officers had latitude in deciding which ones deserved the most attention. I selected youth associations, primarily as a result of two meetings in October 1946 with Russell L. Durgin, head of the Youth Organization and Student Activities Branch in SCAP's CI&E section in Tokyo.

As I noted earlier, Durgin was an "old Japan hand" who had spent many years in the country before World War II on behalf of the International Young Men's Christian Association (YMCA). When I first met him, he had just returned from Yamanashi Prefecture, where he had conferred with prefectural education officials and had talked to two newly established youth associations. Most young men from ages eighteen to thirty, he said, had served in Japan's armed forces. Upon their nation's defeat in World War II, they had returned home disillusioned and bewildered. It was important now to prevent their radicalization, as had occurred after the Meiji Restoration in 1868, when there arose small groups of highly politicized right-wing and left-wing activists. Because 80 percent of Japan's youth, male and female, received little or no secondary education during the war years, it was vital to channel their energies into constructive projects. I promised to do what I could to supplement SCAP's national youth programs in Yamanashi.

I delivered my first address before a youth association in Funatsu, Yamanashi Prefecture, on November 20. It was both sobering and enlightening (see chap. 5). Despite my desire to devote more time to the youth movement, school reform and other duties precluded my doing so for several weeks. Nonetheless, I was able to keep abreast of the movement through reports from the prefectural Education Section. They underscored the rapidity with which new youth associations were being formed. By the end of December 1946, Kofu, Yamanashi's capital had at least twenty. In the same month, twenty-seven representatives of prefectural youth associations met to listen to reports presented by delegates who had attended recently the second Japanese Youth Communication Conference in Tokyo.[4] The majority of Yamanashi's youth associations, according to other information I received, had little time to participate in community affairs.

The Japanese penchant for organization and centralization of any activity bore fruit early in 1947 when some sixty Yamanashi youth leaders laid the groundwork for a prefectural federation of youth associations. The most popular club activity was athletics. No fewer than fifty-one athletic clubs reportedly formed, mostly to play baseball, the nation's favorite sport, but with only males participating, of course. A few clubs centered around tennis or ping pong. Yamanashi's young ladies, who were represented in separate "departments" in the nascent associations, generally did not participate in athletic activities, although one girls' athletic club was reported to be active.[5]

In Yamanashi and other prefectures, the postwar youth movement was often assisted by local members of the Japanese YMCA and YWCA. These Christian-founded associations had existed long before World War II and now enjoyed, not surprisingly, a boost in membership. Members of both were now at the forefront in helping to "democratize" the young people of their country. In Yamanashi early in 1947, some of their leaders sponsored classes to explain to youths the significance of the new Constitution and to suggest ways they could help implement SCAP's adult education program. They were also instrumental in organizing the first all-prefecture youth conference in Kofu on January 19, 1947, attended by several hundred young people. I was forced to decline an invitation to deliver the opening address when I was ordered to attend a CI&E Labor Education Conference in Sendai. Another team officer read my address.[6]

During February, I managed to find time to meet occasionally in my office with youth leaders, both men and women, who sought my advice on various matters. For many, a most troubling question was how young American men and women comported themselves and "commingled." They were products of a society, of course, in which male superiority was taken for granted, and in which social, educational, and economic backgrounds or "status" defined their interactions. The concept of a relatively status-free society, as in America, was difficult for them to grasp and emulate. Group activities by both sexes, especially "dating" American-style, was completely foreign to their Confucian heritage. I was not at all sanguine about their ability to overcome in a short while this and other deeply ingrained cultural traits.

Meanwhile, youth leaders continued to espouse federation. The local YMCA and YWCA leaders had arranged for another, smaller conference confined largely to their current membership. I addressed their meeting in March, when the much-discussed plan of Yamanashi's youth leaders to create an umbrella organization to coordinate their activities and exchange information came quickly to fruition:

About 100 representatives of youth associations in Yamanashi met on March 8, 1947, in the prefectural assembly hall. This was the initial meeting to formally establish a loose federation of all young people's organizations. The federation's aim will be to encourage the development of additional autonomous youth groups in all villages and towns to engage in constructive tasks for the purpose of raising the cultural level of the prefecture.[7]

I had been consulted earlier about establishing a federation and had raised no objection, provided it steered clear of any efforts to affiliate with a political party. A handful of self-styled leaders believed that youth associations—and their federation—should be aligned with either one of two Socialist parties or with the Japan Communist party. A number of signed and unsigned letters to my office had specifically alleged that several "Mr. Sato-sans" were Socialists or several "Mr. Kato-sans" were Communists who were trying to "take over" certain youth associations.

This was not merely a local problem. During the January CI&E and Labor Education Conference in Sendai, several other military government CI&E officers informed me they, too, had encountered politicizing efforts by some youth leaders. SCAP and Eighth Army education officials sought to forestall this. An Eighth Army directive of February 16 specifically forbade youth associations from engaging in partisan politics, and I followed up by issuing a press release on the subject for the local newspapers and radio station. To the best of my knowledge, the ensuing months saw no violation of the directive, although I continued to receive occasional reports about certain individuals who believed youth associations should become politically active.

As March 1947 neared its end, Akaike Hajime joined my staff to serve as a consultant on youth organizations and religion. An elderly gentleman, Mr. Akaike had studied earlier in the century for a year or two in a school in San Francisco under the auspices of the American YMCA. Upon his return, he joined the small YMCA movement in Japan. Eventually, his duties took him to Dairen near the tip of the Liaotung Peninsula in China, after it fell under the control of the Japanese. From there he was repatriated at war's end to Yamanashi Prefecture. His advice on the problems besetting Japan's postwar youth and his assistance in working with young people in Yamanashi proved extremely helpful during the ensuing months.

Although I was unable to spend as much time with Yamanashi's youth leaders and associations as I had originally hoped, by the end of March 1947 I had attained from conversations with numerous leaders, their letters to my office, and reports from the prefectural Education Section, a general profile of the prefectural youth-association movement.

First, there was a strong propensity among all young men and women in a village, town, or city to join an association, on the assumption (generally true but never spelled out in a directive) that SCAP and military government expected all youths, especially males, to do so. Second, memberships revealed a considerable disparity in ages, from as young as fifteen to as old as thirty-five or even forty, based on a traditional belief that only older youths could give proper guidance to younger ones. Third, the first two factors accounted for the large size of most associations, from 80 to 150 members, with a handful reporting enrollments as high as 370, 450, and in one instance, 600.

Fourth, because many schools did not want youth associations to use their facilities, the majority had no satisfactory meeting places except for a room in a large teahouse, or in a Buddhist temple, or in some other building. A few had the good fortune to use one or the other of two new citizens' public halls completed by the end of January 1947.

Fifth, young men and women members of an association sat separately in meetings, with the latter deferring, as was customary, to male leaders. Sixth, all associations sorely lacked funds, a characteristic of all postwar organizations. Assessments ranged from one to five *yen* per month per member, with some groups dependent entirely upon contributions. In one instance, these came from a *tonarigumi* or neighborhood association, with the village elders also providing "excessive advice" on how young people should comport themselves. In some rural areas, the associations raised funds by selling empty tin cans, ashes for fertilizer, and vegetables from farms. (I refrained from asking if any of the last were sold at black-market prices!) Sixth, most active youth associations grouped themselves into departments according to members' interests, such as cultural, physical education (which included general recreation), and women's departments. The women's department enabled young ladies to talk about or study the finer points of flower arrangement, cooking, sewing, and other domestic subjects.

Shortly, I learned of associations with special departments for the study of health and hygiene, juvenile delinquency, agriculture, and fire prevention. Finally, it was evident by the end of March 1947 that many youth associations existed more on paper than in fact. For most rural youths not in school there was little time to attend meetings. Constant work and obtaining the necessities of life, except for a few leaders, were their lot and were made all the more necessary by the continued inflation and the deteriorating economic situation throughout Japan.

Women's Organizations

Advising and assisting Japanese women to develop new and independent democratic organizations was, as noted earlier, another important objective of SCAP's Education Division. Its Women's Education Branch was headed by Ethel B. Weed, a former English major from Western Reserve University in Cleveland, Ohio, and director of public relations of the Women's City Club in Cleveland before she became a WAC first lieutenant during World War II.

It was difficult for the vast majority of Japanese women to become accustomed to exercising their new democratic franchise, despite the support of SCAP directives, the revised Japanese Civil Code and other legislation, and the new Constitution. Women's subordinate status in the nation's social order had long been cemented in a Confucian culture and by tradition. The magnitude of SCAP's problem in raising the social and educational status of women was underscored in a SCAP survey completed in late summer of 1946. Nationwide, it showed, only 23 percent of women had schooling beyond the sixth grade, and only 0.4 percent had attended a university.[8]

Although prewar Japan possessed women's colleges in every prefecture, primarily for training public school teachers, there were no women's universities. Thus any who managed to enter a university found themselves in an all-male institution. Nonetheless, many women cherished a strong desire to participate more prominently in the political life of Japan. This was demonstrated vividly in the first major postwar election of April 10, 1946, when women exercised their new political franchise by winning thirty-nine seats, all from urban areas, in the House of Representatives in the Japanese Diet. It was a heady beginning. Most women of Yamanashi Prefecture were aware of this revolutionary change, but few were prepared to challenge their male "superiors."

Although Eighth Army was recruiting women's affairs officers for military government teams, none had been assigned to my office. Thus I had virtually no time to address newly established women's groups. I met periodically, however, with a representative of the prefectural Education Section who handled women's affairs and with several small groups of women leaders who came to my office. I also asked the local newspapers and radio station to publicize SCAP-prepared articles on the subject of women's new rights in Japan. Even though no women's affairs officer was in sight, circumstances suddenly dictated in February 1947 that I accept an invitation to address a recently established group in Kofu because the wife of Yamanashi Prefecture's governor would be present. The meeting was for the purpose of "advancing women's education and culture."

The event proved quite different from what I expected. We met in a large, elegant room used, apparently, for very special occasions. The polished floor gleamed with *tatami* mats, and every alcove contained a magnificent cloisonné vase filled with carefully arranged flowers.

On each wall hung a delicately painted *kakemono*, with a particularly beautiful one displayed in the room's main alcove. In front of the alcove was a lovely black and gold lacquered table rising only a few inches from the tatami-covered floor. To my surprise there were no more than thirty or so ladies, all attired in colorful kimonos and with their hair elaborately coiffed. The only nonsurprise was the hostess, the wife of the prefectural governor. Upon my arrival, she introduced me to the others present, all wives of ranking prefectural officials whose status was clearly sufficient to warrant an invitation to this august event. If my interpreter's post-meeting observation was correct, the ladies desired a close look at the Yamanashi Military Government Team's civilian CI&E officer, whose name appeared frequently in their local newspapers and about whom they had heard from prefectural officials, school principals, teachers, and other citizens.

My prepared address was on "The Role of Women in a Democracy." I discussed first the development of women's suffrage worldwide and in America, then some of the activities of a women's club in Oregon (to which my mother belonged), such as providing clothes or other aid to the poor, discussing school and other community matters, and listening to an occasional speaker. (I avoided any mention of the club's patriotic efforts during World War II in selling U.S. War Bonds to local citizens to raise money to defeat the Axis powers of Germany, Italy, and Japan, with my mother winning a special award for selling the most bonds!) When I finished, I received soft, perfunctory applause. There were only two or three questions. Clearly, my distinguished audience had something else on its mind.

The "something else" was a tea ceremony. Had I ever witnessed one, the hostess asked? I had not. Surely, she said, I would wish to remain to see how it was done. Fearful of a grave setback to the women's movement in Yamanashi if I said "I have to get back to the office," I replied in the affirmative. Following some rather elaborate preparations which one of the ladies explained as they proceeded, the tea ceremony began with much grace and aplomb. As my notes on this memorable event fail to convey its unique elegance, I quote instead from Basil Hall Chamberlain's classic book, *Things Japanese*, published at the turn of the century:

The tea used is in the form not of tea leaves but of powder so that the resulting beverage resembles pea soup in colour and consistency. There is a thicker kind called *kocha* and a thinner kind called *usa-cha*.

The tea is made and drunk in a preternaturally slow and formal manner, each action, each gesture, being fixed by an elaborate code of rules. Every article connected with the ceremony, such as the tea canister, the incense burner, the hanging scroll, the bouquet of flowers in the alcove, is either handled or admired at a distance, in ways and phrases which unalterable usage prescribes.[9]

Upon completion of the ceremony, amidst delicate applause, there was much whispering among the ladies who had participated in it and the hostess. The subject of their exchanges was conveyed to my interpreter who, in turn, asked me: "Would you be willing to perform the tea ceremony?" Astonished, I demurred. After consultation with the hostess, she said: "They will feel honored if you do. One of the ladies will assist." I was trapped. So, with a gorgeously bedecked lady at my side, I tried to imitate as best I could the ceremony I had just witnessed amidst many smiles, murmurs, and titters. As I, an American in a business suit, completed the unfamiliar rite, my audience expressed its approbation by prolonged, gentle clapping of hands, bows, smiles, and nodding of heads. Then, after the hostess congratulated me on my talk and expressed her appreciation for my participating in the tea ceremony, I took my leave amidst many bows, thank you's, and good-byes. Thus ended my apprenticeship in a highly esteemed Japanese cultural event.

It had been a long afternoon. In a letter to a friend, I described the highlights of the tea ceremony in rather earthy terms, especially my physical reaction to drinking the ceremonial tea. "It tasted," I wrote, "like wet, crushed alfalfa hay which fortunately did not give me dysentery." Furthermore, "I felt like a barbarian intruding on an ancient and exquisitely beautiful mystic rite." Returning to my office, I pondered what to say to the team commander if he inquired about my prolonged absence, and whether he would believe that I had spent most of the afternoon witnessing and participating in an elaborate tea ceremony. Fortunately for me, he was closeted with a couple of visiting Eighth Army officers. In the team's monthly report, I merely noted that I had addressed the "Kofu Educational and Cultural Society."

Parent-Teacher Associations

A third SCAP adult education program called for the establishment of American-style Parent Teacher Associations. The acronym PTA quickly became a Japanese household word. The *Report of the United States Education Mission to Japan*, in recommending the decentralization of the Japanese educational system, had referred rather obliquely to this type of organization. It suggested only that lay educational agencies encourage "the organization of parents and teachers to promote child welfare and improve the educational process" (*Report*, pp. 30–31). Nor did SCAP directives initially mandate PTAs, but SCAP's top educational officials in Tokyo soon signaled the Ministry of Education that the coming decentralization of education in Japan should include at least something akin to them. Not until February 1947, however, did military government CI&E officers receive specific Eighth Army orders to provide assistance in the development of Parent-Teacher Associations, to be democratically established and operated.

In truth, organizations called PTAs began to appear early in 1946, but these in reality were slightly revamped versions of traditional "school supporters" or "school maintenance" societies. These societies met only two or three times a year, as special occasions to enable the parents to listen to the school principal and a head teacher reporting on the school's progress and activities and on any problems that may have arisen. Parents listened respectfully and rarely questioned what their educational peers had to say. Impending decentralization of education would now require parents, in cooperation with principals and teachers, to participate more actively in the educational process. Uncertainty over how to proceed led, I noted, to some variations in establishing new PTAS:

Some schools have established new parents' organizations by districts (*Guns*). Under this arrangement, teachers meet parents in only one district at a time. A few other schools have established special parents' committees who meet with teachers. In a third instance, parents with students in a particular school class have met with their teachers.

Many new parents' organizations have been very active and have gone to great lengths to help alleviate the poverty of local teachers. In addition, a few have engaged in heated controversies with certain leaders of the Yamanashi Teachers' Union.[10]

The verbal clashes with leaders of the Yamanashi Teachers' Union stemmed primarily from a pervasive parental dislike of most of the tactics of Socialists, radical Socialists, and Communists. In the battle for better salaries and other benefits, teachers were required frequently to interrupt their instruction during the school day to discuss or vote on some immediate teachers' union proposal.

Notwithstanding the reports of changes in the functioning of parents' committees, the anchor of tradition was holding fast in early 1947 when I had occasion to address two groups purporting to be PTAs. I wrote as follows in a letter:

> The presidents of two associations were local village headmen who appeared in winged collars and swallowtail coats and addressed their segregated audiences—women seated on the left, men on the right—in an officious manner. After expressing thanks on my behalf for SCAP's many democratic reforms and invoking the spirit of the New Education, each then declared their new PTAs officially "organized."
>
> At both meetings, officers of the new PTA were introduced without the benefit of debate or ballot. All were men. Then I was introduced to give my talk. (Feb. 25, 1947)

At each meeting, I summarized the objectives of the school reforms and focused on the coming decentralization of the Japanese educational system (beginning April 1, 1947) which would herald the new school year. I also cited highlights of the pending Japanese legislation; namely, the School Education Law and the Fundamental Law of Education, which would come into force in March 1947 and would initiate the 6–3–3–4 educational structure.

As decentralization was implemented, boards of education would be established (starting April 1, 1948), first at the prefectural and major city level, and then progressively in smaller cities, towns, and villages. This would require very active PTAs, from whose ranks would come board members responsible for upholding educational standards, certifying the qualifications of teachers, approving textbooks for students, arranging for in-service teacher-training programs, establishing new schools, and approving the establishment of private schools. The Ministry of Education's role would be limited largely to setting educational standards, distributing education funds approved by the Diet, and providing advice rather than dictating how new school buildings should be constructed or what type of textbooks every school should use.

Members of both PTAs, it was evident, were greatly troubled by these forthcoming educational changes. They asked in various ways: "Don't education officials, principals, and teachers know better than we how children should be taught?" The concept of local school boards was strange and unsettling to my listeners. The fact that America had thousands of city, town, or district school boards failed to impress my audiences (in previous weeks, both prefectural education officials and citizens who came to my office had already expressed their apprehensions about local school boards). By March 1947, I was developing some reservations about the feasibility of the boards, especially at the small-town and village level in a rural prefecture. I would have more occasions to discuss the role of PTAs and school boards at conferences in the ensuing months.

Citizens' Public Halls

A fourth adult education program developed by SCAP's Adult Education Branch called for the construction in every community in Japan of a citizens' public hall, or CPH as they popularly became known. The halls, SCAP's education specialists believed, would strengthen grassroots democracy and would not be encumbered by heavy bureaucratic hands at either the national or prefectural government levels. They produced a twelve-page document, dated July 1, 1946, and sent copies to all military government units then in existence, and to all prefectural government education offices through the Ministry of Education. It set forth soaring goals:

A citizens' public hall (CPH) should be opened in all cities, towns, and villages throughout the country where people may assemble to talk, discuss, and read books in order to obtain information about their work and life in general and cultivate friendship.

The CPH is a cultural organization . . . a fountainhead of local progress and development by way of being a link between various associations and organizations.

The initiative should not be taken by official hands but left to civilians who will betake themselves to cooperate with each other, combine their advice and originality, and contribute from their own purse to the support of the institution. . . . The CPH is to be . . . born of the people's wishes and cooperation and supported ideally by their own purse and brain.[11]

Each CPH, the document continued, should consist initially of four departments: general culture, library, industry, and social gathering. Once established, three other departments could be added: physical training, social work, and health and welfare. Facilities "proportionate to scale" should consist of classrooms, a drawing room, an auditorium, a reading room, a specimens room, a place of worship, and rooms for recreation. A children's playground should be adjacent to the halls. The halls should contain variously a movie projector, a magic lantern for slides, wireless sets, corn-powdering and threshing machines, electrical-repair equipment and other tools needed to teach trades, and other items. Finally, the CPH document contained instructions on how to make the halls a "beehive" of community activity.

I was unable to give much attention to the CPH program during my first two months in Yamanashi Prefecture. A report indicated that the first CPH was completed on November 3, 1946, but I had no time to visit it. Re-reading SCAP's CPH document at year's end, it was obvious its author had never visited rural Japan, where citizens and local officials were faced with a variety of pressing needs in an inflation-wracked economy—building more classrooms, raising funds to replace hundreds of missing or cracked school windows, supplementing teachers' salaries, and the like. To the extent a CPH program had begun, all planning and funding were provided directly or indirectly by the Ministry of Education or the Yamanashi prefectural government, with local citizens merely "consulted" on where a CPH should be built. Nonetheless the program moved forward, and a second CPH was completed in January 1947. In the same month, prefectural education and village officials in five *Guns* held meetings and established as their goal the construction of forty halls in Yamanashi.[12]

After the first two halls were built, there was little money to pay for a staff and all of the equipment SCAP's Adult Education Branch deemed essential. After several more were completed, I visited one upon its dedication with the team commander, who delivered a short speech I had drafted for him. Although they were largely bereft of equipment, the CPHs were utilized quickly by youth, women's, and other organizations, thus fulfilling one of the purposes for which they were built.

Educational Exhibitions

A fifth adult education program, but one which often included students of all ages, consisted of periodic exhibitions in the reading room of the Yamanashi Military Government Team headquarters. Its purpose, as noted earlier, was to stimulate local cultural and educational interest and to demonstrate how communities, on their own initiative, could sponsor and prepare an exhibit without a directive or guidance from the national or prefectural government. In short, it was to encourage local decision-making as befitted a democracy.

Three exhibitions had been held in team headquarters prior to my arrival in Yamanashi. Two consisted of SCAP-provided photographs of atrocities committed by Nazi Germany contrasted with scenes of American life. The third featured paintings by a Mr. Yamamoto, a local artist. I soon expanded the program and was fortunate to have as my assistant in this endeavor the Miss Aramaki, mentioned earlier, who demonstrated unusual talent in planning exhibitions, most scheduled for five-day showings, plus the assistance of two enlisted men on my staff. After their initial showing in team headquarters, most exhibits were then displayed in towns in other parts of the prefecture.

In December 1946, in cooperation with a number of primary and middle school art teachers, Miss Aramaki assembled a collection of 400 pieces of student crayon drawings, many of which were mounted in the reading room of the team's library. Committees of art judges were appointed. The local newspapers and the radio station publicized the event. Hundreds of students, teachers, and citizens viewed the collection by young artists of every grade level which depicted their rural surroundings: mountains, forests, farm fields, farm and village houses, village streets, temples, shrines, bridges, and portraits of fellow students. After the judges determined the best entries by grade, age, and gender, the team's commanding officer presented a trove of awards, numbering thirty for primary students and twenty for those in middle school. For us Americans, the talent of so many youngsters was remarkable, none of us having been taught art in our schools as were children in Japan. The exhibition was a fine, morale-boosting event.[13]

This was not the end of this particular exhibit. Through personal contacts in the United States, I sent dozens of the most outstanding art pieces to public schools and/or museums in Portland, Oregon; Chicago, Illinois; Omaha, Nebraska; and Westchester County, New York. School and museum officials were profuse in their thanks for the opportunity of showing the collection, and they sent in return American school art, which was displayed throughout Yamanashi Prefecture in August 1947.[14]

Interestingly enough, only one museum refused to exhibit the Japanese art collection—New York City's Museum of Modern Art. A friend of mine in New York, however, managed to arrange for showings of the art at the elementary school attached to Columbia University, and at the Lincoln and Horace Mann elementary schools also in New York City.[15]

In February 1947 there was a paper-manufacturing exhibit. It was timely because, since the end of World War II, paper for commercial use was severely in short supply. Toilet tissue and screens were both top-priority items for every home and office, and high demand forced citizens to pay a steep price on the black market. The shortage gave a boost to numerous papermaking craftsmen, who produced varying grades of high-quality paper from rice, bamboo, and other products for personal and commercial uses. Two gifted craftsmen volunteered their services for the exhibit. One was Kobayashi Yashijiro of Ichikawa, who discoursed every day on his papermaking tools, his drawings, and the art of papermaking to large crowds of citizens of all ages. The second was Goto Sikichiro, an artist and papermaker from Fukiyama City in nearby Shizuoka Prefecture. He also lectured daily on the finer points of his trade.[16]

In the same month, Miss Aramaki assembled in the team's library another very popular exhibit of archeological artifacts found locally. Several of Yamanashi's archeologists, most of them amateurs, proudly displayed some of their most recent and noteworthy acquisitions in addition to those found in earlier decades and borrowed from small museums. Many of the artifacts, dating back 1,000 or more years, consisted of arrows and hooks carved from bones and rocks by ancient hunters and fishermen, various kinds of pottery, primitive art drawings, and other relics of early life in the area that became Yamanashi Prefecture. The archeologists explained the significance of their collections, which were supplemented by posters and drawings depicting the early civilizations that made them. Several thousand citizens of all ages were willing to stand in line before entering the jammed reading room during this unusual one-week showing.[17]

March featured a handicraft display with hundreds of primary school students contributing items they had fashioned from bamboo. Prize-winning examples of bamboo handicraft were sent to YWCA headquarters in Tokyo, where they were shown for a more extended period. In the same month, the indefatigable Miss Aramaki organized for photography buffs an exhibit titled "Winter Scenes in Yamanashi." Again a committee, consisting in this instance of local artists, reviewed the photos, selected the best, and the team commander awarded prizes to those whose entries were deemed the most beautiful, unique, or possessed of the greatest artistic merit. Mt. Fuji, not surprisingly, was the focal point of many a photographer's camera lens.[18]

Finally, Japanese movie theaters throughout Yamanashi continued during the first three months of 1947 to show special American films for adults and students alike. As noted earlier, special educational documentaries were selected by scap's Motion Picture and Theatrical Branch and were shown free to students (but not to adults) as a "public service" by theater owners. Kofu, in February 1947, added a fifth theater, attesting to the popularity of American, British, and French films as well as Japanese movies in the early postwar period. For thousands of citizens, films offered a brief escape from the harsh struggle for existence in early postwar Japan.

One of the more important American documentary films shown in this period was *Tuesday in November*, depicting how American citizens elected their president, vice-president, and members of congress, as well as officials of state, county, city, and town governments. The effectiveness of the special documentary films was difficult to assess. As in earlier documentaries, when asked about them, students were wont to note mostly how wealthy and comfortable Americans appeared to be— the large homes, the lawns, the modern kitchens, the beautiful schools, and other common items of an affluent society. Many young girls said they aspired someday to own a large washing machine; young boys, an American car. Most adults, when questioned whether they had seen a regular American film, likewise were impressed by America's material standard of living. The democratic message of the documentaries and full-length American films thus often was eclipsed by the vivid contrast between "rich" Americans and "poor" Japanese.

To improve the coordination of the diverse adult education programs, the prefectural government in March 1947 upgraded its social education office to a Social Education Section. The section's mission was defined as the furtherance of such adult education projects as educational films, and the establishment of citizens' public halls, youth and women's organizations, and ptas. Its immediate task was to publicize the four national, prefectural, and local elections scheduled for April, and to assume full responsibility for the ongoing effort to popularize the new Constitution, which would come into force in May.[19]

10

The Conundrum of Religious Freedom

Basic Religious Policies

Except for a discussion of SCAP's directive of December 15, 1945, abolishing State Shintoism in Japan, I had received no detailed briefings on the subject of the separation of religion and the state, now mandated by occupation authorities. By the end of November 1946, the first month of my CI&E duties after joining the Yamanashi Military Government Team, I had dealt with two religion/state violations. One concerned the failure of a village headman to remove completely a *hoanden* shrine, which formerly contained the portrait of the Emperor, from the entrance to a primary school. The second involved a primary school principal who led his students during a school day to a sect Shinto shrine to perform a religious rite (see chap. 5). Soon other religion/state issues arose. They would prove to be more numerous and complex than I had anticipated.

Forced suddenly to familiarize myself more with the background leading to establishing religious freedom in Japan, I found that plans to ensure it flowed from two documents preceding any SCAP directives on the subject: the Potsdam Declaration of July 26, 1945, and the U.S. Initial Post-Surrender Policy for Japan of September 6 of the same year.[1] After the onset of the occupation, SCAP issued before the end of 1945 a landmark Civil Liberties directive on October 4, followed soon by four other directives specifically addressing the subject of religious freedom and/or the separation of religion from the state. The last and most famous of this initial series, issued on December 15 and cited earlier, abolished at one stroke the institution of State Shintoism. It also prohibited indirect as well as direct participation in and support for sect Shinto, which was permitted to exist by public officials at all levels of government, and mandatory collection of funds for any religious purposes—Shinto, Buddhist, or Christian.[2]

Neighborhood Associations and Religious Solicitations

Establishing religious freedom by fiat did not ensure that long-ingrained religious, social, cultural, and political habits of the Japanese could be changed overnight. This was especially true with respect to the activities of neighborhood associations, which existed in every village, town, and city throughout the nation and which often continued to violate SCAP's directives requiring the separation of religion and the state. The nature of these associations and the reasons so many persisted in breaching the religion/state separation requires a brief explanation.

At the lowest level, a neighborhood association consisted of a collection of six to thirteen households (*tonarigumi*) headed by a chief. In rural areas, groups of *tonarigumis* were called *burakukais*. In urban areas, the chief of several *tonarigumis* was the *chonaikai-cho*. These sociological groupings had a long history dating back many centuries in China, where they existed under different names and possessed the character of quasi-government entities. Along with other facets of China's culture, neighborhood associations became an integral part of Japanese society until the Meiji era, beginning in 1868, which witnessed the formation of a national, modern government. Although the associations continued to exist, they were not supported by the central government in Tokyo through 1939.[3]

In 1940, Japan's ruling cabinets were becoming increasingly militaristic as the nation prepared for possible war with the West. The government placed the associations under the control of the Home Ministry, which employed them as the lowest branch of local government in close association with the newly founded Imperial Rule Assistance Association (IRAA), an ultranationalist organization established to replace political parties and convert Japan to a one-party state.

In peaceful eras, neighborhood associations performed useful functions for local, prefectural, and national authorities by disseminating information about new laws and ordinances, obtaining census data, and administering public welfare. Villages and towns especially relied on them to collect money to support local celebrations of the spring equinox and the autumn harvest festival, and for the support of local Shinto shrines and Buddhist temples. As World War II approached and then began, the associations played a vital role in furthering the central government's militaristic and ultranationalistic goals of spreading official propaganda, ferreting out political dissidents, selling war bonds, rationing scarce commodities, and organizing civil defense. It is fair to say that when Allied forces arrived in Japan in September 1945, most Japanese citizens could not conceive how to get things done efficiently without their neighborhood associations.

More Religious Violations

Despite their role in aiding the war effort, SCAP initially did not abolish the neighborhood associations. Its Religions Division in Tokyo was slow to realize that associations continued to violate the SCAP prohibitions against collection of funds for periodic religious celebrations and for supporting local Shinto shrines and Buddhist temples. To be sure, many Japanese citizens understood that the "old way" of raising funds was no longer permissible. They often sent signed or unsigned letters to SCAP headquarters and to military government units and teams citing instances of "wrongdoing," especially the "forcible" collection of money from households. By November 1946, the Yamanashi Military Government Team had received about thirty such complaints.[4] A typical letter (translated in team headquarters) might read as follows:

> At Autumn Shinto festival, some people were forced to make big contribution by leader of our town. Boss of every street made his followers go house to house to collect ten *yen* in the least and 100 *yen* on basis of people's tax, all of which was spent for sake, food, and dramatic party of which people are now complaining.
>
> I beg of you to investigate the matter and give a most severe punishment for social restraint against these supporters of feudalism who forced people to make a religious contribution.[5]

The money collected, the letter added, was also used to pay for the salaries of Shinto priests and for other festival expenses.

That same month, the Japanese government promulgated the new Constitution, which contained in Article 20 a ringing endorsement of religious freedom. The article stated in part: "No person shall be compelled to take part in any religious act, celebration, rite or practice. The State and its organs shall refrain from religious education or any other religious activity." It was thus logical for SCAP to act against neighborhood associations still soliciting funds for religious purposes. SCAP instructed the Japanese government to cease this practice but, interestingly, limited the injunction only to activities on behalf of sect Shinto.[6] On November 26, 1946, Eighth Army headquarters in Yokohama sent the specifics of SCAP's order (directive 90) to all military government teams, districts, and other commands in Japan. It instructed them to "exercise surveillance" and "take immediate steps to publicize the fact that the use of neighborhood associations to collect offerings and distribute amulets and charms for Shinto shrines constituted a violation of SCAP's directive of December 15, 1945, abolishing State Shintoism."

Although the Japanese government at the national and local level as well as military government teams throughout Japan publicized the order, the practice still continued in many areas. In Yamanashi Prefecture, in December 1946, citizens complained of an association fundraising which had raised about 6,000 *yen* from 156 households for a Shinto shrine festival, with the proceeds earmarked for street decorations, shrine accessories such as incense and amulets, and food and drink.

In January 1947, I brought these complaints to the attention of the prefectural Penal Affairs Office. The local police immediately jailed the former *chonaikai-cho* (association head) and began an investigation of the fundraising activities of his four assistants. Meanwhile, several citizens had also come to my office to criticize the activities of the former *chonaikai-cho*. Our conversation indicated that the problem was more complex than it first appeared. Most illuminating was the strong personal dislike my visitors bore toward the "bossy" *chonaikai-cho* and his assistants; in fact, this personal antipathy outweighed their concern that SCAP's directives had been violated.

To my surprise, they indicated that most fellow-citizens wished to proceed with the planned Shinto festival. Did they understand the difference between a forcible and a voluntary contribution for a religious festival, or for the upkeep of a local shrine, I asked? Their replies were ambiguous. What type of punishment did the *chonaikai-cho* threaten against citizens who did not wish to contribute to the festival's expenses? Again, there were vague replies amounting to a simple admission they wished to avoid a confrontation with him. They wanted military government to "correct" the problem by dismissing him from his position.

In the event, the *chonaikai-cho* was soon released from jail and his four assistants were reprimanded by the police. At my request, the three local newspapers and the local radio station gave considerable publicity to this violation of SCAP's directive on religious freedom. I also issued a special press release underscoring the significance of Articles 20 and 89 of the new Constitution mandating the separation of religion from the state. I explained again the difference between a voluntary and involuntary contribution. Yamanashi's citizens, I hoped, would now grasp the importance of religious freedom, especially the need to maintain a wall between religion and the state, as in America.

My expectations were unfulfilled. Almost immediately two additional complaints arose about "forceful" fundraising by former association officials to support local Shinto shrines. Both men had asked for contributions ranging from about 5 to 35 *yen* per household and, according to several letters from citizens, were "intimidating" in their requests for money. I sent the two cases to the prefectural Penal Affairs Office for further investigation and, if necessary, action; I issued another press release on SCAP's directive and restated the provisions of the new Constitution.

Illegal fundraising for religious purposes was not confined solely to citizens residing near a local Shinto shrine. A fourth case arose when several citizens near a small Buddhist temple complained about an official of a neighborhood association and his assistants who were raising money to erect a small monument. Using tax records, they had divided fifty-seven households of the association into six grades, according to ability to pay. Those in the sixth, or lowest, grade were asked to contribute a minimum of 50 *yen*, and those in the highest or first grade, a minimum of 500 *yen*. This time some of the citizens' letters expressed concern lest the fundraising violated SCAP's religious directive. Once more I referred the case to the prefectural Penal Affairs Office, but this time one of its officials made an interesting reply. The complainants, he said, "seriously misunderstood" the "new" village fundraising system, as the solicitors had merely "suggested" rather than "demanded" what each household should contribute. His answer was illogical because the "suggested" payments were based, as usual, on local tax records and thus were essentially coercive. To further clarify the matter, I issued another press release which stated that collecting funds based on local tax records to support Shinto shrines and Buddhist temples was illegal, and I differentiated once more between "voluntary" and "involuntary" contributions. This elicited a letter from the headman of the village where the monument was to have been erected. He expressed regret about the manner of fundraising and promised to desist thereafter.

The foregoing problem was not unique to Yamanashi Prefecture, of course. It was discussed informally at the January 1947 SCAP and military government CI&E and Labor Education conference at IXth Corps headquarters in Sendai attended by all CI&E officers from fifteen military government teams and two military government regions. Several CI&E attendees generally agreed that the most common violation occurred when present or former heads of *tonarigumis* continued the traditional practice of assessing each household an annual sum to maintain a local Shinto shrine and support Shinto festivals.

Several weeks later in Tokyo, I discussed this particular problem with William P. Woodard of the Religions Division of SCAP's CI&E section. He agreed that the "forcible" collection of money for Shinto shrines and festivals was indeed a pervasive problem, given Japan's cultural and religious traditions. He was also aware that SCAP's directive of November 6, 1946 (with the specifics relayed by Eighth Army on November 26 to all military government teams) banning such solicitations applied only to Shintoism and not to Buddhist temples, an omission that he and other SCAP officials were "looking into." To my inquiry if the majority of Japanese citizens might never consent to abandoning the traditional practices of neighborhood associations insofar as they were related to supporting local Shinto shrines and Buddhist temples, Mr. Woodard opined that SCAP and military government teams nonetheless should continue to try to teach the Japanese the importance of separating religion and the state in their social and political activities.

The Case of the Buddhist Chaplain

During late February and March 1947 I received complaints about another unusual religion/state problem which I summarized briefly in a team report:

A Buddhist chaplain from a Tokyo prison has been addressing students in many primary schools on how to prevent juvenile delinquency. The chaplain always ends his lectures by extolling the merits of the Buddhist faith and the value of a talisman, to prevent juvenile delinquency, which he sells to students at a cost of one *yen* each. He sells an average of 150 talismans at each school.[7]

Three concerned teachers, from a school where the chaplain had spoken, had conferred with me on the subject. To allow the students to purchase the talismans, they said, the school principal temporarily suspended classes, believing this action would violate neither SCAP's directives nor the new Japanese laws and Constitution, soon to come into effect, mandating the separation of religion and the state. The teachers desired to know if the principal's action had been "correct."

Claiming to speak for their fellow faculty members in the school, the teachers believed the chaplain had violated SCAP's religious directives. Nevertheless, they also believed that the chaplain's talk had been very constructive, in light of the lack of discipline in the school under the New Education, and especially since SCAP had banned any resumption of the traditional course on morals. Perhaps, they suggested, the chaplain could continue his good work if he cited the merits of all three religious faiths in Japan: Confucianism, Buddhism, and Christianity.

My reply, of course, was no. I tried to assure my visitors, however, that once the New Education was fully implemented, discipline would return to the classrooms and juvenile delinquency would decline. They left unconvinced, I fear, of my assurances. I then instructed the prefectural Education Section to inform the schools that the chaplain should cease his lectures in schools during the school day. The Education Section complied, but in a characteristic manner: According to its instruction, the chaplain could no longer talk to students on juvenile delinquency nor sell talismans to students "by order of the military government," rather than because he had violated the principle of the separation of religion from the state. It was one more instance of prefectural officials separating themselves from an unpopular decision.

Nichiren Buddhist Headquarters in Minobu

In February 1947 I inspected for the first time the headquarters of the Nichiren Buddhist sect in Minobu, Yamanashi Prefecture, the only indigenous Buddhist sect in Japan's history up to this time. My inspection was not in response to any citizen complaints of the activities of its priests, but to determine if Nichirenism's prewar and wartime reputation for inspiring militaristic and ultranationalist feelings still merited concern.

The sect's founder, Nichiren, lived from A.D. 1222 to 1282. Like the founders of most new religions or offshoots of existing ones, he possessed a dynamic personality and preached against the prevalent social corruption and the worship of false gods. His followers multiplied rapidly and his particular type of Buddhism, including divergent sects that eventually arose, had great influence in the ensuing centuries. Compared with other types of Buddhism extant in Japan, Nichirenism was less tolerant and more nationalistic. During Japan's march towards greater military power early in the twentieth century, some of the more noted political zealots were adherents of Nichiren Buddhism.

In preparation for the eventual defeat and occupation of Japan, the U.S. Army's 1944 *Civil Affairs Handbook* on education in Japan, published for American and Allied forces, characterized as follows the inherent danger of Nichirenism:

> Of the various Buddhist sects, Nichiren is the most fanatical. It is the only important [Buddhist] sect of Japanese origin. The thesis that Japan must lead a worldwide revival of Buddhism is imbedded deeply in its theology. Among the more fanatical and violent nationalists of recent years have been a considerable proportion of Nichiren adherents.[8]

To cite one instance of this sect's importance, the Japanese modern era witnessed the rise of a "Blood Brotherhood." Among its thirteen leading members, several were known to be directly or indirectly influenced by Nichiren's teachings. In February and May 1932, they assassinated a Japanese prime minister, a finance minister, and the managing director of the Mitsui Holding Company.[9]

Thus, during my briefings in October 1946, I was asked to "keep an eye" on the Nichiren sect. After assuming my duties with the Yamanashi Military Government Team the following month, however, I learned that the sect had created no discernible problem in Yamanashi or elsewhere in Japan since the onset of the occupation. In fact on October 25, 1946, or roughly a week prior to my arrival in Kofu, the sect had celebrated the 650th birthday of Nichiren, the militant founder, and among the attendees who gathered at Minobu in Yamanashi Prefecture were members of the Japanese Christian clergy.[10] In February 1947, while traveling in the Minobu area on official business, I decided to make a quick inspection of Nichiren headquarters.

As was my custom, I arrived without prior announcement. I was greeted warmly by several robed priests who showed me the main structures associated with the founder of Nichiren. These included the three main buildings or "Three Gates," the "Enlightened Steps" numbering 287, and the mausoleum where the founder was interred. I also walked quickly through its middle school and college. On the basis of my brief observations and talks with several priests, I discerned no evidence of a revival of militarism or ultranationalism. The school and college appeared to be operating in compliance with SCAP's directives on education and religion for private institutions. I would obtain more data on Nichiren headquarters and conduct a more thorough inspection of its educational and other activities later in 1947 (see chap. 18).

11

Political Interlude: Surveillance of the April 1947 Elections

Early Postwar Election Developments

In March 1947 Eighth Army headquarters instructed all military government teams in Japan to prepare to oversee, in their respective prefectures, four national and local elections scheduled for the month of April. Members of the Yamanashi Military Government Team would, of course, participate. The elections would constitute a major step toward decentralizing political power in the nation.

This was not Japan's first postwar election. The first, held in April 1946, witnessed the selection of a new House of Representatives in the Japanese Diet. In the preceding seven months, dating from September 1945 when the occupation began, numerous SCAP directives laid the groundwork for a major change in the country's system of governance. Two were especially pertinent. One was the Civil Liberties directive of October 1945, requiring the government to abrogate all laws and ordinances restricting freedom of thought, religion, speech, assembly, and other measures including the release of all prisoners detained for their political and other beliefs.[1] The second was the sweeping "purge" directive of January 1946, removing or excluding from office seven categories of personnel adjudged as "militarists" or "ultranationalists."[2] In March 1946, General MacArthur announced that the Emperor and the Japanese government would submit to the people later that year a new Constitution granting universal suffrage and other democratic reforms.[3] It would replace the Meiji Constitution of 1890 and would make the Emperor, who had renounced his divinity in January 1946, a constitutional monarch and "a symbol of the state."

Meanwhile, in preparation for the election, the Japanese government in December 1945 revised its 1925 Manhood Suffrage Law (commonly called the election law), which had granted voting rights only to men, age twenty-five and older. The revised law included women and lowered the voting age to twenty years and the age for political candidates to twenty-five years.[4]

SCAP's most significant action preceding the April 10, 1946, election was the January 4 purge directive, which disqualified about 90 percent of the existing membership in the Japanese Diet plus 200 members of the Progressive party, the strongest conservative political party. It also barred from holding public office nearly 400 top bureaucrats in the powerful Ministry of Home Affairs and most ranking public servants who held office between July 1937 and September 1945. It was a tremendous sweep of the political broom (this and subsequent purge actions would eventually make nearly 211,000 citizens ineligible for public office). Meanwhile, new political parties mushroomed (including a revived Communist party) until they totaled about 368, although the majority of candidates for public office for the first postwar election were of moderate to conservative political persuasion and wore traditional party labels.5

To prevent or minimize voting irregularities during the April 10, 1946, election, SCAP instructed Eighth Army headquarters in Yokohama to exercise surveillance of voting precincts twice, on the day of the balloting and on the following day during ballot counting. This was to be done by small military government and other tactical units throughout Japan.

Although each surveillance unit filled out a form to record its observations of the election process and to note any voting or ballot-counting irregularities, this data has never been summarized. SCAP reported that the units visited about 90 percent of the urban and 40 percent of the rural precincts. There are extant, however, some brief observations by an officer on a military government detachment in Yamanashi Prefecture, a rural prefecture with a population of about 850,000. At the voting precincts he visited, he found the demeanor of election officials "businesslike and wholesome." Several days later, after talking to several prefectural intellectuals, he penned a more somber assessment. They believed, he said,

that a true representative vote was not achieved except for two of the five Representatives elected to the Diet from Yamanashi. There had been insufficient time for voters to weigh the issues and the candidates. "Old style" politicians reportedly still possessed the balance of power. Perhaps the best that can be said is that the election was quite fair and about as good as possible given the short time to prepare for it.6

Intellectuals in other prefectures and cities, including Tokyo and some American specialists on Japan, held the same view. Nonetheless, democratic change was in the wind. Nearly 2,700 candidates campaigned for the 466 seats in the House of Representatives, and 306 were elected to the Diet for the first time, including 39 women. General MacArthur quickly invited the ladies to his office, where he congratulated them on their achievement. Another encouraging democratic omen was the 74 percent national turnout of the eligible electorate. A moderate to conservative coalition of Liberal and Progressive party members emerged to form a new government, with Yoshida Shigeru as prime minister.[7]

Preparations for the April 1947 Elections

A more significant political milestone in postwar Japan occurred during the four separate elections held a year later in April 1947, primarily to decentralize political power. In addition to selecting new members for the Diet, Japan's citizens would vote to elect 46 prefectural governors (heretofore appointed by the Home Ministry), 209 city mayors, 1,784 town mayors, 8,522 village headmen, and representatives to prefectural, city, town, and village assemblies.[8]

Prior to the elections, the 1925 election law was further amended in January 1947, and two emerging pieces of Japanese legislation, both effective May 3, would give the elections additional legitimacy. One was a new Local Autonomy Law, which required metropolitan, district, urban and rural prefectures, cities, towns, and villages to come under local public bodies.[9] The other was the new Constitution, especially Articles 93 and 94. The latter article specifically gave public entities the right "to manage their property, affairs, and administration and enact their own regulations within law." In addition, the second phase of SCAP's purge effort, in January 1947, removed thousands more public officials and would-be-candidates from the political scene. In Yamanashi, 478 public officials resigned (in addition to more than 1,000 purged earlier) and a prefectural screening committee disqualified five more.[10]

The April 1947 elections would also witness more thorough military government surveillance. Forty-five military government "teams" had been established throughout Japan in July 1946, replacing detachments, companies, and other tactical units.[11] Large urban centers, such as Kanagawa-Tokyo and Osaka, obviously would field more units than would less populous areas such as Yamanashi Prefecture. In small or moderately populous prefectures, one surveillance unit was usually assigned to each *Gun* or district. In Yamanashi there were nine *Guns* plus the city of Kofu, the prefectural capital. Thus ten surveillance units were assembled, each headed by a commissioned officer or civilian. Six were members of the Yamanashi Military Government Team, and four officers and four enlisted men were borrowed from the First Cavalry Division near Tokyo.[12] I was the sole civilian. In addition to a commissioned officer or civilian, each unit included an enlistee, a Japanese driver, and an interpreter.

Preparations for surveillance before the first election were fairly elaborate. The team's political affairs officer met with prefectural election officials and the prefectural police chief and stressed strict observance of campaign rules and the election law. I issued several press statements on the same subject, which also underscored the obligation of all citizens to vote. These were sent to the local radio station and three local newspapers. On April 3 the team commander briefed the leaders of the ten surveillance units on how to observe and report violations at voting precincts. He designated me to assemble data on any violations and to compile at month's end a final team report. The next day, several surveillance units departed for their assigned *Guns* to visit their first precincts before voting began on April 5 at 7:00 A.M.[13]

As during the April 10, 1946, election, two days of surveillance were required for each election day, to observe both the voting process and the ballot counting. Like most rural prefectures in 1947, Yamanashi's roads were narrow, rocky, and often rutted. I adroitly managed an assignment to a nearby *Gun*, permitting my return each evening to the BOQ for a warm dinner and a comfortable bed. This calculation escaped several newly arrived and temporary-duty officers. They covered the more distant *Guns*, requiring their overnight stay in a remote mountain hotel, sleeping on a *tatami* mat, and consuming Army C-rations for breakfast, lunch, and dinner (unless they wished to chance the hotel's fare and risk contracting a common digestive disorder, then known as "Tojo's revenge").

Team Surveillance and Results of the Four Elections

The purpose of the April 5 election was to elect prefectural governors, mayors of cities and towns, and headmen of villages. Nine surveillance units were scheduled to travel in jeeps, but at the last moment my vehicle broke down, necessitating a switch to a three-quarter-ton truck, seemingly without springs. By the time the polls closed at 6:00 that evening, I had visited 30 of 64 *Gun* precincts in 17 small towns and villages, a number similar to that of most of my colleagues. The next morning we all arose again at dawn to witness the ballot counting.

Two days on Yamanashi back roads proved exhausting and adventuresome, as I noted in several letters:

One officer's jeep experienced two tire blowouts. There being only one spare tire, the second had to be patched laboriously by hand. His jeep also returned with a broken spring. A second officer, traveling in a remote and mountainous area, walked with his companions a half mile to reach two precincts in a village and drove his jeep over a dry riverbed to reach another. A third officer spent a day in bed recuperating from his travels and a sore "tatami" back, very angry with General MacArthur for deciding that surveillance of the election was necessary.

I ached from stem to stern, mostly because of the wrenching ride for two days in a truck. Happily, it was now "deadlined" in the motor pool, awaiting new oil packing for its rear wheels. I was reassigned a jeep the next day.

Only the team's executive officer, a major, had an easy two days. Pulling rank, his surveillance duty in the team commander's 1940 De Soto sedan was confined to precincts in Kofu, Yamanashi's capital, with many paved streets. (April 1947)

As noted, the April 5 election was a major step in decentralizing political power in Japan. Nationally, at least 70 percent of the electorate went to the polls, and in Yamanashi the figure was somewhat higher. The purpose of military government surveillance, to assure that the elections were free and unfettered, was generally achieved, although the number of violations observed and reported were considerably more than eventually reported by SCAP. This was because many violations proved to be inadvertent, rooted as they were in Japan's traditions and respect for status. I noted my impressions after visiting thirty precincts:

Citizens established voting precincts in many places: small shops, Buddhist temples, schools, theaters, and town or village offices. Election officials, all males, were dressed up for the occasion with some wearing winged collar shirts and swallowtail coats. They were seated as befitted their age, status, and position. The Superintendent of a precinct invariably sat in the center of a row of chairs, flanked by three poll watchers on each side, and his chair and table were larger than anyone else's. Another important official, the Recorder of Minutes, likewise occupied a large chair and table. In some villages, all officials sat crosslegged on a small, elevated platform with the Superintendent's seat slightly higher than those of the poll watchers.

There was no doubt that all precinct officials had arrived on time, there being an abundance of clocks and watches on display to attest to the opening of the polls precisely at 7:00 A.M. and their closing at 6:00 P.M.

For numerous outlying villages, election day and the arrival of a military government official accompanied by an enlisted man, a driver, and an interpreter was a major event. It brought all voting to a halt as the local citizens, including young women with babies on their backs, gossiped about the Army truck and its occupants. All appeared very friendly.

Polling officials were very polite. As I approached them, they would rise in unison and greet me with a bow. It was difficult to ask a low-ranking poll watcher if any voting problems had arisen, as the Superintendent of the precinct or the Recorder of the Minutes would rush over to provide an "official" answer.

Other officers reported similar observations and experiences. There was general agreement that the April 5 election went smoothly, but all noted some infractions of the election law or procedures. Most common was the failure of some election officials to post outside of the polling areas the names of candidates for office and their political affiliations. In addition, at numerous precincts, a local policeman sat in a chair next to the poll watchers—looking, no doubt, for an opportunity to flex the muscle of the law. The police were told to leave the polling areas, which they did, undoubtedly with some embarrassment. At one precinct, election officials had placed a large chair next to that of the superintendent. It bore a sign reading: "Reserved for the Military Government Officer." I asked for the removal of the chair and the sign, informing the baffled officials that, while General MacArthur had indeed asked military government to oversee the voting, his order also forbade surveillance officers from sitting with poll watchers and officials. Strange are the ways of democracy, they must have thought!

On April 6 during the ballot-counting all members of Yamanashi's surveillance units were shown numerous invalidated ballots in every precinct. Most were marked improperly, indicating that some men and women voters did not know what to do, most likely, according to our interpreters, because of their inability to read the instructions or the names of the candidates. A few voters demonstrated their new freedom by writing in the name of Emperor Hirohito or General MacArthur to serve as Yamanashi's governor. One wrote in the name of the commander of the Yamanashi Military Government Team to serve as a village headman. At one precinct, the superintendent showed me a ballot on which a citizen, identified by the interpreter as a woman, had written: "I don't think any of the above candidates are qualified to be mayor." What, he asked gravely, should he do with this insulting ballot? "Nothing," I replied, adding that in Japan's new democracy, citizens could express themselves in unusual ways. Of 330,866 ballots cast, about 5 percent were declared invalid. A common but not serious violation was the failure of some precinct officials to seal ballot boxes properly.[14]

The April 5 election in Yamanashi Prefecture resulted in the reelection of the prefectural governor and Kofu's mayor, and the election of 124 small town mayors and village headmen, the majority of whom ran as political Independents. A minority ran as members of the Liberal, Social Democratic, Democratic, People's Cooperative, Communist, or other parties. Several mayorality contests witnessed fierce campaigning by Communist candidates, but all were defeated. Yamanashi's largely rural citizens distrusted the "Reds." On April 15, four run-off elections selected one town mayor and three village headmen. Independents won three contests; the Liberal party, one. Only two military government surveillance units were needed to oversee the voting and ballot-counting.[15]

On April 20, Japan's citizens voted for the first time for a new 250-member House of Councillors, which replaced the appointive House of Peers established under the 1890 Meiji Constitution. Yamanashi selected two, one Social Democrat and one Independent. Our ten prefectural surveillance units discerned no important voting problems. The next day the units observed only a few improperly sealed ballot boxes. Surprisingly, precinct officials reported they had seen an inordinate number of invalidated ballots. When they completed their tallies, a total of 12 percent of the 289,331 ballots cast in Yamanashi were found to be invalid, indicating again that voters were probably unable to read correctly the ballot instructions or were confused about the candidates and their party affiliations.

In Tokyo, the Japanese government quickly announced that a high rate of invalid ballots had also been cast nationwide. This impelled the Home Ministry to order all of Japan's election officials to increase the distribution to homes of handbills explaining more clearly the voting procedures and listing more prominently the names of political candidates for the upcoming elections of April 25 and 30. Eighth Army asked all military government surveillance units to remain aloof from this special information activity.[16]

Yamanashi's ten units were on the road again in late April, when Japan voted for 466 members of the House of Representatives. Yamanashi selected five—two Social Democrats, one Democrat, one Liberal, and one Independent. Then, on April 30 the nation's voters elected representatives to serve in their prefectural, city, town and village assemblies. Yamanashi selected 41 prefectural assemblymen, the majority of them Democrats, 31 assemblymen for Kofu City, the majority of them Independents, and 3,250 town and village assemblymen plus 6 assemblywomen, the majority also Independents. The election of the six ladies was indeed a historic event. The number of invalidated ballots now dropped steeply, to only 1 percent of 314,023 ballots cast for the House of Representatives, but rose slightly to 4 percent of the 370,469 ballots cast for the prefectural, city, town, and village assemblies. Also significant for a rural prefecture like Yamanashi was that women constituted 50.6 percent of the electorate during the five election days (including the run-offs on April 15), close to the national average.[17]

Throughout April 1947, we members of the Yamanashi Military Government Team's ten surveillance units, comprising forty individuals, more than earned our pay. Thirteen- and fourteen-hour days (which included two Saturdays and two Sundays) were common, and the team's jeeps suffered frequent tire blowouts, broken springs, and other damage while traveling over washboard roads. Much liniment was used on aching backs and muscles. At least two officers, having indulged too heartily in the fare of remote hotels, contracted Tojo's revenge, but the team's medical officer quickly restored them to health. Despite some traveling delays, the units visited about two-thirds of all prefectural precincts.

At the national level, the House of Representatives election was the most important, with the liberal Social Democrats demonstrating unusual strength by winning 143 seats. The totals for other parties were: Liberals, 131; Social Democrats, 124; People's Cooperative, 31; other parties, 20; and Independents, 13. The Communists won only four seats, one less than in April 1946, underscoring their lack of public appeal despite their large expenditure of funds and their zeal in campaigning. In the House of Councillors, the Social Democrats also came out on top, garnering 47 seats, and the Communists the fewest with three seats. The average age of the new councillors was younger by ten years than the former House of Peers, and for new house members it also dropped considerably. A coalition of Social Democrats, Democrats, and the People's Cooperative emerged to form a new government under Katayama Tetsu, a Christian. His cabinet would last only until February 1948, because of an ideological struggle between the left and right wings of the Social Democrats, and worsening economic inflation.[18]

As the elections proceeded, the Yamanashi Military Government Team received a steady flow of signed and unsigned letters, numbering at least 150, from citizens reporting election law or campaign violations. Some citizens came directly to my office. I submitted all complaints to the prefectural Penal Affairs Office for investigation. The Penal Affairs Office received additional reports of campaign and election infractions which they combined with those from the team, and they soon released a detailed list of verifiable offenses:[19]

Type of Violations	No. of Cases	No. of People
Pre-election violations	9	11
Buying votes (with rice, sake, cinema tickets, and yen)	29	68
Illegal house visits	23	36
Illegal voting	4	4
Sending letters, using name cards, illegal expenditures, etc.	150	150
Creating election disturbances	7	9
School teacher taking advantage of position	1	1
Injuries caused by election	1	1
Other unspecified violations	4	4
Totals:	228	284

Of the 284 citizens cited for election violations investigated by police, about one-third were convicted. Most were fined, but some received jail sentences. The most flagrant violation was by a candidate who made many house-to-house calls, leaving his name card and upwards of 500 yen at each house. He distributed an estimated 60,000 yen in this manner. Curiously, this was the only violation in Yamanashi

Prefecture cited in SCAP's report for April 1947. So much for the reliability of SCAP's reporting on the elections in Yamanashi.[20]

The majority of violations were not serious. They arose from ignorance of the new campaign rules and the new election law as well as from the propensity of numerous candidates to campaign in a traditional manner. Such gestures as sending personal letters to residents and leaving name cards while making house-to-house visits were newly prohibited during the April 1947 elections.

The election brought to light an illegal hoarding of war supplies by a successful candidate for a seat in the prefectural assembly. According to my notes (May 1947) I was tipped off by a citizen who asked that his name not be made public, and I immediately asked a first sergeant on the team with experience in intelligence to investigate. Working with an interpreter, he found the citizen's allegation to be true. The evidence was turned over to the prefectural Penal Affairs Office, and police soon uncovered fifty-seven drums of oil and gasoline and other wartime supplies which the new assemblyman had hidden at the time of Japan's 1945 surrender. He was quickly arrested, indicted, convicted, and sentenced for illegal hoarding—and he lost his seat in the prefectural assembly.

An immediate postelection problem arose when one of Yamanashi's six newly elected village assemblywomen came to my office. She complained that during village assembly meetings the village headman completely ignored her presence. Whereupon I asked the headman to see me.

He arrived the next day, wreathed in smiles. His manner clearly was that of an old-fashioned bureaucrat. Was it true, I asked, that he had difficulty seeing the new assemblywoman and hearing what she had to say? With several bows and still smiling, he offered an intricate explanation which, laboriously translated, made it appear there had been only a "slight misunderstanding" between the two of them. Whereupon I read to him several articles of the new Constitution which underscored the equality of all Japanese citizens. I instructed him to remember these articles the next time he convened a meeting of the village assembly. Furthermore, the Yamanashi Military Government Team did not wish to receive any more reports about his "undemocratic" behavior. There were no more complaints from the newly elected assemblywoman.

During and after the elections, I also received periodic reports of the "undemocratic" behavior of some police officers, who were wont to exhibit a "haughty" attitude towards voters, allegedly "ordering them around" instead of explaining to them the nature of their infractions of the election law. Also, they occasionally "threatened" those known to have written to or visited team headquarters to register a complaint. This was not surprising. Since the onset of the occupation, military government units and the later teams, constantly supplemented SCAP's efforts to democratize the nation's police and other law enforcement agencies. In Yamanashi, the team's public safety officer, who earlier had served as a law officer in Honolulu, Hawaii, had written and translated in late 1946 a pamphlet titled *Police and the Public*. He had also lectured groups of police on their new role in democratic Japan and had issued press releases on the subject for the local radio station and newspapers.[21]

As mentioned earlier, the team commander had asked me to record election violations noted by surveillance units and to compile a final team report. This duty completed, I was asked to speak in May to prefectural law-enforcing authorities on their new democratic responsibilities. I delivered one address before forty members of the prefectural Penal Affairs Office, and a second before all local police chiefs, citing specific examples of police abuses during the April elections. To both groups I quoted Article 15 of the new Constitution, which stated in part: "All public officials are servants of the whole community and not of any group thereof." Press releases, also aimed at the public, addressed responsibilities of citizenship. The press releases stated in part: "The power of citizens to elect candidates to office is a public trust. It can be preserved only by learning about political candidates and voting intelligently." The lectures and press releases were part of a continuing educational campaign to change traditional police attitudes and behavior.[22]

To sum up, the April 1947 elections for candidates to national and local offices, as members of ten military government surveillance units in Yamanashi Prefecture observed them, constituted a major effort by SCAP headquarters to transfer political power from the Japanese government in Tokyo to the prefectures, cities, towns, and villages. SCAP's Civil Liberties directive and the two initial purge actions greatly facilitated this process. The latter was especially important by ultimately disqualifying more than 200,000 former, current, or potential candidates for public office, including substantial numbers from Yamanashi, tainted with the brush of "militarism" or "ultranationalism." And it opened wide the door of opportunity for a new and younger group of citizens, women as well as men, to seek roles in public service, especially via the ballot box.

The consensus of the leaders of Yamanashi's ten surveillance units was that the 1947 elections were unusually free and unfettered. The majority of campaign and election-law violations were minor rather than major. In Yamanashi and nationally, more than 70 percent of the electorate voted, with women casting fully 50 percent of the ballots.[23] According to scores of letters from and conversations with Yamanashi's citizens, plus reports from other prefectures, military government surveillance during the elections contributed importantly to preventing any serious intimidation of voters or deliberate irregularities at the voting precincts.

The election of six women to rural village assemblies in Yamanashi was a remarkable political and societal breakthrough, given the fact Japanese women had never been allowed to vote or hold public office until April 10, 1946, when they won thirty-nine seats in the Diet's House of Representatives. Nationally, of 232,864 officials elected to public office in April 1947, women won 818 seats as follows: House of Councillors, 10; House of Representatives, 15; prefectural assemblies, 22; city assemblies, 94 (including 16 in Tokyo); and town and village assemblies, 677. Negano Prefecture elected the most women to office, with 47; Saitama Prefecture was second, with 35; and Gumma Prefecture was third, with 27.[24]

Although the process of decentralizing political power in Japan in the postoccupation years would undergo considerable attenuation, the four April 1947 elections nonetheless remain a landmark in establishing a basic political democratic structure not only in Yamanashi Prefecture but throughout the nation.

12

Inauguration of the Educational Structure

Early Problems

April 1, 1947, the beginning of a new school year, was a major landmark in postwar Japanese education. It witnessed the official establishment of a six-year primary and a three-year lower secondary school system. Three-year upper secondary schools and four-year colleges and universities would make their debuts during the 1948–49 and 1949–50 academic years, respectively, to be followed by the establishment of two-year junior colleges. These changes accorded with the recommendations of the 1946 *Report of United States Education Mission to Japan* and the mandates of the March 1947 Japanese School Education Law, the Fundamental Law of Education, and other implementing legislation.

Despite the apprehension of many prefectural education officials, parents, and older male students, I had discerned in previous months a fair degree of support for that aspect of the New Education mandating educational opportunities for girls and young women equal to those of boys and young men, not only in secondary schools but also in colleges and universities. Although most of Yamanashi's "higher" primary schools already provided schooling through the eighth grade (those fortunate to enter the traditional middle schools did so beginning in their seventh school year), the education of many students in highly rural communities often ceased at the end of the sixth grade if their families needed them to labor on farms and in small factories and shops. Now with compulsory education through the seventh grade during the 1947–48 school year, and through the ninth grade two years hence, there would be a substantially higher enrollment of students in the already crowded prefectural schools. How could they possibly be accommodated in such a short time?

In most instances, prefectural and local officials established new lower secondary schools as adjuncts to existing primary schools. Hastily remodeled buildings were also used. Another plan was to convert parts of the eleven traditional middle schools (seventh through eleventh grades for boys; seventh through tenth grades for girls), into lower secondary schools, as their grade structure would place the majority of the students in these institutions (seventh through ninth grades) by the beginning of the 1949–50 school year, when nine years of compulsory education would be required.

Not surprisingly, the plan elicited strong opposition from middle school students, their families, faculties, and alumni—in short, the prefectural elite—as it demoted the greater part of their prestigious institutions to lower secondary status. Such a drastic change was virtually unthinkable among those who had graduated from them. After much hand-wringing, only one of Yamanashi's eleven middle schools was directed, finally, to accommodate a new lower secondary school during the 1947–48 school year.

A second problem was assigning the principals and teachers for the new lower secondary schools. Again, class consciousness was a significant factor in the selection process:

> The committee in charge of faculty nominations to the new lower secondary schools is composed predominately of former primary school principals and teachers. Thus, most of the new principals are those whose social and educational backgrounds reflect that of the committee. A few middle school teachers have been appointed as principals of the lower secondary schools. Unless an offer to become principal is received, the vast majority of teachers in the traditional middle school schools have no desire to work in the new lower secondaries.[1]

A third problem in establishing the new lower secondary schools was the lack of textbooks. Whereas Yamanashi's primary schools had received by April 1947 new textbooks on Japanese language, mathematics, and science, the new lower secondary schools had received textbooks only on the Japanese language and the social sciences. It was June before texts on mathematics and science arrived, the delay attributed, according to SCAP's Education Division, to a severe nationwide paper shortage—although it was obvious to SCAP and military government personnel that a large black market in paper existed to supply the proliferating newssheets, magazines, and booklets authored by long-suppressed writers, trade unionists, and new adult groups. Black-market paper also enabled the Japan Communist party's newspaper, *Akahata*, to expand its circulation.[2]

A fourth problem, as in the previous year, was the poor quality of most textbooks. In June 1947, shortly after the beginning of the new school term, I compiled the following list of textbook shortcomings on the basis of conversations with principals, head teachers, and faculty members: (1) some or parts thereof appeared to have been hastily written; (2) most looked more like pamphlets than books; (3) the quality of paper was poor and the pages tore easily; (4) the print was too small; (5) they contained too few maps and illustrations; (6) Japanese literature texts needed more poems, fables, and local history; (7) they lacked adequate "measuring scales" for the study of mathematics; and (8) parts of some allegedly contained too much "old, prewar thinking" and insufficient "democratic" thought. Also, the study of *kanji* was still inordinately time-consuming, even though the required number for use in school had been reduced to 1,850 characters by the Ministry of Education on November 3, 1946. The new social studies course in various grades likewise remained a most troublesome subject for teachers.

The social studies courses introduced into the curriculum during the 1946–47 school year were designed to explain to young boys and girls the close relationship, past and present, between their life and their environment: the nature of farm-life versus city-living; how climate and soil determined the type of clothing people wore and the food they ate; the impact of different modes of transportation; the role played by post offices, telephone companies, banks, railway stations, factories, fire departments and village offices in a community; and how Japanese life compared with life in other countries. The course encouraged visits by students to the aforementioned places, where officials explained the nature of their duties and answered student questions.3

There were successively advanced social studies textbooks for each class. Although primary school students, when asked, soon chorused they liked their social studies course "best of all" (primarily, it seemed, as it afforded them an opportunity to visit frequently during the school day the nearest railway station, post office, etc.), most teachers were puzzled by its lack of specificity. In fact, early in the 1947–48 school year, many school faculties suspended efforts to teach the course until they received more guidance on how to present its contents to their students.

The new school year also witnessed an important first step in shifting some of the control over education from the Ministry of Education to prefectural assemblies. In Yamanashi, as elsewhere, the latter were empowered for the first time to prepare prefectural school budgets, establish or abolish public primary or lower secondary schools, provide supplementary funds for school faculties, pay travel expenses to teachers attending conferences, and underwrite the cost of the school nurse.

These problems, and the progress of the new lower secondary schools, as well as numerous other subjects were discussed at two CI&E conferences held during the first and second weeks of June 1947, respectively. The first was held at IXth Corps headquarters in Sendai for the CI&E officers and their assistants from the fifteen military government teams (including the District of Hokkaido) within the IXth Corps' area of responsibility, and the second was limited to CI&E personnel assigned to the eight prefectural military government teams within the Kanto Military Government Region. With some exceptions, both conferences had the same agenda rendering the second one unnecessary. This duplication of effort indicated the lack of coordination between IXth Corps and SCAP's CI&E section, which had arranged the Sendai conference, and the Kanto Military Government Region, which had planned for the conclave in Niigata.

Present at the conference in Sendai were two SCAP education officials—Dr. Helen Heffernen, a specialist on primary school education, and Ethel Weed, a specialist in Japanese women's organizations. Dr. Heffernen underscored the importance of parental influence on preschool and school-age children, and the need for parents to understand some of the basic facts of child psychology, mental and physical health, and the development of children's personalities. She also addressed the special problems of farm women.

Miss Weed discussed the new status of women as defined in the revised postwar Japanese Civil Code and the new Constitution, their activities in the labor movement and in political life since the April 1947 elections (in which 818 women had won seats in the Japanese Diet and in prefectural, city, town, and village assemblies), and the activities of some of the new women's organizations. She cited the achievements of several noted postwar women journalists, especially Ichikawa Fusae, then one of the most famous women leaders in Japan, plus others. She urged all military government CI&E officers to encourage and assist as much as possible the new "democratic" women's organizations as well as those for professional women, such as nurses.

More School Inspections

At the Sendai and Niigata conferences I had learned that within the Kanto Military Government Region I was the only CI&E officer without an assistant, all the rest having at least one and in some instances, two. In addition, several teams had a women's affairs officer on their staffs. I remonstrated strongly to my military government CI&E superiors on my need for at least one CI&E assistant, explaining that I was also serving as the labor education officer on the Yamanashi Military Government Team. Whether because of my appeals or by chance, I received an assistant in late June 1947 who was a graduate of a university and a U.S. Navy Japanese language school. He appeared remarkably fluent in the Japanese tongue, and I immediately assigned to him, with the team commander's approval, the task of labor education, thus relieving myself of much but not all of this responsibility. As my assistant was quite young, inexperienced and quickly manifested a lack of discipline, the team commander enjoined me to maintain a watchful eye over his activities.

In July, I received additional part-time assistance when Dr. Rollin C. Fox, the Kanto Military Government Region's civil information and education officer, made his first three-day visit to Yamanashi Prefecture. He was a highly experienced educator. A former teacher, school principal, and superintendent of schools in three separate districts in New York State, he had also served for three years during World War II as a principal and then superintendent of schools in the Manzanar Japanese Relocation Center in California. He offered valuable advice not only to me but to prefectural education officials, principals and school faculties with whom he conferred on how to restructure more effectively the Japanese school system and improve the administration of schools. As a "roving educational ambassador" for the eight military government teams in the Kanto Military Region, he would come to Yamanashi Prefecture several more times and also played a leading role in subsequent education conferences. His periodic visits enabled me to spend more time on my other CI&E duties.

Meanwhile, I continued to visit and inspect public schools. Supplementing my efforts to explain the merits of the New Education was the Fuzoku Primary School, attached to the Yamanashi Men's Normal School, which possessed a fairly young and aggressive head teacher and a very capable eighteen-member faculty. To demonstrate various new and advanced teaching techniques, it had begun to hold periodic one-day teaching clinics. The first was held in March 1947, with 500 teachers in attendance, followed by additional one-day teaching clinics in May and June.4 Others were held later that year and in 1948. A major objective was to demonstrate how students could be taught other than by rote. The head teacher and his faculty published a guide for innovative teaching of the Japanese language, science, mathematics, social science, and fine and practical arts.

Another beacon of progress was the Yatsushuri Lower Secondary School, with a principal and faculty attuned to improving teaching techniques, and with the dual advantage of new facilities and moderate-size classes. It was soon designated by the Ministry of Education as a "model showcase" lower secondary school, to facilitate the spread of ideas and practices of the New Education.

Other schools began to demonstrate progressive attributes. After a question-and-answer session with older students in several classes at the Isawa Primary School, I recorded: "The faculty has done its job well in acquainting students with the many changes taking place in Japan. The youngsters showed a surprising grasp of the various articles in the new Constitution." At the Suruhashi Primary School, I noted that the faculty was "particularly outstanding" in the use of a wide variety of teaching aides in the classrooms. New charts, maps, and graphs were being "used generously throughout the school."

Social studies continued to be troublesome for most teachers, but occasionally I encountered one who grasped how it should be taught. The Kajikawaza Primary School possessed a teacher who had "done good work in developing and using teaching aides for . . . the social studies course." The school was also above average in maintaining good administration and teaching standards.5

Coeducation and Other Educational Adjustments

Without doubt, one of the surprising successes of the 1947–48 school year was the acceptance of coeducation, a reform nearly all prefectural officials, parents, principals, and most faculties, except for some women teachers, had initially opposed. "It has been adopted in all of the primary schools," I reported in May 1947, "and the majority of the new lower secondary schools likewise have put it into effect." Most of the latter schools, however, opted for classroom commingling of the sexes only through the compulsory school year (i.e., the seventh grade). They continued to teach boys and girls in separate classrooms in the eighth and ninth grades. There was a broad consensus among principals and teachers that coeducation was working better than expected. Some women teachers, when queried, believed it had "tamed down considerably" the behavior of boys in the upper primary school grades.

As noted earlier, coeducation had long been practiced in the first three grades, with girls sitting next to girls and boys next to boys at their two-seat desks in the same classroom. Now, new and interesting seating arrangements blossomed in some schools. In some instances, teachers placed a boy next to a girl at the two-seat desks. In the fourth through seventh grades, there were other seating arrangements. Most common was the placement of boys on one side of the room, girls on the other. A second variation found boys and girls seated in alternate rows. A third placement had boys and girls sitting alternately behind each other. To the recurring question—"How are students seated in America?"—I explained how my classmates were seated alphabetically by name, although this system often varied. For example, if two troublemaking students were seated one behind the other, the teacher would not hesitate to give them desks some distance apart. I avoided offering a preferred seating arrangement, stating each school should make its own decision.

There was sufficient anxiety about seating arrangements to impel several educators to come to my office to confer about this momentous problem. One fairly young head teacher from a distant school arrived with a tally sheet showing an excess of girls in several classrooms. How should this problem be handled, he asked? If several girls sat one behind the other, would this not violate the spirit of the New Education? Some girls complained if there was no boy in front of or behind them. His tentative solution was to rotate the girls' seating to assure none would be deprived of the "learning experience" of sitting in front of or behind a boy. I gave the proposal my blessing.

There also arrived a highly conscientious male teacher whose third-year class had four more girls than boys. Using an elaborate sketch of the two-seat desks in his classroom, he explained how he had devised a seating scheme whereby each of the four girls was given "equal time" every week sitting next to a boy. Showing me his precise daily calculations over several months, which were figured out to the minute, it was apparent he had expended an inordinate amount of time in making his compilations. I complimented him on his conscientiousness but suggested politely that his effort was well beyond the requirements of the New Education in assuring coeducation in his classroom. He appeared greatly relieved when I opined that his elaborate record-keeping was no longer necessary.

Despite observable improvements in Yamanashi's primary and new lower secondary schools early in the 1947–48 school year, some schools still faced formidable difficulties. This was underscored by a visit to the new Yuda Lower Secondary School and Yuda Girls' Middle School, both private institutions, in late 1947. Located in Kofu, the main building housing both had been badly damaged in the July 1945 bombing raid. It was in the new lower middle school where I found a class of 120 students—a record—although a rebuilding program was well under way. For public schools in and outside of Kofu, the rebuilding costs were spiraling out of control. In December 1947, prefectural education officials estimated that the 900,000 *yen* cost of rebuilding a school in April of that year had now tripled because of soaring expenses for labor and materials.[6]

As numerous schools complained frequently of their inability to get glass to replace thousands of cracked, broken, or missing window panes while others managed to obtain all they needed, I directed prefectural officials to devise a more equitable system for rationing this short-supply item.

Another problem associated with the New Education, cited through March 1947 and still manifest during the new school year, was the unruly behavior of students, mostly boys but also some girls. This could be attributed partially to the continued presence of so many young, relatively inexperienced women teachers in the primary schools whose education had been drastically shortened during World War II.

Many still interpreted the New Education as a license for their pupils to do as they wished in order to "develop their inner selves." Other teachers attributed the breakdown of discipline to the continued absence of the traditional morals course, permanently banned by SCAP because of its militaristic content. Thus, in December, more than a year after assuming my CI&E duties, I noted how "the pendulum has swung from one extreme to the other. Until the end of World War II, school discipline was strictly enforced; today there is an excessive lack of it." Many teachers remained convinced some new type of morals course, possibly highlighting teachings from Christianity, Buddhism, and Confucianism, was the answer to restoring discipline in the schools. With the separation of religion and state, decreed by SCAP directives and enshrined in new Japanese legislation and the new Constitution, this was no longer possible, of course.

There was still considerable student and teacher absenteeism during the 1947–48 school year because of health problems and economic hardship. The reliance of families on their children, especially those engaged in farming, remained high. Teachers struggled with inadequate textbooks, teachers' manuals, and reference materials. Small wonder some schools had very abbreviated learning days. In January 1948, at one distant primary school I observed: "Students began school late in the morning and were sent home by noon." A few days later at a new lower secondary school I reported how the school's sole project for the day "was the viewing of a movie, then the students went home." I also noted "neither school possessed weekly classroom schedules." Schools in the more distant corners of Yamanashi Prefecture were especially handicapped in understanding and applying the tenets of the New Education. A long and bumpy journey to the Hirano Primary School led to the following observation:

This is one of numerous schools located in a mountainous area and so isolated none of the faculty members have ever had an opportunity to attend a prefectural teachers' meeting or conference. . . . The cost of transportation is prohibitive. . . . Travel allowances would cover only a small part of the teachers' expenses. This particular problem has been aggravated in recent months by the rise of transportation costs.[7]

I conveyed my findings on absenteeism and conference attendance to prefectural education officials who, in turn, discussed them with prefectural school inspectors. Little was done about the first problem except to exhort all teachers to do their best under the prevailing circumstances. The second problem was partially resolved when prefectural authorities allocated extra travel allowances sufficient for a few teachers to attend a conference. I also asked prefectural education officials to establish a more uniform system of student fees for young students participating in the school lunch program, which began in February 1947. A more uniform fee system began in September when all schools reopened after a short summer vacation period.

The New Upper Secondary Schools

January 1948 witnessed a special three-day CI&E conference at the Kanto Military Government Region headquarters near Tokyo. In attendance were all CI&E officers within the IXth Corps (i.e., in northern Honshu), and education officials from SCAP, Eighth Army and, of course, the Kanto Military Government Region. The conference had a full agenda with lecture and discussion panels on in-service teacher training, primary and secondary schools, experimental schools, higher education, school administration and finance, youth associations and women's organizations, and the civil information program. CI&E officers and a few women's affairs officers participated in the panel discussions.[8] In addition to the formal agenda, there was considerable discussion on the establishment of upper secondary schools (the third step in the new 6–3–3–4 educational structure) beginning April 1, 1948. Overall, I found the exchange of views at this conference far more useful than the sessions in Sendai and Niigata in June 1947.

Establishing new three-year upper secondary schools in Yamanashi—also popularly called senior high schools—proved to be difficult. Highlights of the planning process follow:

Three meetings of a preparatory committee for the establishment of the upper secondary schools were held during the month. A special committee of eight members also attended a special meeting in Tokyo held under the auspices of SCAP's Education Division and the Ministry of Education concerning various upper secondary school matters. Tentatively it has been agreed to establish twenty-four of these schools (including three private ones) in Yamanashi. The prefectural government is disposed to let localities settle the most crucial and controversial problems. For example, Yamanashi has three towns of about 12,000 population, with each containing one boys' and one girls' middle school. What remains to be settled is whether to use one or both schools in the three towns for upper secondary purposes.

It also appears that in all three towns, a lower secondary school should be combined with an upper secondary school. Also awaiting a decision are the number of branch schools needed in Yamanashi for part-time schooling for students beginning April 1, 1948.[9]

Meanwhile, I met periodically with the prefectural education chief, school inspectors, and principals to discuss the coming educational change. In February, Rollin Fox again came to Kofu to assist me. In a day-long meeting with the Committee on the Establishment of Upper Secondary Schools, Dr. Fox outlined his views on administration and curricula. He also explained the merits of a five-day week—currently all Japanese ran a five-and-a-half-day week.

Among the various problems associated with establishing the new upper secondary schools, three appeared most intractable. The first was financial, as most communities would have to raise the major portion of the necessary additional funds, given the limitations of the prefectural school budget (lower secondary schools were still largely financed by the Ministry of Education). The second problem, noted earlier, was the great reluctance of traditional middle school students, faculties, and alumni to surrender their cherished historic school identities. The third was whether to accept coeducation from the tenth through twelfth grade. With respect to the last problem, Yamanashi's six girls' middle schools appeared even more determined than the five boys' middle schools not to lose their special status and characteristics. Consequently, prefectural education officials decided to delay any co-education at the upper secondary level until at least the beginning of the 1950–51 school year.[10]

Concurrently, prefectural education officials, principals and representatives of the prefecture's men's and women's normal schools, and the Cultural Department of the Yamanashi Teachers' Union were also discussing how to provide more effective teacher-training courses. These discussions in May and June 1948 (which were in effect "negotiations" because of the inordinate power of union representatives) led to a decision to establish a special Education Institute which would focus initially on upgrading the skills of the primary school teachers.

April 1, 1948 witnessed the opening of new upper secondary schools throughout Japan. In Yamanashi Prefecture

twenty-two public and three private upper secondary schools were established. A number of the new schools were not able to accommodate all of the students who applied to attend them. Initial figures show 151 boys who qualified for admittance could not be enrolled for lack of space.

In addition, 124 boys and girls were not admitted because of their failure to pass the qualifying examinations. All former girl middle schools (converted to upper secondaries) were able to admit all girl applicants.[11]

To assure a wider range of educational opportunities, the new upper secondary schools planned to offer either college and university preparatory subjects, or such vocational courses as agriculture, commerce, carpentry, and engineering. These courses had been taught formerly in special vocational institutions, such as the agricultural and technical colleges and the numerous youth schools which also offered primarily vocational training.

Not surprisingly, the political and educational influence of Yamanashi's five boys' and six girls' former middle schools remained manifest. All eleven of them, plus three new upper secondaries, would offer only college preparatory courses while the others would include a varied fare of vocational subjects. Virtually all of the principals and teachers in middle schools retained their positions, and the majority of principalships of new upper secondaries were drawn from the ranks of former middle school teachers.

Accompanying this major restructuring of secondary education was a pervasive concern, however, that standards would drop. This would happen, Yamanashi's predominately male educational elite was convinced, when all boys and girls would be promoted to their tenth year if their grades were reasonably satisfactory and if they passed a test far less dependent on memory and thus less stringent than had previously been required to enter a middle school. Most girl students and women teachers, on the other hand, supported the American concept of "equal" educational opportunity.[12]

Coeducation was another major concern, and would not be attempted in the new upper secondaries until the 1950–51 school year. "Opposition to coeducation," I wrote in the team's June 1948 report, "remains strong as expressed by all parties concerned: boy students, girl students, teachers, and parents." Yamanashi Prefecture was simply not ready for the daily commingling in the same classrooms of sixteen- to eighteen-year-olds. There were also very practical reasons for postponing this democratic innovation because of the disparities in former middle school recreational facilities, the need for separate male and female toilet facilities, and the absence of a school bus system to transport girls to former boys' middle schools, and vice versa, or to other newly established upper secondary schools.

The teaching load of faculty members in the new upper secondary schools was another issue not yet settled when the new school year began on April 1, 1948. Traditionally, former middle school teachers were expected to teach only fifteen to eighteen hours per week, and primary (and presently new lower secondary school teachers) about twenty-five hours per week, although few adhered strictly to these schedules because of the turbulence created in the schools by the war's aftermath and by postwar educational reforms. Now the question was asked: should faculty members in the new upper secondaries be entitled to the lighter teaching load which they enjoyed in their former middle schools? At the outset of the new school year, the answer was yes. But debate on this issue was continuing.[13]

Part-time and Correspondence Study

In the past, as mentioned earlier, many thousands of students, mostly boys and young men, who could not enter a traditional middle school but were eager to obtain more education enrolled in youth schools, which numbered at least forty-seven in Yamanashi Prefecture. The ones I visited or inspected were very small, were housed in rudimentary structures, and possessed little laboratory or vocational equipment. There also existed a "higher" Yamanashi Technical College and an Agricultural College which had both full-time and part-time students. A youth-school normal school, separate from Yamanashi's two regular men's and women's normal schools, provided the teachers for the youth schools. Understandably, students and teachers in these vocational institutions were greatly concerned about their futures in the new 6–3–3–4 school structure. In talking with them from time to time, I found it most difficult to maintain their morale and convince them their educational opportunities would be enhanced rather than diminished under the New Education.

In October 1947, the Ministry of Education, prodded by SCAP, announced that all youth schools would be abolished on April 1, 1948, the beginning of the 1948–49 school year. In Yamanashi Prefecture this evoked a strong response from hundreds of youth school enrollees. They formed a "Laboring Students League" with 200 of them attending a meeting in Kofu on November 25. Several prefectural leaders of the Socialist and Communist parties were on hand to assist the students in voicing their discontent. Also on the rostrum was the head of the Youth School Department of the Yamanashi Teachers' Union. A Communist speaker alleged that the 6–3–3–4 school structure would leave working, part-time students bereft of educational opportunities. Further, the new structure was only "for the monied and privileged classes and operates at the expense of the working people." By the time the meeting of the new Laboring Students League ended, it had elected eighteen officers to serve in various positions.[14]

After adjournment, several attendees presented a petition and a "manifesto" on the specific problems of youth school students to the governor of Yamanashi, the president of the Prefectural Assembly, and the commanding officer of the Yamanashi Military Government Team.[15] Meeting with several of the league's leaders shortly afterwards and also in the ensuing weeks, I conceded there would be some initial pain for part-time students as the school structure was phased in. I emphasized, however, that the new structure would provide better opportunities for part-time participation in vocational and correspondence courses in the new secondary schools, and that graduation certificates would likewise prove more valuable than those presently awarded by the existing vocational and the youth schools. I sensed I did little to allay the concerns of my listeners. By late 1947 and early 1948, it was increasingly evident that the new secondary schools would not possess by the beginning of the next school year the requisite teachers and equipment for the much-needed vocational courses for students who could not attend a secondary school full time.

The unpreparedness of the New Education to provide adequate correspondence and part-time study was confirmed at the onset of the new school year beginning April 1, 1948, which also witnessed, as has been noted, the establishment of twenty-four upper secondary schools. Nationwide, the opportunity for correspondence study was considerably less than planned for former youth school students because the Ministry of Education had allotted only 2,685,840 *yen* for the program. In Yamanashi Prefecture, enrollment in these courses was limited to 100 and 200 students in the lower and secondary schools, respectively. Each attendee would be assessed a standard fee for each course to help defray costs.[16]

For the initial correspondence courses offered at the Kanoiwa Lower Secondary School, 96 students signed up, and at the Kofu First Upper Secondary School the total enrollment was 186. Each student paid an enrollment fee of 20 *yen* and a tuition fee of 75 *yen*. Because the Ministry of Education had not yet distributed newly prepared correspondence texts, the students at both schools were limited to studying only the Japanese language and mathematics. Instructors mimeographed the lessons. After several weeks, the necessary textbooks were available for courses in radio engineering, English as used in trade, and other vocational subjects. A special *Correspondence Education Bulletin* issued by the Japanese Research Institute in Tokyo provided guidance for instructors.[17]

The bulletin included results of a survey of the first student enrollees in correspondence courses at the secondary schools. They represented twenty-four occupations. Farm youths, numbering 37, composed the largest group, followed by 16 who listed themselves as clerks, and 8 who listed themselves as lumberers. Other students identified themselves as plasterers, roofers, electricians, cocoon inspectors, railway workers, or other occupations. Except for young ladies who aspired to be nurses, all of the other enrollees were young men. There was no breakdown by age of those studying at the lower secondary school level, but a sampling of those in the upper secondary school showed that 151 ranged in age from 16 to 24 years. Twenty-three listed their ages as 21; fifteen were between ages 25 and 29; and the two oldest were ages 37 and 48.

For part-time study 2,800 students applied, mostly young men and a few young women. Designated to serve this program were thirteen new upper secondary schools and fifteen branch schools, the latter consisting of classrooms in small, renovated buildings.[18] Again, plans could not be translated immediately into reality. All of the instructors had not been selected. Worse still, funds to support part-time schooling had not yet been appropriated. Not until June 1948 was any money forthcoming—4 million *yen* from the Ministry of Education and 12 million *yen* from the Yamanashi Prefectural government to cover the first year's cost of teachers' salaries, renovation of and rent for branch classrooms, and other operating expenses. Once the money was in hand, part-time instruction began on July 20, more than three and a half months after the new school year began.

Given the schedule, such shortcomings were unavoidable: "Too much reform in too short a time," I noted. The rationale for all the haste in phasing-in the programs, according to SCAP and military government CI&E officials, was to secure the 6–3–3–4 educational structure as soon as possible, since the occupation might end sooner than expected.

Licensing of Private and Trade Schools

The beginning of the 1948–49 school year called for stepped-up licensing of private and miscellaneous trade schools in compliance with the March 1947 School Education Law and other pertinent legislation. Although the traditional youth schools (which taught mostly trades) had been abolished officially by the Ministry of Education during the previous school year, those that could not immediately meet new and higher standards were permitted to remain open.

The licensing of private schools, which had existed long before World War II and of which there were relatively few, did not appear to be a serious problem. Licensing of upgraded trade schools, however, proceeded very slowly. As indicated, a fair number of the former youth schools still functioned in the hope of raising more money and becoming licensed. "It has taken pressure to get local education officials to take an interest in this matter," I wrote in May 1948, "and to enforce the law governing many of these inadequate institutions."[19] That so many still attracted students was further testament to the zeal of Yamanashi's young people to obtain some additional education and training, no matter how meager, above the higher primary school level, (i.e., the eighth grade).

During June 1948, as the unpreparedness of the lower secondary and the new upper secondary schools to teach vocational subjects, and the inability of most former youth schools to meet higher standards in the near future became glaringly evident, I ceased badgering prefectural officials about their licensing. Scant as the schools' offerings were, students had an opportunity to study further the Japanese language and agriculture, sericulture, technology (called "engineering"), fisheries, veterinary science, commerce, and the like. Upgrading these schools clearly would remain a slow process.

The Five-Day School Week

Concurrently with the foregoing reforms during the 1947–48 school year, an experimental five-day school week in eight new upper secondary schools was also begun. The concept had been discussed by SCAP educationists, but Rollin C. Fox of the Kanto Military Government Region gave it his strong support. In his view, a shortened teaching week offered two important advantages: it would ensure more efficient use of available school time and facilities, and it would free teachers on Saturdays to engage in independent study or attend in-service training and other educational meetings.

Although I admired Dr. Fox's great expertise as a public school administrator, and though I appreciated his positive impact on Yamanashi's prefectural education officials, principals, and teachers, with whom he met periodically from July 1947 onward, I disagreed with his advocacy of a five-day school week, despite its convincing merits on paper.

From my perspective, it promised to exacerbate the existing turbulence in the present school-reform program, and most teachers would use their "free Saturdays" not for self-improvement but to shop for life's necessities in their inflation-wracked economy. It was also clear that prefectural education officials, principals, teachers, and parents did not wish to forego their traditional five-and-a-half-day school week. Once the occupation ended, I was convinced, this particular reform would be abandoned immediately.

Because of Dr. Fox's high prestige among local administrators, I publicly supported the five-day school week experiment. I had no desire to emulate a CI&E colleague in another prefecture in the Kanto area, however, who had "ordered" a five-day school week for the entire public school system (it may have been mandated in other prefectures also). The experiment in Yamanashi continued throughout the 1948–49 school year but was never adopted on a prefecture-wide basis.

Two More CI&E Conferences

The spring of 1948 witnessed two more military government CI&E conferences organized by the Kanto Military Government Region. The first was held in Maebashi, the capital of Gumma Prefecture, on March 22–23, and the second at Urawa, the capital of Saitama Prefecture, on June 7–8. Both were convened by Dr. Fox, as the Kanto Region's CI&E officer, with welcoming remarks delivered by the commanding officers of the military government teams and prefectural governors of Gumma and Saitama Prefectures, respectively. Each conference was attended by seven military government CI&E officers, one women's affairs officer, and seven Japanese representatives. The latter consisted in March of prefectural government education chiefs, and in June of other noted educators, one from each of the prefectures represented at the conference. Each military government CI&E officer and a Japanese representative made joint presentations.[20]

The panels at the two separate conferences discussed many educational reform activities: information programs, the new upper secondary schools, youth associations, new women teacher-consultants, women's community activities, PTAs, teachers' unions, and the like. Speakers at the June conference included two members of SCAP's Education Division, Dr. Virginia A. Carley, a specialist in higher education, and Donald M. Typer, head of the Youth Association and Student Activities Branch who had participated with me during a major two-day youth conference in Yamanashi in late March 1948.

The restructuring of Japan's institutions of higher education stimulated the most debate. SCAP's near-term objective, said Dr. Carley, was to convert all normal schools into four-year institutions and to ensure that each of Japan's prefectures would possess at least one national university (see p. 178).

At both conferences there was a strong consensus that it would take many more years and considerably more money before all of SCAP's educational reforms would be accepted permanently by the Japanese people.

13
Further Reforms in Teacher Training

Practice Teaching and Refresher Courses

The implementation of the first phase of the new 6–3–3–4 school structure on April 1, 1947, which marked the beginning of the 1947–48 school year and witnessed the establishment of new lower secondary schools, inevitably focused more attention on Yamanashi's three normal schools. They would be the source of new teachers not only for the new lower secondaries but also the new upper secondaries scheduled to begin operations on April 1, 1948.

I had not spent much time with Yamanashi's normal schools pending clarification by SCAP's Education Division of its plans for revamping Japan's system of higher education. By the onset of the 1947–48 school year, additional details were available for establishing a more egalitarian system of colleges and universities. Existing normal schools were destined to become four-year teachers' colleges. Until this change went into effect, however, normal schools were expected to follow guidance, provided primarily by the Ministry of Education, on how to streamline and democratize their curricula.

The disparities in educating men and women in normal schools were several. In Yamanashi Prefecture the men's regular normal school in Kofu was by far the largest. It possessed 618 students and a faculty of 33. The women's regular normal school in Kanoiwa, not far from Kofu, had 357 students and a faculty of 25. The Yamanashi Youth-School Normal School, also in Kofu and scheduled to be phased out eventually, was the smallest, with 219 students, mostly men and a few women. Its faculty numbered 18.[1]

The disparities were reflected not only in the number of men and women enrolled in these schools but also in practice-teaching requirements. Students in the men's regular normal school spent three weeks each in the attached Fuzoku Primary School and in a new Fuzoku Lower Secondary School (both experimental), and four weeks in one of fifteen designated prefectural primary schools, for a total of ten weeks. Students in the women's regular normal school spent one week in a kindergarten, seven weeks and three weeks, respectively, in the Fuzoku Primary School and a new lower secondary school, and one week in one of fifteen designated primary schools, for a total of twelve weeks.[2]

The youth-school normal school practice-teaching requirements called for ten weeks for men and eleven weeks for women as follows: for men, two weeks and four weeks, respectively, at the Aikawa Primary School and the new Aikawa Lower Secondary School, and four weeks in one of six designated youth (also called vocational or trade) schools; for women, eight weeks at the new Kanoiwa Lower Secondary School, and three weeks at one of three designated youth schools. Upon graduation, they would teach in one of the prefecture's numerous youth schools.

A more concerted effort to upgrade the qualifications of hundreds of very young, mostly women teachers in the primary and new lower secondary schools, began in August 1947. During the war years, many had not even attended a normal school, and those who did had received very abbreviated educations. Consequently, they held only provisional teaching certificates. They were now asked to spend eight days of their brief vacation period in August to take refresher classes in eighteen separate primary schools. Classes included lectures and discussions focusing on the new Constitution, the School Education Law and the Fundamental Law of Education (both enacted at the end of March 1947), educational psychology, and the new teachers' manuals. (Similar upgrading activities were held concurrently in other prefectures.)[3]

Using guidelines from SCAP's Education Division, I offered advice and assistance for this special summer-school effort to the prefectural Education Section, and to the principal and faculty members of the two regular normal schools who arranged and carried out the upgrading program. Then, preparatory to resuming school in September, the normal school principal, apparently on instructions from the Ministry of Education, revised the curricula of the two regular normal schools for third-year students. He divided the study area into two broad fields, literature and science, and also introduced a few elective courses. Shortly there were three classes in literature, one in science, plus several electives for these students.[4]

Establishing an In-Service Training Program

Soon after the end of the brief 1947 summer school recess, I asked Rollin Fox of the Kanto Military Government Region to come again to Yamanashi and assist in formulating a long-term in-service teacher training program. He arrived in October and spent several days meeting with prefectural education officials, school inspectors, normal school faculties, principals and teachers, representatives of the Yamanashi Teachers' Union, and the main local Education Association.5 As previously, Dr. Fox's lectures and discussion sessions on how to institute a permanent in-service teacher training program at both the primary and secondary school levels won high acclaim from Yamanashi's educators.

I held follow-up sessions with the aforementioned educators throughout November. Two long-term problems now took center stage. One was the considerable reluctance of the former boys' and girls' middle school teachers to be included in the same type of in-service training as for teachers in the primary and lower secondary schools. The second problem would prove to be more difficult. This was the determination of the leaders of the Cultural Department of the Yamanashi Teachers' Union to substitute their own plan throughout the prefecture for the in-service teacher training program. While the first problem was resolvable, the second triggered protracted debate among Yamanashi's educators.

An uneasy consensus finally emerged that regular in-service teacher training could be achieved best by establishing an Education Institute. The consensus then fractured over who should have control of the institute: the prefectural Education Section which promised to finance it, the regular men's and womens' normal schools which would provide the instructors, or the Cultural Department of the Yamanashi Teachers' Union. There was also protracted debate over the institute's proposed curriculum, with union representatives arguing strongly for a particular course of study which, it was suspected, might contain some Marxist political overtones.

The debate between the contending factions extended into February 1948, when more definitive planning for the Education Institute began. By then, the main players in this struggle for educational influence and control were the prefectural Education Section and the representatives of the Yamanashi Teachers' Union. Mr. Yamaguchi, the prefectural education chief with whom I conferred frequently, explained that negotiating with union leaders created for him "a most difficult situation." Nonetheless, by month's end the two sides agreed to convene a ten-member committee, five from each side, on how to establish the institute. The committee agreed to have the institute work closely with ten primary and nine lower secondary schools, recently designated as "showplace" experimental schools (albeit several, according to my information, were only marginally above average). The prefectural Education Section agreed to provide an initial 600,000 *yen* for the institute and for the cost of holding training sessions at the experimental schools. A preliminary plan stated in part:

> The institute will be staffed by either part-time or full-time instructors. Special courses will be given without cost to teachers on such subjects as social studies, Japanese language, geography, etc. As present teachers' contracts provide for 20 days of free study time per school year, many teachers will spend this time at the institute.[6]

Meanwhile, representatives of the two regular normal schools, who would provide the instructors, again interjected themselves into the struggle over control of the institute. They were again rebuffed strongly by the Teachers' Union.[7] The bargaining power of the normal schools remained weak, in my judgment, as its president was quite elderly, conservative, and not inclined to advance strongly proposals on his own in the area of educational reform.

As planning for the institute continued, other contentious issues were slowly resolved early in 1948. One was the cost to the prefectural Education Section, a figure not readily ascertainable as the two regular normal schools, which would provide the instructors, were still largely supported by the Ministry of Education. The other was the location of the institute. After considerable debate, the conferees decided to place it in a building near the men's regular normal school in Kofu. Shortly, a director was appointed, as were several instructors. A tentative agreement was also reached on a curriculum. In monitoring these developments, it was impossible to avoid the following assessments:

> The Education Institute is primarily the creation of the Yamanashi Teachers' Union with prefectural education and normal school officials ostensibly "cooperating." Among the institute's objectives is to have fifty teachers at a time engage in educational research of dubious value.
> Until prefectural government and other officials are able to exert more influence, the union will dominate the institute. The fact that nearly every

principal and teacher is a union member or distantly affiliated with it creates a dilemma in developing a truly independent, professional teaching organization.[8]

Whatever the institute's possible failings, it promised to make some commendable changes. It would condense heretofore separate domestic arts courses for women into a single course called "Home," leaving more time for women to enroll in more advanced courses in language and social studies. The institute also appeared strongly supportive of having teachers continue to observe exemplary teaching practices at some of the ten designated primary and lower secondary schools.

The institute finally opened in June 1948, but only twenty-seven teachers enrolled for the 20-day, in-service refresher courses. One reason for the lower-than-expected attendance was financial. Many teachers could afford neither the cost of commuting daily to and from Kofu nor the cost of living in the city temporarily. A second reason, not openly admitted, was psychological. Rather than viewing the Educational Institute as an opportunity to enhance their professional status, many young teachers construed their enrollment as a stigma, underscoring their poor teaching qualifications. It illustrated once again an unexpected gap in attitudes between Japanese and American teachers.[9]

A critique of the institute's first month of operation, based on opinions of its faculty and students, highlighted several shortcomings. First, enrollment was too small, indicting a need for more active recruitment; second, too many courses were being taught concurrently; and third, there was not enough time for students to discuss their readings among themselves and with faculty members.

All of the young teachers agreed that the most helpful part of in-service training was observing better teaching techniques and listening to successful teachers explain their methods at the Fuzoku or other designated experimental schools. This was also the view of most of the 124 other poorly trained teachers who did not attend the institute but visited briefly the experimental schools. Finally, all officials and faculty members associated with the institute agreed there should be a minimum of fifty students enrolled, as originally planned.[10]

About a week after the Education Institute's June 1948 session, Rollin Fox again visited Yamanashi Prefecture. Fully apprised of the influence of the Yamanashi Teachers' Union in educational affairs as well as the union's influence in other prefectures, he sought my assistance to curb union activity in professional matters. These matters, in his view, rightfully belonged to the local education associations. I agreed, but saw no way for military government as it functioned in Japan to direct teachers' unions to stay out of professional education activities. In fact, SCAP's Education Division was likewise powerless to curb the intrusion of the Japan Teachers' Union into educational affairs, given the still highly pro-labor policy of General MacArthur.

Prior to Dr. Fox's arrival, I had again conferred by phone with a member of SCAP's Education Division on this matter; he conveyed his and the division's dismay over union activities. Presently, he said, there was no legal way to curb it. Although I had informed Dr. Fox of the SCAP's views on the subject, he still believed military government could and should reduce the union's influence. Even my commanding officer had difficulty convincing this fine educator of the CI&E's limits of authority on this particular issue.

Concluding there was no serious conflict with the union-dominated Education Institute's in-service teacher training program, which had drawn only twenty-seven students in June, the principal and faculty of the two regular normal schools proceeded with plans to hold their second annual in-service session for primary and lower secondary school teachers in early August 1948 (the first, it will be recalled, was held in early August 1947 in eighteen schools). This time, to assure maximum attendance, lecture and discussion sessions were scheduled in seven geographical areas. Thus the vast majority of teachers were spared lodging and transportation costs. Furthermore, a number of educators from the Ministry of Education would be on hand at various schools to lecture and lead discussions on educational psychology and on teaching more effectively the Japanese language, mathematics, and other subjects.[11]

About 900 teachers signed up, although actual attendance reportedly was somewhat less. Because this in-service program did not focus exclusively on reeducating the youngest and most poorly educated teachers, they felt no particular stigma attached to attending the sessions. In the same time-frame, from August 3 through 9, and also under the aegis of the two regular normal schools, about 400 upper secondary school principals and teachers also participated in their annual separate in-service training sessions in Kofu and two other schools.

Meanwhile, the Yamanashi Teachers' Union's Education Institute scheduled (during the same week in early August 1948) its own second in-service training program for the more poorly educated teachers.

Once more attendance was quite low, for the reasons cited in June—the cost of traveling to and from Kofu or of living briefly in the city, and the stigma attached to attending the institute—and also because of the simultaneous scheduling of the schools' in-training sessions.

According to several reports, teachers who attended the in-service teacher training programs (under the auspices of the two regular normal schools or the union's Education Institute) considered them worthwhile. In lectures or discussions with teachers over the preceding months, I always encouraged Yamanashi's educators to take advantage of these programs emphasizing that in the United States, they were always viewed as necessary for career and professional enhancement. Both the regular normal schools and the Education Institute were greatly assisted in their educational endeavors in the summer of 1948 when each received a collection of about 700 new volumes (on various aspects of education and other subjects) and subscriptions to professional magazines.[12]

Yamanashi's Educational Association

Because of Dr. Fox's deep concern that the Japan Teachers' Union headquarters in Tokyo and its adjunct, the Yamanashi Teachers' Union, had usurped the functions of professional Japanese education associations, I prepared for him in early July 1948 a special report on the subject. It focused on why the former Great Japan Education Association (it had dropped the word "Great" in early 1946) and its prefectural affiliates were not yet capable of asserting leadership in instituting democratic educational reforms in Japan (See note 11, chap. 3). I also cited the complex nature of the association which, as in the past, had separate branches for active and retired primary and secondary (i.e., middle school) principals and teachers, albeit the latter was basically a separate organization.

Despite SCAP's purge of the association's principal leaders for militaristic or ultranationalistic activities during the immediate prewar and wartime periods, it was uncertain, I continued, whether the postwar Japan Education Association had been entirely dissolved and reorganized in accordance with SCAP directives. As for the association's affiliate in Yamanashi,

it remained ineffective because (1) it was reorganized after the war by self-appointed leaders without an election; (2) its present leaders comprised only a small group of elderly conservative principals and teachers who demonstrated little ability for educational reform and who possessed a hearty dislike of the Yamanashi Teachers' Union; and (3) its ineptness had enabled the Cultural Department of the Yamanashi Teachers' Union to assume virtually all of the functions once performed by the association.[13]

In addition, a number of the local association's reports to my office indicated that its property and financial records were a tangled web.

The determination of the Yamanashi Teachers' Union to play the dominant role in prefectural educational affairs was further underscored when it established its own "Education Association," to which many if not most rank-and-file principals in primary and lower secondary schools payed dues of five *yen* per month, apart from their union dues. This tactic further diminished the immediate prospect for the emergence of a truly independent, American-style professional education association with reasonably young leadership. Dr. Fox accepted these observations unhappily but indicated he would do his best in the forthcoming months to reestablish in Yamanashi and other prefectures a more professional association.

My report to Dr. Fox suddenly seemed premature near the end of July, when the head of the nearly moribund Yamanashi Education Association announced a reorganization of the association, launched a vigorous membership drive, and raised annual dues from 60 to 80 *yen*. He urged all educational retirees, those still in the schools, PTA members, and other citizens interested in education (and disenchanted with the Yamanashi Teachers' Union) to join.

Very soon thereafter, an association representative claimed to have recruited thousands of new members, although I was skeptical of this figure. Nonetheless, several spot checks during school visits and meetings of educators in my office indicated that some principals and teachers who disliked the Yamanashi Teachers' Union and were aware of Dr. Fox's views had indeed joined and paid dues, although none appeared to have participated thus far in the associations's activities, such as they were. Some teachers, uncertain as to what to do, were now paying dues to the union, to its new Education Association, and to the "reorganized" old Japan Education Association. It was another example of the confusion in postwar educational reform, especially in a predominately rural prefecture.

Despite the renewed activism of the old Education Association, I did not expect it to diminish seriously the influence of the Yamanashi

Teachers' Union in the foreseeable future. The union's leaders in Tokyo as well as in Yamanashi were too strongly entrenched, and its activities under SCAP's labor policies were legal. Meanwhile, SCAP's plan to decentralize education in Japan took another step forward on July 5, 1948, when the Japanese Diet enacted the Board of Education Law. From my perspective, this major step towards educational decentralization would provide an additional opportunity for leaders of the Yamanashi Teachers' Union to maintain their influence over prefectural education.

Converting Normal Schools to Teachers' Colleges

Concurrently with the foregoing developments, Yamanashi's educators were also bracing for major changes in their traditional normal schools. These changes, along with other subjects, were discussed at some length on June 7–8, 1948, at a CI&E conference in Urawa, the capital of Saitama Prefecture, convened by Rollin Fox. Chairing the discussions on normal schools and higher education was Virginia A. Carley of the Higher Education Branch in SCAP's Education Division.[14]

Dr. Carley reiterated SCAP's policy at this time to convert all of Japan's normal schools into four-year institutions and upgrade their curricula. Japan's educationists, she noted, had produced no new materials on pedagogy and psychology since about 1938, when the nation stepped up its military preparedness. Hence there was a particular need for normal schools to teach courses on the growth and development of children, and on child and social psychology. Normal schools and other colleges and universities were over-specialized. Courses in the humanities should be taught along with those in science and mathematics. A new booklet for normal school faculties, prepared by the Ministry of Education with the guidance of SCAP, would be distributed shortly on the subject of general courses on education.

Dr. Carley also reiterated SCAP's plan for ensuring the establishment of at least one university in each of Japan's forty-six prefectures (large cities already had more than one). In some prefectures, like Yamanashi, she said, four-year normal schools, renamed teachers' colleges, might be able to merge with their prefectural agricultural and technical colleges to form the nucleus of a university. She underscored the need to

make higher education less elitist and to reduce the inordinate influence within Japanese government and business held by the graduates
of a few important universities in the largest cities, especially Tokyo
University.

Such were the objectives expressed by one of SCAP's leading educators in mid-1948 for normal schools and higher education in Yamanashi and throughout Japan to further the nation's democratization.

14

Private Schools and the School for the Handicapped

A Christian Girls' School

Not until after the beginning of the new school year on April 1, 1947, was I able to devote much time to monitoring and inspecting a few of Yamanashi Prefecture's private schools and the special school for the handicapped. Fortunately, as I was still without an assistant CI&E officer, there were relatively few such schools. The purpose of my inspections was, of course, to determine if they were operating in compliance with SCAP directives, new Japanese government education legislation enacted at the end of March 1947, and other clarifying ordinances.

During the 1930s and until the attack on Pearl Harbor on December 7, 1941, Yamanashi Prefecture possessed about twenty-one small private schools. By war's end in September 1945, however, most of these had ceased to function. I managed to visit several, including a Christian girls' school (*Eiwa Jo Gakko*) founded by Canadian Methodists in 1899; a middle school and college of the Nichiren Buddhist sect near Minobu in the Mt. Fuji area; and two of three Korean schools established by local Korean citizens shortly after the occupation began in September 1945.

The Christian girls' school located in Kofu created no difficulties whatsoever. In fact, the first Yamanashi Military Government Detachment greatly assisted in rebuilding the school and the house of its principal after both were seriously damaged during the July 1945 B-29 bombing. Some team members assumed that a flourishing Christian girls' school with its largely western-style curriculum and teaching methods would have an exemplary influence on efforts to reform the Japanese education system. This assumption was not realized in subsequent months, however, as it never served as a "showplace" school where Yamanashi's public school teachers could visit on a regular basis to observe western teaching practices. Nonetheless, because two of the school's graduates were the most able bilingual Japanese employees on the team, and because its principal and teachers were frequent attendees at periodic Christian services conducted by U.S. Army chaplains at team headquarters, there existed considerable empathy between team members and members of the school's faculty.[1]

The Nichiren Buddhist Schools

I inspected briefly for the first time the headquarters, middle school, and college of the Nichiren Buddhist sect near Minobu in February 1947. I conducted a more thorough inspection of the sect's educational institutions and other activities in November 1947. On both occasions I discerned no violations of SCAP's directives on education and religion (see chaps. 10 and 18).

Korean Schools

Although the Korean community in Yamanashi Prefecture established only three very small Korean schools soon after the occupation began, the illegal operation of these private institutions, especially their all-Korean curricula, would eventually occupy my intermittent attention. Their existence was already a major problem for some military government personnel in Japan's largest cities with a high concentration of Koreans, where numerous private Korean schools were operating. As early as December 1946, there were confrontations in some of Japan's largest cities between Koreans and the Japanese government over the former's insistence that they be recognized as foreign nationals with the right to establish their own educational institutions. This dispute would lead in 1948 to the occupation's first serious disturbances.

The Korean school issue in Japan had its antecedents following Japan's defeat of China during the war of 1894–95, which gave Japan a foothold in Korea leading to its annexation in 1910. As a consequence, increasing numbers of Koreans were brought to Japan, most of them forcibly, to work in its mines and factories and in other laboring positions. Their numbers increased dramatically shortly before and during World War II, until the war's official end in September 1945, when there were about 2,400,000 Korean residents in the country. Under SCAP's repatriation program for foreign nationals, approximately two million Koreans decided to return to South Korea, albeit many of these, disillusioned with the chaos in their newly liberated country, soon elected to return to Japan. By the beginning of 1947, about

600,000 Koreans were still in Japan (only a few hundred went back to Communist-ruled North Korea).

Meanwhile, SCAP had issued a directive on November 20, 1946, stipulating that Koreans who refused repatriation to their homeland would be treated as Japanese citizens. This was also the view of the postwar Japanese government. From the outset, however, the new interim South Korean government (it did not become officially the Republic of Korea until August 15, 1948) took an opposing position, insisting that any Koreans still in Japan should be treated as foreign nationals, similar to other United Nations personnel. Koreans in Japan fervently agreed. To demonstrate their independence from SCAP's directive and the new Japanese law governing private schools, they established during the first two years of the occupation (September 1945–September 1947) about 578 private schools in Japan, mostly primary, with a small number at the secondary level. Students were taught by about 1,500 Korean teachers. The Koreans further exhibited their foreign national status by teaching primarily the Korean language, history and culture, and mathematics. Many schools were housed in makeshift buildings with little or no equipment, below even minimum physical standards.[2]

There were only a few thousand Koreans in Yamanashi Prefecture and, except for their inclusion in statistics on health, repatriation, and black-marketing, their political activities were not cited in a Yamanashi Military Government Team report until June 1947:

> The Koreans in this prefecture held a mass meeting on June 10 for the purpose of discussing the promotion of a Korean Provisional Government in South Korea, the political situation in the homeland, organizing women's and cooperative unions, and a taxpayers' association. About 600 attended. The gathering was orderly.[3]

In August 1947, a news report indicated that the Yamanashi branch of the League of Koreans in Japan (*Choren*) held a meeting on August 15, 1947, to celebrate the second anniversary of Korea's independence. There were about 2,300 attendees.[4]

Meanwhile Yamanashi's small Korean community was struggling to maintain its three small private schools. I was aware of their existence but with many other CI&E matters on my agenda, I had not yet visited or inspected them. Near the end of 1947, however, Mr. Yamaguchi, the prefectural education chief, told me his office was having difficulties with the three schools. This followed the issuance of a new directive from the Ministry of Education requiring all Korean schools to comply with Japanese education laws as they applied to private schools. Enforcement of the directive would begin at the onset of the new school year on April 1, 1948.

A few days after my meeting with Mr. Yamaguchi, two members of the local Korean community came to my office to complain of harassment by a prefectural school inspector who had threatened their schools with possible closure for failure to comply. With considerable emotion, they asked me to restrain the inspectors. Emphasizing their many years of persecution by the Japanese, they strongly asserted their right to teach their youngsters the Korean language and other Korean subjects. Yamanashi's Koreans, they added, were very poor and did not have sufficient funds to build good prefectural school buildings.

I explained to them why a SCAP directive and new Japanese education legislation on private schools required Koreans to comply with certain minimum standards of education. The teaching of the Japanese language was considered essential if they and their families elected to remain permanent residents of Japan. Otherwise, the children would grow up as strangers in their adopted country. Private schools, of course, were free to teach the Korean language and some Korean subjects, but basically they should adhere to the new postwar Japanese education curricula. America I explained, was a country of many races, but all children in private schools learned English and American history. In addition, schools had to meet minimum standards with respect to buildings, classrooms, and equipment.

My listeners were unpersuaded and clearly unhappy with my refusal to accede to their request. SCAP's Education Division had already been wrestling with this problem for many months, and as periodic confrontations on the issue continued between the Koreans and Japanese authorities in the larger cities throughout 1947, an eventual showdown appeared inevitable. The tensions were exacerbated by the fact that the leadership of *Choren*, the largest of several Korean groups, was dominated by Communists and worked closely with the Japan Communist party. This reduced an initial sympathy for the Koreans among SCAP and military government personnel.[5]

As the spokesmen for Yamanashi's three Korean schools continued to defy both the SCAP directive and the Japanese legislation governing the operation of private schools, I finally inspected two schools. It was a disheartening experience. The schools were merely mud huts with thatched roofs, and neither had a playground. Twelve or fifteen students were inside, and the schoolroom had only a few chairs and some elevated planks that served as desks. Each faculty consisted of a principal and a male teacher (other teachers reportedly were absent). They were not pleased to see me. I conveyed essentially what I had told the two Korean visitors to my office; namely, that they had to abide with SCAP directives and new Japanese education laws governing the operation of private schools. Both principals and the teachers displayed much anger and belligerency about the Japanese laws and insisted Koreans had a right to do as they wished, given years of mistreatment by the Japanese. I said I understood their feelings. Nevertheless, they had to operate in accordance with provisions governing the operation of private schools in Japan or they would have to be closed. Their attitude clearly was defiant.

The Korean School Riots

While the Korean school issue in Yamanashi Prefecture simmered, it was gradually coming to a boil in Tokyo and several other large cities. On January 20, 1948, the Ministry of Education had again ordered all Korean schools to obey the laws governing private educational institutions and mandated the use of Japanese textbooks on April 1, the beginning of the 1948–49 school year. Some Korean schools finally complied, but many others did not. Consequently, under heavy pressure by SCAP, the ministry on April 20 ordered the closing of all Korean schools operating in violation of the laws.[6]

Among the schools not complying were the three in Yamanashi Prefecture. Mr. Yamaguchi, the prefectural education chief, was highly distressed over this. Desiring to avoid a confrontation with local Korean leaders, he asked me to issue the school closing order. After conferring with the team commander on the matter, I phoned a member of SCAP's Education Division for guidance. SCAPS's position at the moment, I learned, was to let the Ministry of Education assume responsibility for carrying out its education policy on private schools. (The latest instructions from Eighth Army headquarters to military government teams on this volatile issue had not yet been received.) Consequently, I informed Mr. Yamaguchi that the situation required the prefectural government to enforce the laws with respect to Yamanashi's Korean schools.[7]

Meanwhile, violence had already erupted elsewhere in Japan over the school closing order. On April 15, five days before the ministry's order, Japanese police apprehended seventy-three Koreans in Kobe for creating disturbances over the closings, and several days later, in Okayama on southern Honshu Island about 8,000 Koreans demonstrated, gaining the release from prison of a Korean leader who had vigorously opposed any school closings. On April 23 in Osaka, where closings had already caused disturbances, several thousand Koreans invaded the Osaka prefectural building but were finally driven out by about 5,000 Japanese police. The next night, in Kobe again, 500 Koreans stormed the Hyogo prefectural headquarters building to protest the April 20th edict. Many of the participants succeeded in locking up for six hours the prefectural governor, the chief of police, and the city mayor. They forced the governor to rescind the prefectural school–closing order, an action that led to the governor's immediate resignation.[8]

At this juncture, General MacArthur decided to intervene. He authorized U.S. Eighth Army Brigadier General Pearson Menoher, commander of the Kobe Military Base, to declare a limited state of emergency in the city and to deputize all of the city's Japanese police under the U.S. Provost Marshal. General Menoher also instructed all Japanese officials to reaffirm their school-closing order and to arrest Koreans who opposed it. It was no secret that leaders and many members of the Korean opposition were members of the Communist-dominated *Choren*. On April 26, Lieutenant General Eichelberger, Eighth Army commander in Yokohama, arrived in Kobe for a first-hand look at the explosive Korean-Japanese confrontation.

Surprisingly, in Tokyo where there were about twenty-three Korean schools, disturbances were not quite as severe, although fourteen of the schools defied the Ministry of Education's order to register and operate their private schools in conformance with Japanese law. The other schools promised to abide with the ministry's order.[9]

Meanwhile, all of the evidence gathered by SCAP, military government, and Japanese officials in the cities where the disturbances had occurred indicated they had been orchestrated by the Communist leaders of *Choren* and the Japan Communist party. The evidence also showed that Korean Communists especially were trying to influence the outcome of the first free elections in Korea scheduled for May 10.

In Yamanashi Prefecture, meanwhile, the problem of its three Korean schools had not yet been resolved. The day after the rioting in Kobe, I met again with Mr. Yamaguchi and other prefectural education officials and asked them if they were prepared to act against the three Korean schools still operating illegally. The officials were reluctant to make a decision. Whereupon I instructed them either to register the private schools in accordance with Japanese law or, if this were not possible, to close them.

Almost immediately after the education officials had left my office, my commanding officer received a phone call from Eighth Army headquarters ordering team members to keep out of the Korean school problem until further notice. (Similar calls were made to military government teams throughout Japan.) The caller provided no explanation for Eighth Army's injunction. I learned the reason the next morning when I phoned a member of SCAP's Education Division. He said the main consideration for remaining aloof temporarily from the Korean school problem was the upcoming May Day celebrations by workers throughout Japan. As in many countries in the world, these would be held on May 1. In addition, SCAP now believed it was also desirable for military government personnel to avoid controversy over the Korean school issue until after May 10, the date for a national election in South Korea to create a national assembly preparatory to establishing the Republic of Korea.

The May Day celebrations in Japan's main cities came and went. Then on May 7, the Ministry of Education, after extensive talks with Korean leaders in Tokyo, announced a revised policy for Korean schools which would permit them to increase optional courses in Korean language, history, literature, and culture, although certain Japanese courses would still be required. The ministry briefly relaxed the deadline for compliance. In Yamanashi Prefecture, Mr. Yamaguchi came to my office to give me further details of the ministry's revised policy. He was greatly relieved by this turn of events.[10]

Soon thereafter, the prefectural education chief informed me that his office was continuing to talk to local Korean leaders about the three schools. The discourses were quite amicable, and a final decision would be made about the future of the schools on June 5. Again no action was taken after the Ministry of Education decided to give Koreans still more time to upgrade their facilities throughout Japan. Thus the problem continued to simmer during the ensuing weeks, although it was destined shortly to trigger another outburst of Korean activity.[11]

The catalysts for the new round of disturbances began with elections on May 10 in South Korea, under the supervision of United Nations personnel, creating a national assembly. This was followed by the formal establishment on August 15, the third anniversary of the defeat of Japan, of the Republic of Korea with Syngman Rhee as president. General MacArthur flew to Seoul to participate in the ceremonies. This inspired the Soviet-backed Communist regime north of the 38th parallel to establish on September 9 its own Democratic People's Republic of Korea in Pyongyang under Kim Il Sung. Its institutions were modeled after those in the Soviet Union. The two events heightened tensions and resulted in renewed clashes between the Communist-led *Choren* in Japan and Japanese police in some of Japan's largest cities, and more defiance by *Choren* members against Japan's education laws. SCAP and military government officials now backed more firmly the Japanese government's enforcement of SCAP's directive categorizing Koreans residing in Japan as citizens of the country, and Japanese laws as they pertained to private schools.[12]

I had departed from Japan less than a fortnight when the new disturbances began, although I followed the events as best as I could upon arrival in the States. Suffice it to say that another year elapsed before the final denouement of the Korean-Japanese clashes, with the status of Korean schools fueling the historic hostility. On September 9, 1949, with the full support of SCAP (who concurrently launched a "Red Purge" requiring the dismissal of all Communist teachers in Japan), the Japanese government ordered the dissolution of *Choren* and three other left-wing groups. The four organizations were characterized as anti-democratic and terrorist and were charged with refusing to obey the orders of occupation authorities. *Choren* appealed to SCAP to reverse the order, but to no avail. Accordingly, the Japanese government finally confiscated *Choren's* assets and closed all schools still under its jurisdiction.[13]

With the outbreak of the Korean War on June 25, 1950, SCAP took additional actions against certain Koreans in Japan who were considered security risks. Not until after hostilities ceased, following the signing of an armistice agreement on July 27, 1953 (fifteen months after the end of the occupation of Japan), was there some amelioration in the relations between the Koreans and the Japanese in Japan. The problem of the status of the Korean schools in Japan gradually eased, although it was not fully resolved.

School for the Handicapped

Yamanashi Prefecture had one school for the handicapped; namely, for those who were blind, deaf, or unable to speak. Although this was a prefectural rather than a private school, both SCAP and Eighth Army education officials made a special effort to improve the lot of these disadvantaged boys and girls and young adults.

In November 1946, shortly after I assumed my CI&E duties, a IXth Corps official and I visited the very rudimentary facilities of this school in Kofu and urged prefectural education officials to improve its living and studying facilities. This was finally accomplished in June 1947 when deaf and mute students moved to new quarters in a part of Yamanashi's Medical College (now destined to be closed by the Home Ministry), and blind students to a section of the prefectural hospital. The change was a major improvement. At this time, students of both sexes numbered eighty and ranged in ages from seven to thirty years. The faculty, augmented by recent hirings, consisted of ten full-time and part-time members. With the assistance of the team's medical officer, Captain Jakofsky, prefectural authorities quickly began providing the handicapped students with more medical care and arranged for a full-time nurse.[14]

The eighty students comprised only a part of the total number of handicapped persons in Yamanashi. As in many countries of the world, most families in rural and mountainous areas believed that having a disadvantaged offspring was a badge of shame. In a few extreme cases in Yamanashi and elsewhere in Japan, parents hid such children, locking them in a room or shed. It was occupation policy to try to change this attitude.

The Japanese Diet's enactment of the School Education Law on March 29, 1947, had mandated compulsory education for all handicapped children, ages six through twelve. This necessitated a nationwide survey of the numbers in this age group and, thereafter, all those above the age of twelve. Counting was a slow process. Not until August 1947 did I receive the total number of handicapped persons in Yamanashi: 407 blind and 612 deaf and mute individuals for a total of 1,019. Of these, about 300 fell within the age group (6 to

12) requiring compulsory education. A few parents who had been reluctant to send their handicapped child to a special school were finally persuaded to do so.[15]

In November 1947, the facilities for handicapped students were further improved by providing a larger building next to the Yamanashi National Hospital. A kitchen, better classrooms, and two dormitories, one for boys and men, the other for girls and women, had been renovated or constructed. Vocational training for certain students was enhanced by the school's acquisition from local textile manufacturers of three silk-threading machines to enable them to learn a trade.

There was one traditional vocational course for older students that I believed should be discontinued. This was *hari* or "needle cure," known in America as "acupuncture." During another visit to the school I watched briefly a class where the course was being taught:

> A blind student was teaching *hari* to several other students. Many Japanese still believe in this old but unscientific and useless practice. I discussed the matter with the school's principal who said steps will be taken eventually to eliminate this course from the curriculum. The teaching of *hari*, I have learned, is found in most schools for the handicapped in Japan.[16]

The technique of acupuncture originated in China about 200 B.C. and was introduced in Japan about A.D. 573. My skepticism was reinforced by the opinion of Captain Jakofsky, the team's medical officer, who placed no credence in the practice. By chance, two Japanese members of the team's administrative staff had recently sought relief from particular ailments from a local acupuncturist with dubious results. One, a lady, was treated for an infected toe and, after the treatment worsened the infection, it was quickly cured by an antibiotic prescribed by Captain Jakofsky. The second staff member, a male, took several acupuncture treatments for recurring headaches. When I queried him about the result, he said his headaches suddenly disappeared. In the judgment of Captain Jakofsky, the acupuncture treatment had so severely irritated his skin that he no longer noticed the headaches. Such was the prevailing view towards acupuncture of most American physicians in the 1940s.

Despite my suggestion to the principal of the school for the handicapped that acupuncture should be removed eventually from the school's curriculum, it was still being taught when I departed for the United States in late August 1948.

Little did I realize that many years later my standard American medical encyclopedia for family use would contain the following statement: "Acupuncture has been most effective in such disorders as arthritis, neuralgia, headaches, and other metabolic functions. . . . In recent years, it has also been employed as an effective anaesthetic in surgical operations."[17]

Although many American health-insurance organizations today will not pay for acupuncture treatment unless it is performed by a duly accredited medical or osteopathic physician, its efficacy in curing or alleviating some human ailments no longer appears in doubt.

15

The School Lunch Program

February 1947 witnessed the beginning of another CI&E task in Yamanashi Prefecture. This required oversight of a SCAP-sponsored school lunch program. Conducted on a nationwide basis, it would continue for many months.

The decision by SCAP headquarters to supplement the diet of young Japanese students, especially in towns and cities, followed the shipment beginning in 1946 of U.S. food to Japan to ameliorate the hunger of millions of the nation's citizens. The reasons were both practical and humanitarian: to forestall any social unrest that might undermine the occupation's objectives, and to prevent any large-scale epidemic that could affect adversely the health of American and Allied personnel.[1]

As with other SCAP-initiated activities and reforms, the administration of the nationwide school lunch program was the responsibility of the Japanese government, with American and Allied personnel providing advice and supervision. School lunches consisted of a variety of American foodstuffs and some Japanese rationed food. The major cost of American food imports for schools was underwritten by the Licensed Agencies for the Relief of Asia (LARA), a special agency created for this purpose.[2] SCAP officials spent several months planning the program in cooperation with six Japanese ministries (Education, Home, Public Health and Welfare, Finance, Agriculture, and Forestry) before it began implementation in Tokyo and in the heavily populated adjacent prefectures of Kanagawa and Chiba.[3] In January and February 1947, school lunches began to be served gradually in other urban schools. Students in farming areas were excluded, on the premise they had easier access to fruits and vegetables. In Yamanashi Prefecture, only the schools in Kofu and a few large towns were declared eligible initially to participate. Students in grades one through eight were served the special lunches twice a week, then, with the onset of the new 6–3 school system on April 1, 1947, the servings were extended to students in grades one through nine.

Shortly before the nationwide school lunch program began, an Eighth Army directive enjoined all CI&E officers to exercise inventory surveillance of imported LARA food items. Another responsibility was to answer the many questions of prefectural education officials, principals, head teachers and faculties about establishing lunch facilities in schools: What should be the size of a school kitchen? Was a brazier or a stove preferable for heating skim milk and soup? Was coal, lignite, charcoal, or wood the best fuel? Should schools hire only part-time or full-time employees? In short, how did schools in America operate their lunch programs?

Unfortunately, neither I nor my military government colleagues had any personal experiences with school lunch programs. In the America of the 1920s, 1930s, and very early 1940s, when we team members were in primary and high schools, we brought our lunches to school or, if we lived nearby, we went home for lunch. Some schools had lunch rooms with chairs and tables and a canteen where students could purchase a limited array of items such as candy bars and soft drinks. Cafeterias where students could purchase a part or all of their lunches with money provided by their parents existed only in schools in America's largest cities. Consequently, I was not able to provide much expert advice to Yamanashi's educators on how a food-service system for students should be established and administered.

Nonetheless, I tried to make constructive suggestions. Expenses could be kept to a minimum, I counseled, if schools hired only a few part-time employees and solicited assistance from newly formed PTAS. Most schools did this, with "mother's committees" soon volunteering their services during midday to help prepare and serve the twice-a-week lunches. Mr. Yamaguchi, the prefectural education chief, needed some manpower and a truck or two to transport LARA food supplies from railroad boxcars to the schools. I recommended he ask for transportation assistance from other prefectural agencies. In addition, I suggested that some of the lunch costs could be defrayed if schools sold the empty containers used for shipping foodstuffs from America. Some local businesses, I soon learned, were willing to pay a good price for these very durable storage receptacles.

Soon most schools eligible to serve luncheons had established a kitchen and had acquired the necessary braziers, pots and pans, bowls and cups, and other utensils, plus a small staff of part-time and volunteer workers. The initial LARA food items consisted of dried skim milk, chocolate drink, citrus juices, and soup mixes, as well as canned nuts, sugar, and salt. Shortly other LARA shipments also included chocolate and vanilla items, preserved butter, packed strawberries, dried fruits, and dessert powders. Former Japanese Army and Navy food stocks provided additionally several varieties of canned meats, rice, and bean paste. Occasionally, fresh whale meat and other fish were included in the luncheon diet. Also, many students brought local vegetables. My initial report on the school lunch program in Yamanashi Prefecture in March 1947 told of a good start:

> A total of 18,227 students in eighteen schools are now being fed an average of two lunches per week. The cost of serving warm lunches ranges from 50 to 90 *sen* per student with an average cost of 70 *sen*. Those who eat cold supplementary lunches are assessed only two *sen* per meal. Cost differentials for students who consume warm food is contingent on the amount of vegetables they bring from their homes. Some items, particularly fish and meat, are imported from Saitama and Hokkaido Prefectures.
> The eighteen schools include the Yamanashi schools for the blind, the deaf, and those unable to speak. Twelve schools are presently able to serve warm luncheons, but six still lack cooking facilities.[4]

In April 1947, several additional schools were declared eligible to serve lunches, and soon there were eighteen more for a total of thirty-six.

Meanwhile, reports of occasional pilfering of food items necessitated increased inventory surveillance of LARA supplies. I monitored their unloading from railroad boxcars to trucks and, in addition, examined the warehouse where they were stored temporarily. Also, during school inspections or visits, my interpreter checked the LARA supply records in schools where luncheons were served. Rather quickly I turned the surveillance task over to a technical sergeant on my staff who, with a bilingual Nisei corporal, carefully checked the English language manifests of incoming LARA shipments against the Japanese warehouse and school-storage records.

This did not end the pilfering of the foodstuffs, however, especially of such popular items as chocolate drinks, citrus juices, and dried fruits. School inspectors and local police were asked to investigate reported thefts. There was one highly publicized arrest of a citizen who not only received a rather severe jail sentence but also universal opprobrium for stealing school lunch supplies, a crime considered far more reprehensible than engaging in black-market operations. Two principals, whose schools' food-storage rooms had been broken into at night, came to my office to proffer their resignations. I refused to accept the resignations. The pilferings, in my judgment, underscored the severe economic hardship of many very desperate citizens and did not reflect unfavorably on the administrative proficiency of the two principals.

School lunches were discontinued during the brief traditional school holiday period in August 1947 but were resumed in September. Twenty-one tons of new supplies were on hand. The cost of a food item per student, meanwhile, had risen considerably, as follows (in *yen* and *sen*): canned meats, 3:80; canned juice, 3:00; powdered milk, 3:00; and dried fruit, 2:80. Temporarily, an insufficient quantity of supplies allowed the serving only of heated powdered milk in schools outside of Kofu. Upon the arrival of more supplies in November, canned meats, juices, and dried fruit were again added to the menus of schools earmarked to serve school luncheons.[5]

The most difficult decision I had to make while monitoring Yamanashi's school lunch program was to deny special requests from teachers for permission to take home a few LARA food items. Many teachers or close members of their families had critically ill infants or preschool children who desperately needed, they believed, some citrus juice, skim milk, or chocolate drink. I had to reject such requests lest public knowledge that these or other imported food items were made available to children of preschool age open a pandora's box of hundreds of such pleas. That some school principals occasionally permitted this practice appeared to be confirmed in several anonymous letters to my office which made precisely such allegations. Because these breaches of eligibility were rare, I did not ask the local police to investigate them.

By mid-1948, shortly before I returned to the United States, about 28,000 students in thirty-six primary and lower secondary schools in Yamanashi Prefecture were still receiving the special lunches twice a week.[6] Nationwide, about 4,750,000 students were participating in the program.[7] Judging from conversations with prefectural officials, principals, teachers, citizens, and from dozens of letters that flowed into the offices of the Yamanashi Military Government Team, it is doubtful if any single SCAP-sponsored program was appreciated more by parents than the feeding of Japan's youngsters. It further embellished the reputation of General MacArthur as a humanitarian, and it was a significant factor, in my view and that of many other military government officials, in assuring the continued cooperation of the vast majority of the Japanese people in the occupation. As an American, I was proud that so many of my fellow citizens contributed willingly through various organizations to make possible the purchase of substantial quantities of LARA foodstuffs.

16

Expansion of the Labor Education Program

New Labor Education Duties

Following General MacArthur's order prohibiting a threatened national labor union strike on February 1, 1947 (see chap. 8), the activities of Japan's many unions, which included unions for most of the nation's teachers at all levels of education, were less volatile in the immediately ensuing months. Nonetheless, the danger remained that unionists would further weaken economically a still-prostrate nation. This possibility impelled members of SCAP's Labor Division to devote more resources and manpower to educate union leaders on the one hand, and government and management officials on the other, on how to engage in more democratic and constructive collective bargaining to settle disputes primarily over salaries, benefits, and working conditions.

In January 1974, during a CI&E and labor conference at IXth Corps headquarters in Sendai, military government CI&E officers were asked to assume the additional duty of labor education officers and provide more information to labor and management on how to resolve labor disputes through arbitration, conciliation, and mediation. This task became more time consuming in the spring of 1947. In Yamanashi Prefecture I initially shared this duty with Captain John Kopke, the team's labor officer, but because he too had additional team responsibilities, the labor-education task fell primarily on my shoulders, especially after the nationwide May Day labor parades and celebrations.

Following the near nationwide labor walkout on February 1, 1947, all military government teams in Japan were enjoined to monitor closely labor's annual demonstrations on May 1 and report any disturbances. In Yamanashi Prefecture, the two largest worker's groups assembled in Kofu, the prefectural capital, and Otsuki. In Kofu, unionists marched to the front of the prefectural government building and presented to Governor Yoshie Katsuyasu fifteen resolutions on worker's needs. In response, the governor promised "to make every effort to carry out . . . the resolutions if they are in my power to do so. Other matters I will refer to the various ministries in Tokyo." He said he was happy that the labor movement in Japan "was now following a healthy course."[1]

A number of union orators considered the governor's promise insufficient and promised to conduct a campaign of "no confidence" in him. Their dissent had no impact on Yamanashi's chief executive, however, as he continued in his post in the ensuing months.

During May and June 1947, Captain Kopke and I were asked to review six separate union allegations against employers who reportedly tried to influence the union or, in some instances, discriminate against employees who engaged too vigorously in union activities. It was very difficult to judge the validity of the allegations. In the event, the prefectural Labor Relations Committee or the prefectural Government Labor Office managed to resolve most of these cases in accordance with the guidelines in the Trade Union Law and the Labor Relations Adjustment Law of March 1 and October 13, 1946, respectively, and in the Labor Standards Law promulgated on April 5, 1947, to become effective September 1 of that year. Our main contribution was to issue press releases highlighting some of the provisions of the new Japanese labor laws which specifically prohibited employer influence or discrimination against unionists.[2]

In a rural prefecture like Yamanashi, there were ample reasons for workers to file complaints against employers. Why they did so only infrequently was not difficult to comprehend. The new American-style unionism could not quickly replace the deeply rooted tradition of employer paternalism in the hundreds of small businesses, plants, and factories throughout the towns and villages. Substantial numbers of employers and workers remained insulated from postwar Japanese labor legislation and from Article 28 of the new Constitution which gave workers the right to organize and bargain collectively.

Nowhere was this insulation more manifest than in the seventy to eighty silk-spinning mills, mostly small, located in the more remote parts of Yamanashi. To familiarize myself with their operations, I inspected two of them early in June 1947. Both were located in partially landscaped and wooded areas suggesting an ambience of pleasant working conditions. Although the mills' interiors and machines appeared rudimentary, they were remarkably clean. Most of the employees were young girls, ages fifteen through nineteen, with sixth- to eighth-grade educations, who resided in nearby dormitories.[3]

Mill officials who escorted me on my inspection of the facilities boasted of the care provided to the young girls. They had free room, food, and medical services. The largest portion of each girl's salary was sent directly to her family, leaving her with a small allowance to spend as she wished. Normally, the girls worked eight to ten hours per day, six days per week, but occasionally more if silk orders required them to do so. They received no overtime pay. Supervision was strict to "protect their morals." They were free to visit with their families only on specified days several times a year.

In truth, the girls were indentured employees of the two mills, and they and the owners and managers of the two mills appeared oblivious to new Japanese labor legislation, such as Article 48 of the Labor Standards Law, which prescribed a 48-hour working week and mandated no less than four holidays per month. Neither military government nor the prefectural Labor Relations Committee had received a complaint thus far about the working violations from either the girl employees or their families.

The absence of any complaints about the still semifeudal operations of the silk mills could be ascribed to at least four factors: the working and living conditions of the girls were less harsh than those of millions of other citizens in postwar, poverty-stricken Japan; their salaries augmented the cash income of their families; their relatively low educational level; and their general isolation from the torrent of SCAP-imposed social, economic, labor, political, educational, and other reforms. It was unrealistic to believe the young girls could demand their own union and bargain collectively with their employers over working hours and benefits in a manner similar to large trade unions in urban areas.[4]

Accordingly, I informed the owners of the two silk mills and the prefectural Labor Relations Committee that the mills were operating in violation of the impending Labor Standards Law. My records do not indicate how soon "corrective action" was taken but, as with educational, religious, and other reforms, it may be assumed that traditional employee practices in many small factories would not be changed immediately.

The First Labor-Management Institute Conferences

The visits to the two small silk mills were an illuminating and worthwhile preparation for a SCAP-arranged series of Labor-Management

Institute Conferences scheduled for July 1947 in many prefectures. In Yamanashi, they would be held successively, first in Kofu and then in six towns. Most of the participants would be Japanese, but Captain John Kopke and I would participate. Consequently, I met in late June to discuss an agenda with several officials in charge of labor affairs in the Yamanashi prefectural government and with members of the local Labor Relations Committee. A major purpose of the conference series would be to explain and clarify, especially for labor and management attendees, the key provisions of present Japanese labor laws and the "rights" of labor and management in the workplace.[5]

Captain Kopke's participation in these seven separate conclaves was cancelled, however, following the sudden arrival in late June of my first civilian assistant, who had served a very brief duty tour with another military government team. He was a graduate of a university and a navy language school, and so had developed considerably fluency in Japanese. He was still in his early twenties, however, and had no previous administrative experience. Nonetheless, he appeared fairly bright, so I proposed and the team commander agreed to assign him the duty of labor education officer, working under my supervision. This would enable me to spend more time on my varied CI&E responsibilities. A health problem precluded his familiarizing himself immediately with the subject of labor-management affairs, so he received "on-the-job training" during the seven separate conferences which began on July 15 and ended ten days later.

The first conference opened as scheduled in Kofu, and identical one-day sessions followed successively in Nirazaki, Ensen, Yomura, and three other towns. The purpose of holding the conferences at seven separate locations was to enable as many prefectural union and management representatives and citizens as possible to learn how labor-management disputes could be settled in a "democratic" and "responsible" way, rather than by marching, holding huge demonstrations, and shouting slogans, as most Japanese unionists were still wont to do.

The agenda for each of the seven conferences listed lectures and discussions on the following subjects: The Purpose of Labor Laws; Labor Unions; The New Labor Standards Law; The Present Situation of Enterprises and Labor Unions; The Theory of Labor Unions and Management; and Labor Surveillance Under Current Conditions. Japanese participants consisted of representatives of the Yamanashi

Labor Relations Committee (which included one professed Communist), management, local trade union officers and members (unionists comprised about 65 percent of the 125 to 150 attendees at each of the seven meetings), primary and secondary school union members, unorganized workers, other professions, and prefectural employees. My new assistant and I participated as neutrals, favoring neither the cause of labor nor management.[6]

Following the first all-day conference in Kofu, a new SCAP purge of citizens deemed to be former militarists and ultranationalists disqualified two key management representatives who were not, unfortunately, replaced immediately. Thus the proceedings had to continue briefly without a strong voice on behalf of management. Titles of recent Japanese labor periodicals were distributed at this first and at subsequent meetings.

For the regular participants, including interpreters, the holding of the conferences at seven different geographical locations over an eleven-day period was very strenuous. Only twice did my assistant, my interpreter, and I have the luxury of traveling over Yamanashi's rugged roads in the team commander's De Soto sedan; mostly we went by jeep. During my presentations at each of the seven conferences, I gave a general survey of the American labor movement, the nature of labor legislation, the function of the U.S. Department of Labor, the role of labor unions in a democratic society, and related information. I also stressed why labor unions should be social and economic organizations and not, as Communist and radical Socialists believed, adjuncts of a political party.

Japanese labor and management representatives emphasized their respective problems under postwar Japanese labor laws and some of the difficulties each had experienced thus far in complying with the new legislation.

My assistant usually followed with a short discourse on other aspects of democratic unionism, using a paper prepared by SCAP's Labor Division. He delivered it in Japanese, which turned out to be a distraction, as the all-Japanese attendees seemed more fascinated by his ability to speak the language than by the substance of his remarks. He acquitted himself quite well, although my completely bilingual interpreter found it necessary to correct him occasionally when he erred in translating certain American labor words and phrases into Japanese.

During all seven conferences, I was asked by attendees to explain in considerable detail not only how various labor unions functioned in America but also the intricacies of collective bargaining. Several Japanese labor activists appeared to enjoy asking me repeatedly about a very recent development in labor legislation in the United States. This was the Taft-Hartley Labor Law, enacted by the U.S. Congress on June 23, 1947, over the veto of President Truman. The law dealt with past "excessive rights and activities" of American labor unions and limited their power in many ways.[7] All top American labor leaders and strongly pro-labor politicians branded the new law variously as "anti-union," "labor-busting," and "reactionary." It was no secret among occupationaires that all key members of SCAP's Labor Division, most of whom were drawn from the ranks of labor, shared the same attitude toward the law which had been widely publicized in Japan's relatively free press.

Immediately after the enactment of the controversial law, SCAP and military government officials were advised that, as the Taft-Hartley Law was the "law of the land," it should not be publicly criticized. Consequently, I gave questions about it short shrift and said in varying ways that it appeared to be "corrective legislation." I noted that even some American unionists believed the law was necessary because their leaders failed to consult with them on all issues they negotiated with management. Once the worst labor "excesses" ended, the law probably would be repealed. I used the law as an example of how a "democratically elected U.S. Congress" frequently passed legislation opposed by particular groups or organizations.

At the end of the seven separate labor conclaves, I summarized briefly my impressions of the status of labor-management relations in Yamanashi Prefecture in a letter to a friend:

Except for union leaders, workers' education has not progressed very far. Knowledge of new Japanese labor legislation, especially matters pertaining to collective bargaining procedures and how "democratic" trade unions should function, still appears negligible.

In addition, a recent survey of educational facilities in different unions in this prefecture revealed that only 11 of 111 separate unions had a small reading room or library for the use of workers to enable them to read about their union rights. Consequently, during the seven conferences I emphasized constantly to union leaders the importance of making union literature available to workers. (July 1947)

A Joint CI&E-Labor Conference in Tokyo

The urgency with which SCAP and Eighth Army's military government officials regarded the labor-education effort for Japan's millions of unionists was further underscored when they arranged a joint CI&E-Labor conference in Tokyo in mid-August 1947. This was only three weeks after the end of seven labor-management conclaves in Yamanashi and other prefectures in the last half of July.

The intervening twenty-one days were very difficult. I had to catch up on my CI&E duties, shelved temporarily during the seven labor-management conferences, but I also had to exercise oversight of my new civilian assistant's activities. This proved to be a troubling distraction. His personal behavior often irritated his uniformed colleagues on the Yamanashi Military Government Team. Notwithstanding his intelligence, he lacked discipline, was uninhibited, was unnecessarily argumentative, and did not try to conceal his very liberal political opinions. In the BOQ he was wont to declaim loudly on the inadequacies of President Truman, whom he considered too "right-wing," and the virtues of Henry A. Wallace (Truman's former secretary of commerce, fired in September 1946 for criticizing openly the president's foreign policy as being too "anti-Communist." Wallace also denounced the "anti-labor" nature of the newly enacted Taft-Hartley Labor Law).

Concerned about my new assistant's seemingly "leftist" political leanings, the team commander asked me whether he should continue to work in the sensitive labor-education position.[8] As I badly needed his services in order to concentrate on my CI&E duties, I assured the commander that our new team members' political "pop-offs" were typical of young college and university graduates, and that he had been firmly instructed not to criticize the new Taft-Hartley Labor Law when talking to prefectural officials, unionists, and citizens.

The team commander agreed to take a "wait and see" position with respect to our new employee, but he asked me to supervise him closely. This I promised to do, albeit I had no control over his statements outside of the team's office. When he suddenly proposed taking a jeep to inspect the "feudal" working conditions in prefectural shops and factories (Captain Kopke, the labor officer, had already visited many of them), I confined him to his office to acquaint himself more throughly with the considerable literature on the history of American and Japanese unionism. As noted earlier, until his arrival in Yamanashi, his knowledge of the two subjects was virtually nil.

After this reprieve, our very young labor education officer accompanied Captain Kopke to two prefectural meetings, one with a labor group, the second before a labor-management conclave. Before the labor group, he discoursed on the purposes of labor unions and collective-bargaining procedures; before the second, on American labor laws. He used SCAP-prepared materials for both meetings. Captain Kopke believed he kept him reined in, although there was no way he could vouch for what he said in Japanese.

Very shortly, my new assistant and I entrained for Tokyo to attend, beginning August 18, a three-day CI&E and labor education conference. In addition to SCAP and Eighth Army officials, the conference was attended by all CI&E and labor education officers on the forty-five prefectural military government teams, eight military government regions (including Hokkaido) and I Corps and IX Corps in Kyoto and Sendai, respectively. With fully 150 attendees, this was the largest meeting of its type since the onset of the occupation in September 1945.

Although the lecture and discussion periods were interesting and useful, most valuable were the informal exchanges with my military government counterparts and SCAP officials during coffee breaks, luncheons, dinners, and no less than three evening cocktail parties at the Peers Club or atop the Radio Tokyo building.

Several of us "in the field" conveyed to SCAP officials the unique problems we encountered in our work, and they in turn enlightened us on the background of certain educational, religious, or labor reform policies and on the nature of internal agency debates that were an inevitable part of crafting reform directives and policy guidance in our areas of specialization. I took pains to explain to SCAP officials my "rural prefectural view" that it would take quite a while to overcome many traditional educational, religious, labor and other attitudes before the Japanese would accept permanently the many reforms being foisted on them so rapidly.

During the three-day conference, it was troubling to note there were still a number of uniformed military government CI&E officers with little or no higher education who had not yet been replaced by qualified civilians. In contrast, all eight military government teams, including the one in Yamanashi Prefecture, which were under the nominal supervision of the Kanto Military Government Region, possessed a civilian CI&E officer plus one or more civilian assistants, each of whom had college or university degrees plus considerable experience in public education, public administration, or related fields. The majority of military government labor officers, however, were still in uniform, and many, so far as I could determine, were unenthusiastic about their assignments. As noted earlier, they considered General MacArthur's wide-ranging program, especially his support of labor unions, as "for the birds" because "the Japs started the war so we don't owe them anything." This attitude was also held by several of my uniformed team colleagues who had fought the Japanese in the Pacific. Some had not forgotten the fanatical Japanese *banzai* assaults and wartime atrocities, which were reported daily in news stories about the ongoing war crimes trials in Tokyo, Yokohama, the Philippines, and elsewhere. During the conference's third day when all CI&E and labor education personnel met together, a member of SCAP's Labor Division averred that labor education was now more important than school reform because of the inordinate and still-growing influence of members of the Japan Communist party in labor unions. This, he said, was especially true in the large Congress of Industrial Unions of Japan (*Sanbetsu*). His outspokenness sharply contrasted with SCAP's earlier reticence during the January 1947 CI&E and labor education conference in Sendai.

When asked why SCAP did not "crack down" on Communists, a speaker gave the familiar reply that the Japan Communist party was legal and that it was easier to exercise surveillance of "Reds" operating "above ground" than if the party were outlawed and operated "underground." Furthermore, SCAP and Eighth Army did not possess the manpower resources to maintain an effective check on underground Communist activity. These circumstances mandated a need for a strong labor education program to convince rank-and-file unionists in Japan that the authoritarian "Communist way" of doing things was not "democratic."

Also addressed was the Japan Communist party's ability to publish a growing profusion of newssheets, magazines, and tracts on labor subjects despite a chronic, nationwide paper shortage. One SCAP speaker explained:

For reasons not yet known, about 70 percent of the paper allocated by the Japanese government to trade union magazines is going to the Communist newspaper *Akahata*. In fact, this now thrice-weekly newspaper will soon become a daily. How the Communists manage to get such a high percentage of the paper is being investigated. Because of this misallocation, trade unions receive more labor information from the Communists than from SCAP's Labor Division.

Some of us attendees on military government teams or in SCAP headquarters were not mystified by the "paper misallocation." It was easy to surmise there were left-wing Socialists and possibly Communists or Communist-sympathizers in Japanese government agencies who had a hand in allocating paper to newspapers and magazines. Additionally, there was reliable intelligence that the Soviets subsidized covertly many of the activities of the Japan Communist party. Several uniformed labor education officers opined that "pinkos" in SCAP's Labor Division might also have something to do with the paper misallocation, although I considered such a possibility most unlikely. In any event, both CI&E and labor education officers were urged to ensure the widest possible distribution of SCAP-prepared labor information and to stress why "democratic" rather than "Communist-type" unionism was in the best long-term interests of Japanese workers.

With regard to the Taft-Hartley Labor Law of June 18, 1947, SCAP labor officials did not disguise their dismay over the law, but all conferees were instructed again to support the law in their meetings with Japanese unionists and other citizens.

A sequel to the CI&E and labor education conference diverted me briefly from my CI&E duties. Ten days after my assistant and I returned to Kofu, the team commander received a letter from a SCAP intelligence office inquiring about the political views of my assistant. During the conference, the letter stated, he frequently declared that the Taft-Hartley Labor Law was "reactionary" and questioned the obligation of labor education officers to support it. He allegedly made other political statements that raised questions about his patriotism.

Highly disturbed, the team commander summoned me to his office to review once more my assistant's behavior. Still unwilling to resume the double task of CI&E and labor education officer, I urged the commander, and he very reluctantly agreed, to give him one last chance. Whereupon I warned my assistant his job was on the line. I composed a three-and-a-half-page report on his behavior and political philosophy for the team commander, who sent it via Eighth Army to SCAP intelligence. In essence, my report emphasized my assistant's youthfulness and political immaturity but absolved him of an affinity for Marxist-Leninist doctrine. The report also underscored the hearty dislike for the Taft-Hartley Labor Law felt by all of SCAP's key labor specialists.9

The team commander accepted my assessment and also warned our young labor education officer to abide strictly with SCAP and military government guidance in discussing trade union issues with the Japanese. This ended the matter for the ensuing five months. Then, after another serious indiscretion, he was abruptly transferred to another military government team and assigned to a less politically sensitive post. Fortunately, near the time of the labor officer's departure in February 1948, an experienced full-time civilian information officer joined the Yamanashi Military Government Team. The information office quickly implemented a stronger information program designed to teach the Japanese not only about democratic trade unionism but about many other ongoing SCAP reforms.

The Power of Teachers' Unions Expands

Meanwhile, as part of my CI&E duties, I tried to maintain a close watch on teacher unionism. After the April start of the 1947–48 school year, most of the uneasiness Japanese teachers felt during the previous school year about their membership in unions had still not been dispelled. One problem was their feeling that unions were for common laborers, and that membership in unions detracted from the dignity of their profession. Further, most were disinclined to question orders or guidance from their union leaders. Nevertheless, they retained their union memberships for essentially economic reasons, as the unions remained at the forefront of efforts to obtain better salaries, benefits, and working conditions from both the national and prefectural governments. The absence of credible prefectural education associations, whose prewar and wartime leaders had been decimated by SCAP's purges, created an educational vacuum the unions eagerly filled.

Policies of prefectural teachers' unions, with few exceptions, still followed the guidance of their leaders in Tokyo. They underwent some modification, however, in the spring of 1947 when there occurred a significant rapprochement between the two main competing unions. It began when the largest and most radical Council of All-Japan Teachers

Union (*Zenkyokyo*), representing mostly primary and lower secondary schools teachers, installed in Tokyo more moderate leaders.

The new leadership urged a merger with the more moderate National Federation of Teachers' Unions (*Kyozenren*), representing teachers primarily in secondary schools. These two were then joined by a small Teachers Union of Universities and Specialized Colleges (*Daigaku Kosen Kyoso*). As a consequence of discussions between the three unions, their leaders agreed during a June 8 conference in Nara, the ancient capital of Japan, to merge into one large union: the Japan Teachers' Union (*Nikkyoso*). On the eve of the merger, membership in the militant union numbered about 278,500, and in the moderate union, about 98,500. Membership in the union of universities and specialized colleges consisted of only a few thousand.[10]

The new Japan Teachers' Union quickly established a 62-member executive committee, with only two declaring themselves Communists. The rest considered themselves political Socialists, although the Communists would continue to exercise considerable influence in the new union's prefectural chapters, despite a general dislike of the "Reds" by the vast majority of Japan's teachers. The conclave at Nara agreed to pursue ten long-range goals: (1) the reform of the the educational system and construction of a new Japan; (2) support for the new 6–3 phase, which had begun on April 1, 1947, and of the coming 6–3–3–4 educational structure; (3) freedom and democratization of all research activities; (4) a living wage for all teachers; (5) a stable cost of living; (6) national funds for nursery schools; (7) the liberation of women and youth; (8) unification of all teachers; (9) strengthening the working classes by cooperating with other labor unions and groups and people's organizations; and (10) continued dismissal of fascist war criminals from the educational field.[11]

Military government CI&E officers were kept abreast, of course, of these changes. In Yamanashi and other prefectures, however, the new teachers' "unity" did not alter the social and educational distinctions among prefectural educators, nor the identity of the heretofore individual unions. For example, the prefectural government still met separately on new contracts during late spring and summer with union representatives of the primary, lower secondary, and normal schools, and representatives of upper secondary teachers (i.e., those teaching in former middle schools). Furthermore, the contracts eventually written at the prefectural levels followed, as previously, the models developed by the Japan Teachers' Union in its negotiations with the Ministry of Education in Tokyo.

The Yamanashi Prefectural Teachers' Union, still representing primary, lower secondary, and normal school teachers, and the Yamanashi Prefectural government signed a new contract on September 9, 1947. It contained thirty-one articles. The major provisions, most of which were not new, called for (1) a four-hour teaching day and a 42-hour week; (2) twenty days of free study time and twenty days paid vacation time annually; (3) a standard of fifty pupils per class; (4) specific rules for transferring or dismissing teachers; (5) the right of twenty-eight teachers to work full time annually on union affairs. In addition, the prefectural government would commit itself to help establish an Education Institute to improve the qualifications of teachers, and a sanitarium for teachers with tuberculosis. The prefectural government pledged to regard all teachers, even some who refused to join, as union members. It agreed not to negotiate with other teachers' groups without the union's consent.[12]

In October 1947, Yamanashi's upper secondary (formerly middle school) teachers signed a separate contract with the prefectural government. Although its articles were similar in many respects to those contained in the Yamanashi Teachers' Union Contract with the prefectural government, there were several important differences. For example, it called for smaller classes and a three-hour rather than a four-hour teaching day, and it did not specify the number of teachers who would be permitted to work full time on union affairs.[13]

As Yamanashi Prefecture did not have any ranking colleges or universities, the two foregoing contracts covered most of the prefectural public school teachers although, as mentioned, a small number of teachers still refused to join either union. Implementing contract provisions was another matter, however, primarily because of the lack of sufficient prefectural funds. Discussions between the two sides continued in subsequent weeks, and in mid-December 1947 a short conference attempted to deal with several of the most intractable problems. These included reducing average class sizes (building additional classrooms and schools was very costly), devising a formula for equalizing salaries between men and women teachers, obtaining additional money for traveling expenses; establishing a suitable marriage allowance, and assuring payment of a special winter allowance.

By month's end, agreement was reached on a formula for determining equal salaries for women (effective January 1, 1948) in order to abide by the new Labor Standards Law. In addition, the prefectural government found the money to provide an immediate 500 *yen* winter-subsistence payment.[14]

The vast majority of Japanese males in the prefectural government and in the schools remained unenthusiastic over the concept of equal salaries for women engaged in work similar to men. As SCAP's policy since the onset of the occupation was to assure social and legal equality of women under the new Constitution and in postwar Japanese laws, I had followed this particular demand with considerable interest. I recorded my experiences thus far on behalf of Yamanashi's distaff citizens:

> Surveillance will be necessary to ensure that the new equal-salary plan remains in effect. Experience has shown that a similar salary-equalization plan was instituted for middle school teachers in April 1947. A recent check has disclosed, however, that allowances or ability differentials have been allotted to men teachers to the extent that the salary-equalization plan has been nullified.
>
> The new salary plan will again apply to middle school teachers as well as to teachers in the primary and new lower secondary schools. In fact, the method for determining salary increases has already gone into effect. Hereafter, the prefectural Education Section will consult with the Yamanashi Teachers' Union about any future salary increases.
>
> It is hoped the above changes will eliminate to some extent the favoritism displayed heretofore by prefectural education officials and *Gun* school inspectors, who formerly were sole judges in determining teachers' qualifications and salary increases.[15]

By January 1948, the beginning of the last three months of the 1947–48 school year, the influence of the Yamanashi Teachers' Union in prefectural education affairs was more dominant than ever. Although the officials of the prefectural Education Section met frequently with union representatives, the latter more often than not, by all accounts, managed to have the final say on a variety of educational matters that often arose: appointments, transfers, or dismissal of school principals; the distribution of the more able teachers in prefectural schools; appointments or transfers of school inspectors; distribution of supplemental funds to purchase more charcoal for Yamanashi's two coldest *Guns*; and the like. Mr. Yamaguchi as education chief, and other prefectural officials as well, understandably deplored this erosion of their authority.[16]

My continued inspections and visits to schools in early 1948 indicated many improvements since I began my CI&E duties in late 1946. Nonetheless, chronic postwar educational problems remained, such as disorder in many classrooms, frequent absences of teachers (often for reasons of health or family problems), and uncertainty on the part of many teachers about how to teach their courses with new textbooks. In February 1948, I discussed these matters twice with Mr. Yamaguchi and other officials and also with school inspectors. They were all cognizant of these shortcomings but were hesitant to deal too strictly with under-performing teachers because of the need to "clear everything" with the Yamanashi Teachers' Union.

The union, in fact, contributed occasionally to the teacher absentee problem. "The practice of giving school faculties only a half-day's or one-day's notice to decide some union issues," I reported, "has resulted in frequent suspension of classes to meet the union's deadline for an answer."[17] Consequently, I instructed union leaders to stop interrupting the daily work of school faculties, and I emphasized that the teaching of students should take precedence over union business. In defense of the practice, local unionists said the demand for rapid decisions usually came from the leadership of the Japan Teachers' Union in Tokyo. Because the school interruptions were, in my view, so unwarranted, I compiled a special report on the union practice for the Kanto Military Government Region, IXth Corps headquarters in Sendai, and Eighth Army headquarters in Yokohama. I also sent the report to the SCAP Education Division. My effort to halt the school interruptions proved only partially successful.

The attempt to curb the union's excesses not only in Yamanashi but in other prefectures in the Kanto Military Government Region had the full support of Rollin C. Fox, the region's CI&E chief who ardently desired to get the Japan Teachers' Union and its prefectural affiliates out of educational decision-making. Especially disturbing was the clearly illegal provision in the contract between the Prefectural Education Section and the Yamanashi Teachers' Union allowing twenty-eight teachers to work full time on union affairs. In March 1948, Mr. Yamaguchi confirmed that twenty-eight teachers were so engaged. Unfortunately, as this provision was also in the contract between the Ministry of Education and the Japan Teachers' Union in Tokyo, military government could do nothing. As noted earlier, neither SCAP's labor nor education officials planned to nullify the provision despite its conflict with Article 89 of the new Constitution (which prohibited the expenditure of public funds for the use, benefit, or maintenance of any institutions or associations not under the control of public authority) as well as with other Japanese legislation. A member of SCAP's Education Division advised me by phone that it was now up to the Japanese government to test the provision in Japan's newly reformed courts and to have it declared unconstitutional.[18]

Small wonder, then, that Mr. Yamaguchi would not contest the provision in the prefectural-union contract in Yamanashi, inasmuch as it had been agreed to at the Tokyo level. In fact, he considered the use of twenty-eight teachers employed full time by the union as probably the best of undesirable alternatives. "If fewer than twenty-eight were employed." he reasoned, "other teachers periodically would be summoned suddenly to help out on union affairs, thus disrupting more classes." Education chiefs in some other prefectures, he observed, had arrived at the same conclusion.[19]

Also requiring rectification were the union's financial practices and accountability. All union members paid dues of ten *yen* per month. "Except for one union official with whom I discussed the matter." I noted, "no principal or teacher has any idea what happens to the union funds." A similar situation obtained when teachers and principals paid five *yen* per month to a new Education Association established by the union, or dues to the "reformed" prefectural chapter of the prewar and wartime Japan Education Association. Thus, I concluded, "instilling teacher and principal curiosity about financial matters is one occupation objective not yet achieved."

Teacher Unionism Early in the 1948–49 School Year

The new school year began on April 1, 1948. The immediately ensuing months witnessed the continued strong influence of the Japan Teachers' Union in educational affairs throughout Japan. In Yamanashi, as has been seen, the union was the dominant force leading to the creation and operation of a new Education Institute, although most of the funding came from the prefectural government. At the national level, following brief teachers' strikes in Osaka and a threatened strike in Gumma Prefecture (Gumma was in the Kanto area), the Japan Teachers' Union managed to extract from the Ministry of Education an agreement in principle to raise teachers' average salaries to 2,920 *yen* per month, similar to that of all government employees.[20]

The foregoing agreement had a ripple effect which in May led to brief teachers' strikes in Kyoto and Hyogo Prefecture, also for the purpose of obtaining the new average salary level. The Yamanashi Teachers' Union did not call a strike but pressured the prefectural government to match the higher salary scale and to accede to other demands. In this instance, the Yamanashi Labor Relations Committee stepped in to adjudicate the dispute.

Stoking the fires of discontent among teachers and other unionists in Yamanashi in May 1948 was Nosaka Sanzo, the head of the Japan Communist party. Upon his arrival, he "inspected" the work of local Communists, held meetings with representatives of a widow's league, a repatriation society, the local League of Koreans in Japan, and a farm tenants association. He conducted a round table on the "price raising" of farm and other commodities. In honor of his visit, his Communist and Socialist supporters put up posters in Kofu and other towns urging the replacement of the present Japanese government headed by Prime Minister Ashida Hitoshi (who had been designated on February 23, 1948, to succeed the Katayama government and had installed his new cabinet on March 10).[21]

June witnessed more short teachers' strikes throughout Japan with threats of strikes to come. Students in upper secondary schools and other secondary and higher schools were also caught up in the political activism and staged brief nationwide walkouts on June 23–24. In Yamanashi, only 110 or so upper secondary students and 800 students of the Yamanashi Technical College participated in the two-day walkout. The chief grievance of the technical college students was a proposed tuition increase from 400 to 1,200 *yen* per year. "There is considerable reason to believe" I reported, "that the student walkouts . . . were urged by the Communist student groups in Tokyo and within the Yamanashi Technical College." The still-soaring economic inflation throughout Japan was, of course, a major reason for the unrest among students, teachers, and other unionists.[22]

July 1948 witnessed more nationwide labor turbulence, especially among the two and a half million members of the Government and Workers Union, which included teachers in public schools and higher education and those employed in communications and by the national railway system. The hand of the Japan Communist party, as usual, was conspicuous. In Yamanashi Prefecture, it convened a "Labor School Conference" in Otsuki from July 1 through 10 to "educate" the public. Several Communist party members from Tokyo joined prefectural Communists to deliver lectures and lead discussions. As noted below, this particular conclave was apparently timed deliberately to coincide with two separate three-and-a-half-day adult education conferences in the towns of Ichikawa and Yamura in Yamanashi, in which I participated to discuss adult education and related subjects, such as democratic collective bargaining between labor and management.

The Communist-arranged Labor School Conference in Otsuki clearly had other purposes, as its agenda devoted only one session to Labor Problems. The program also listed: International Problems, The National Economy, Cultural Problems, Farm Problems, and Women's Problems. Attendance was moderate, averaging about 75 per day (the two adult education conferences each drew nearly 150 per day). Several officials of the Yamanashi Teachers' Union attended the sessions in Otsuki, but it was not possible to determine how many other prefectural educators were present.[23]

During the first part of July, prefectural education and union officials were locked in a series of discussions on raising the pay of faculty members of the Yamanashi normal schools and the technical college which had recently fallen below that of the primary and secondary school teachers. Specifically, the union wanted to eliminate the wage differential between prefectural normal school graduates and other higher schools. It also demanded a 200-*yen* raise per month for all public school teachers in order to create a salary scale similar to what had been achieved recently in Chiba Prefecture (in the Kanto Region). On July 19, the normal and technical school faculty members held a one-day strike in support of their demands. In truth, the prefectural government could do little to eliminate any wage differentials, as the money for normal and technical faculty members came from the Ministry of Education.

Although the prefectural government was not able to match Chiba Prefecture's new salary scale for public school teachers, it agreed to a complicated scale of salary increases: (1) an overall one-grade raise averaging 50 *yen* retroactive to December 1947; (2) a second one-grade raise retroactive to June 1948 (3) a third one-grade raise beginning September 1948, and (4) disbursement of 1,500,000 *yen* from the prefectural special budget to adjust salaries between June and

September 1948. These last-hour compromises forestalled a threatened short strike by the public school teachers.[24]

Unfortunately, Yamanashi's prefectural government did not possess the funds to meet these new salary commitments. Mr. Yamaguchi and other officials strongly urged military government and SCAP to support uniform salaries nationwide, to preclude the recent situation whereby the Yamanashi Teachers' Union demanded the highest salary scales, equal to those offered in a nearby prefecture. A contrasting view was held by SCAP's education officials and also by military government, including myself, that as Japanese education became more decentralized, differences in the cost of living between cities and more rural areas for teachers and other workers should be reflected in salary scales. This, I said, would be true democracy as in America, where states, counties, towns, and cities were free to determine the size of their respective educational budgets.

The one-day strike on July 19 was the last, not only for normal and technical school teachers in Yamanashi but also for other educators and government employees in Japan. In Tokyo, after conferring with his top political, economic, legal and other advisers, General MacArthur concluded that Japan's fragile economic condition, as at the end of January 1947 when he blocked a planned nationwide labor strike scheduled for February 1, was again seriously threatened by labor unrest. On July 22, he instructed Prime Minister Ashida to revise the National Public Service Law, which had become effective only on July 1, 1948, to forbid public servants in Japan "to strike, or engage in delaying or other dispute tactics which tend to impair the efficiency of governmental operations." All Japanese employees, the letter continued, "should realize that the process of collective bargaining, as usually understood, cannot be transplanted into public service." The letter drew a sharp distinction between those engaged in public service and private enterprise.[25]

The prime minister duly carried out the instructions through Cabinet Order 201, dated July 31, 1948. Not until December 3 of that year, however, was the Cabinet Order translated into an amendment to the new National Public Service Law. Thus ended the right to strike granted by the Ministry of Education to the two major national competing unions when they merged on June 8, 1947, to became the Japan Teachers' Union or *Nikkyoso*.

An immediate consequence of General MacArthur's letter to the prime minister was the resignation of James Killen, chief of SCAP's Labor Division who had succeeded Theodore Cohen as the division's chief in May 1947. Killen opposed any prohibition on the right of teachers or other government employees to strike. In contrast, all members of the Yamanashi Military Government Team breathed a sigh of relief, as did the vast majority of military government personnel in other prefectures. So, too, did most teachers in Yamanashi Prefecture. Many of them during visits to my office and in letters to the Yamanashi Military Government Team expressed gratification that they could no longer be "ordered" to hold strikes when directed by the Yamanashi Teachers' Union, which followed the lead, with few exceptions, of officials of the Japan Teachers' Union in Tokyo.

In fairness to the leadership of the Yamanashi Teachers' Union, they had acted with moderation for many months, especially after they ousted two avowed Communists from their highest counsels. Despite the enormous pressures from the Japan Teachers' Union, there had emerged more local decision-making. The prefectural union's power in mid-1948 resided in a 52-member Consulting Committee, and its decisions were carried out by a 32-member Operations Committee. Thus many more teachers were now obtaining experience in the give and take of committee discussions and had even been emboldened occasionally to question orders from the national union in Tokyo. Such periodic displays of independence were encouraging.[26]

Nonetheless, the manipulating hand of the Japan Communist party in Tokyo and in prefectural teachers' unions remained too obvious to ignore. In fact, the party's influence in the Japan Teachers' Union would rise further in the ensuing months, even to the point of assisting university students to form the All Japan Federation of Student Self-Government Associations (*Zengakuren*) in September 1948.

Twelve months later, in September 1949 (after my departure from Japan), to prevent further undermining of occupation reforms, General MacArthur ordered wholesale purges of Communists, not only in Japan's educational institutions, but also in government, labor, politics, and industry. The "Red Purge" was the consequence of Japan's Communists overplaying their hand and demonstrating unequivocally that their ultimate goal was not in support of democracy, but in foisting their own brand of centralized totalitarian rule upon the still war-weary Japanese people.

17

Expansion of Adult Education Programs

Acceleration of Adult Reforms

As in school, political, and other occupation reforms, the months following March 1947 also witnessed an acceleration in programs for youth associations, women's organizations, PTAs, citizens' public halls, and education exhibits, albeit the last was aimed at students as well as adults. The expeditious pace of reforms arose from an assumption, voiced frequently by ranking Eighth Army and SCAP officials, that the American and Allied occupation of Japan might be of shorter duration than anyone had envisaged at war's end in September 1945.

A hallmark of the speed-up in adult education programs was a significant increase in conferences. The increase was especially manifest in the Kanto Military Government Region encompassing eight prefectures. Military government CI&E and occasionally SCAP education officials participated. The conferences were arranged variously by SCAP's CI&E Section at IXth Corps headquarters in Sendai, the Kanto Military Government Region and, beginning April 1947, by a newly established prefectural Social Education Section, upgraded from a social education office that had existed heretofore in the prefectural Education Section.

The initiative in establishing Social Education Sections in all prefectures, not merely in the major cities and in prefectures with large populations, came from SCAP's Adult Education Branch. Its desire for this type of office nationwide, communicated through the Ministry of Education resulted in a stepped-up effort to transfer more rapidly responsibility for adult education to prefectural governments and local citizens. Given the occupation's objectives in this area, it was a logical move aimed at lessening dependence on SCAP and military government. In Yamanashi Prefecture, the new section's main purposes were "to accelerate adult projects such as educational films, the formation of youth associations and women's organizations, and the construction of more citizens' public halls.[1]

The Social Education Section's two initial projects were political: publicizing the importance of four separate national and local elections throughout Japan scheduled to be held in April 1947 (see chap. 11), and the new Constitution, slated to come into force on May 3. I gave high marks to the section's efforts in both areas, especially the latter. "Hundreds of posters, many based on drawings contained in SCAP's Political Affairs Bulletins," I observed, "have been used in di-agramming the Constitution's significance." In addition, it persuaded adult organizations and schools to produce many posters in towns and villages for use on Constitution Day. Then, following Constitution Day observances in Yamanashi and throughout the nation, the new Social Education Section sponsored a series of twenty-four lectures explaining the highlights and significance of Japan's new democratic charter.[2] Although I participated in this information program, some of my time in April 1947 was also devoted to election surveillance and other CI&E duties.

Youth Association and Women's Activities

Yamanashi Prefecture youth associations began to receive more at-tention after March 1947, with the addition to my staff of Akaike Hajime, a long-time worker in the Japanese YMCA movement. Mr. Akaike's new capacity was as a consultant on Youth Organizations and Religion. In April 1947 there were about 200 youth associations with a membership of about 75,000.[3] The figure suggested that in Yamanashi's towns and villages, a majority of youth, male and female, had joined an association. New associations were still being formed.

I managed to work into my April schedule an address before a freshly minted youth association in Sugahara on the subject of Japan's new Constitution. After my address, the now-familiar questions were asked: "What can youth do when working for bad employers?" and "How do young American men and women play together?" and (from teachers) "Why are America and the West more scientific than Japan?" In replying to the latter question, I attributed the scientific lag to the nation's isolation from the West under the Tokugawa regime from about 1638 to 1853 when U.S. Commodore Matthew C. Perry arrived and negotiated a treaty with Japan, opening the country to commercial intercourse. There were also unusual questions such as: "If women are equal to men, how can there be a head of a household?" and "How do American women spend their time in leisure?"

During May and June, Mr. Akaike and I held two separate meetings, each attended by representatives of almost fifty youth associations. I found these sessions rewarding in that they revealed the extent to which some democratic practices had penetrated many of the small towns and villages. Representatives from a few communities said their parents displayed a surprisingly supportive attitude, but in other communities parents still frowned upon youth activities. Citizen participation among the young was encouraging:

> Many youth associations participated very actively in politics prior to and during the April 1947 national and local elections by holding meetings where both young and old could listen to speeches by political candidates. A few associations reported they are now invited to meet with village or town assemblymen and have been asked to advise or assist in handling local village problems.[4]

Raising revenue was not easy for most youth associations, but by late spring 1947 several began receiving contributions from town or village offices. The sums ranged from 100 to 1,000 *yen* per year. One association received a gift of 20,000 *yen* towards establishing its own building. Several common problems noted earlier remained. One was the disparity in ages of association members. They still ranged in age from about fifteen years to as old as thirty-five or more. The reasons were cultural. One was the assumption that those under twenty or even twenty-five were too immature to assume any leadership roles. Mr. Akaike and I suggested again that associations maintain an age bracket of fifteen to twenty-five years to provide greater opportunity for youths to assume responsibility for their own activities.

A second common trait hindered occupation efforts towards assuring equality between the sexes. This was the propensity of associations to maintain a "women's department" for young distaff members who pursued their own "women's interests." As the American-style commingling of young men and women in various activities was simply not in the Japanese tradition, I did not insist upon it. A third issue was the cultural legacy of uniformity. After receiving about fifty copies of youth association constitutions, I found most to be nearly identical. "They are all modeled," I reported, "after a sample constitution sent by SCAP's Education Division through the Ministry of Education to all prefectural governments during the summer of 1946."[5]

Finally, there was still manifest the Japanese penchant for central-ization. On March 8, 1947, about 100 representatives of Yamanashi's youth associations met to establish a federation. It remained largely a "paper" association until July, when the prefectural Social Education Section recognized it officially and met with a delegation of ten young men and women to discuss the subjects of age differences, and their coeducational, social, political, and other activities.[6]

Adult women's activities remained in high gear. By the end of April 1947, women's organizations claimed to have about 10,000 mem-bers in Yamanashi. As with youth associations, when a new women's group was organized in a town, village, or city, most women in the particular area, usually in the vicinity of a primary school, joined it. Their objectives were similar: education, social welfare, and the raising of the status of women. During the month, I addressed one group on "The Development of Women's Organizations in America," a second on "Women's Activities in America," and in May, at the inauguration of a prefectural Federation of Women's Associations, on "The Place of Women in a Democratic Society."[7]

During May I dealt with another important women's rights case brought to my attention by Mr. Yamaguchi:

> It concerned a public school teacher of twenty-two years of age who left the school and her home when she refused to marry a prospective groom her father had picked out for her. She had fallen in love with another man, and she joined him. Twice the father forcibly returned her to her home. As she was also a very good teacher, Mr. Yamaguchi was greatly distressed by the incident, and he asked my assistance in resolving it.
>
> Because the father was clearly violating the spirit and letter of SCAP direc-tives, the new Constitution, and new Japanese laws with respect to citizen's rights in Japan's new democracy, I ordered the teacher to be released im-mediately from her home and allowed to return to school. This resolved the matter. The prefectural education chief appeared especially pleased to get a good teacher back into her school and he was able to say his action was taken "by order of the military government."[8]

In June, Eleanor Lee, a women's affairs officer with the Kanto Military Government Region, made her first visit to Yamanashi Prefec-ture and spent two days meeting with prefectural women leaders. My assistance was limited to arranging a series of meetings for her.

She appeared well qualified for her task. A former WAC, she had graduated from the University of Cincinnati and had a Master's degree from Columbia University. She had taught art and, during World War II, had served as an instructor for the U.S. Army Information and Education Program. Like Rollin Fox, she was a self-reliant and very capable military government education officer. She would come henceforth to Yamanashi Prefecture periodically to confer with Yamanashi's women leaders and speak to women's groups, leaving me free to concentrate on my other duties.

The July and September 1947 Conferences

For military government CI&E personnel throughout Japan the summer of 1947 was especially busy. The period witnessed a series of conferences on many subjects requiring the participation of CI&E officers and their assistants. In Yamanashi Prefecture the expanded prefectural Social Education Section (upgraded from an "office" in April), scheduled in coordination with my office two successive conferences, each of three-and-a-half days' duration. The first was held in Kofu, on July 2–5, and the second in Otsuki, quite some distance from the prefectural capital, on July 7–10.

The agenda for both was identical. Lectures and discussions encompassed youth associations, women's organizations, PTAs, citizens' public halls, and the 6–3–3–4 educational reform plan. Also discussed were scientific, vocational, correspondence, and physical education programs; university extension, art, music, labor education and religion; and the new Constitution. Governor Yoshie opened the proceedings with introductory remarks followed by talks from Kofu's mayor and a representative from the Ministry of Education. Except for me and my assistant, all of the participants were Japanese.[9]

Citizen attendance in Kofu and Otsuki numbered between 150 and 200 each day. My summary of the proceedings stated in part that topics dealing with youth associations and PTAs generated very lively discussions between youth leaders and their elders on the one hand, and parents and teachers on the other. A discussion of the characteristics of a good elementary school proved most valuable as many teachers and school principals were present. The subjects of vocational education, and art and music festivals, while discussed with less vigor, likewise interested the audience and drew many questions.

Perhaps no single subject was more troubling to the attendees than SCAP's ban on religious education:

The belief that some form of moral training should be given students in school remains the paramount view of the Japanese. How moral virtues, usually regarded as religious, can be instilled in students outside of a religious frame of reference remains an inexplicable problem for nearly all teachers.[10]

I was quite impressed by the competence displayed by the prefectural Social Education Section and the citizens in Kofu and Otsuki who planned and arranged the two conferences. "Speakers, participants, and the public," I noted, "joined in the give and take during the discussion periods." Also, "various chairmen ably and fairly presided over each meeting and at no time did the sessions develop beyond the capacity of a chairman to control the proceedings." In brief, the conferences "did justice to the democratic process."

Upon the completion of the two separate conferences, I had to prepare for a series of Labor Education conferences in Kofu and six other towns during July 15–25 (see chap. 16). Then on July 28–29, a two-day women's conference convened in Kofu attended by about 700 women representatives of women's organizations in Yamanashi. Again, the prefectural Social Education Section made most of the arrangements. My role was limited to delivering the opening lecture of the conference. Other lecturers were Eleanor Lee of the Kanto Military Government Region, several suffragette leaders from Tokyo, and the latter's counterparts in Yamanashi who displayed considerable initiative in arranging for the housing of visitors, and for publicity, exhibitions, and entertainment.

Lecturers and participants discussed women's rights under the new Constitution, recent revisions of the Civil Code, the New Education, and PTAS. A skit on "democratic organizations" was presented and two films from SCAP's Information Division were shown. Exhibitions included one illustrating how to conduct a democratic meeting, and a second on how to prepare meals with imported foods. A highlight of the conference was the presence of six women who had won for the first time in history seats in Yamanashi's village assemblies during the national and local elections of April 1947.[11]

July proved to be my busiest month thus far as a CI&E officer. I delivered twenty-four lectures: fourteen during the twin adult-education conferences, seven during the labor-management conferences, one during the two-day women's conference, and two for the team's enlisted men. The last was an additional team duty which the team commander assigned to me soon after my arrival in Yamanashi. This was in compliance with the U.S. Army's Information and Education Program requiring, when possible, a weekly lecture and discussion period on current events for enlistees. My CI&E colleagues in the Kanto Military Government Region, I learned eventually, had roughly the same workload as mine during the same month.

The major conference of August 1947, held in Tokyo, featured the presence of all CI&E and labor education officers on Japan's forty-five military government teams, eight military government regions, I Corps and IXth Corps, and officials from Eighth Army headquarters and SCAP's CI&E Section and Labor Division. The purpose of this three-day conclave has already been discussed (see chap. 16).

September witnessed another series of adult education conferences in Yamanashi Prefecture. Early in the month there were four separate one-day sessions in four towns where I delivered several lectures. The city of Kofu and the town of Otsuki were bypassed on the premise that citizens in other parts of the prefecture should be given an opportunity to attend and participate in the proceedings. The agenda was a familiar one: youth associations, women's organizations, PTAs, citizens' public halls (of which only four had been built thus far), and educational reform. The last featured a special lecture and discussion on the technique of visual education.[12]

During a lecture and discussion session on youth associations, a new proposal won the quick concurrence of both youth and adult representatives. This was the need for a suitable "coming of age ceremony" for young men and women who reached the legal age of twenty. "Giving thanks for twenty years of life and receiving a certificate of adulthood," I reported, "is presently a cherished aim of young and old alike." Shortly, the prefectural Social Education Section was soliciting the advice of teachers, assemblymen, assemblywomen, women leaders, and others on devising a ceremony annually in all prefectural villages, towns, and cities.[13]

A session on PTAs sparked more debate than previously over the issues of parental dues and contributions and the extent parents should assist in planning education for their youngsters without infringing on the responsibilities of principals and teachers. With respect to women's rights under the new Constitution and Japanese legislation, there was considerable discussion of how women could achieve economic independence, particularly when they became widowed. In addition, in a prefecture like Yamanashi, the women's rights movement had to surmount two major hurdles: the lack of cultural opportunities in the scores of small towns and villages, and the traditional attitude of men toward women. Neither problem could be resolved in the immediate future. Finally, there was much discussion about the need to simplify Japanese wedding and funeral ceremonies, with women participants generally approving such a change. In fact, representatives of several women's organizations said they had already taken steps towards these twin objectives.[14]

The leaders of Yamanashi's small but well-educated YWCA, assisted by several YWCA leaders from Tokyo, also convened two conferences in September. The objectives of both were to discuss ways to improve education and enhance the status of women. The first covered a four-day period and was attended by about fifty women primary and middle school teachers. Its agenda listed the following subjects: Democracy and Education; the School Education Law; the Fundamental Law of Education; the new Constitution; Physical Education; Music; Moral Training; and the Christian Bible, with the last subject optional. The second YWCA-sponsored conference featured an address before a huge audience in the prefectural assembly hall by Mrs. Tamaki Uemura, one of Japan's most prominent YWCA leaders who had just returned from the United States. She spoke on American public opinion regarding Japan. Except for meeting briefly with a few of the YWCA leaders in my office, I was not involved in planning either of the two programs.[15]

Additional Meetings and Conferences

During the last three months of 1947 I continued to devote a fair amount of time to conferring with officials of the prefectural Social Education Section about the problems and progress of youth associations and women's organizations. In these two areas of adult education I was gratified again to receive frequent outside assistance.

With respect to youth associations, members of the prefectural Social Education Section and youth leaders finally agreed to a suitable "coming of age" ceremony for young men and women. The agreement was publicized and all communities throughout Yamanashi were urged to conduct such ceremonies annually. During the same month I disappointed several of Yamanashi's youth leaders, however, by not agreeing with their urgent request to direct the prefectural government to construct a large youth hall and recreation center. I underscored the government's severe financial difficulties and counseled that it would be far wiser if the government used its limited funds to construct several more citizens' public halls, which could also be used by youth groups.[16]

December witnessed the arrival in Yamanashi, at my invitation, of Donald M. Typer, SCAP's chief of Youth Organizations and Student Activities. During his stay of several days, Typer met with representatives of sixty youth associations, members of Yamanashi's YMCA and YWCA, leaders of several PTAS and women's groups, and officials of the Social Education Section. He too wanted prefectural officials to establish a special youth hall and training center, but I deemed the proposal impractical given the prefectural government's lack of money to establish and operate one and the need for more citizens' public halls.[17]

In October and December 1947 I arranged again a series of meetings for Eleanor Lee of the Kanto Military Government Region who conferred with and proffered advice to members of the women's department of the Yamanashi Normal School, principals of all-girl upper secondary schools (formerly middle schools), women teachers engaged in vocational guidance, forty women physicians, and women officials in the prefectural Social Education Section.[18] Both Typer and Lee were very energetic and highly conscientious in their efforts to bring democracy to the Japanese.

Local YWCA members again demonstrated their leadership qualities early in November when they arranged a one-day conference in the prefectural assembly hall featuring outstanding women. These were Magdalene Barot, a YWCA representative from France who spoke about the life of young people in postwar Europe, and three Japanese women from Tokyo: Tamayo Miyagi of the House of Councillors, Dr. Yoshi Tateishi of Meiji University, and Aiko Kume, a lawyer. This session was followed by a two-day conference of Yamanashi's women leaders, also in Kofu, during which Dr. Tetsu Aranuku was the featured speaker. As in previous conferences, attendees discussed the new Japanese Constitution and the planned amendments to the Civil Code and the Code of Criminal Procedure.[19]

More Educational Exhibits

April through December 1947 also witnessed a continuation of educational exhibits in the library of the Yamanashi Military Government Team headquarters. The exhibits intended not only to expand the educational horizons of adults and students but also to demonstrate how local citizens could sponsor such exhibits without relying on instructions from national or prefectural government agencies. As previously, I had the assistance of the very capable Miss Aramaki, who was the major organizer of the exhibits, and three enlisted men on my staff at that time.

April featured a week-long exhibit of books sent by American primary students as a gift to the students of Yamanashi Prefecture. Concurrently, there was another special showing of American books (largely on education but also on literature, history, and other subjects) donated to Yamanashi and other prefectures by the U.S. Education Mission. These books supplemented an initial collection of 400 English language volumes sent by SCAP's CI&E Section to all military government teams in late 1946. Although several thousand students and adults viewed these latest acquisitions, few came thereafter to the team's library to use them. The reason was fairly clear: the struggle for existence absorbed most of their spare time and, compared with Japan's urban areas, there were few with a reading proficiency in English. In addition, the team's library was open only five days a week and never in the evenings.

Eclipsing the popularity of an earlier archeological exhibit was one in May on the cause and prevention of schistosomiasis or "snail fever," a common disease in Japan that was particularly acute in Yamanashi. Triggered by extremely small parasitic worms hatched inside a certain species of fresh-water snails, the worms, also called "flukes," entered the human body through drinking water or externally when men, women, and children worked barefooted and and bare-armed in rice paddies. After parasitic infection of the liver and other vital organs began, the afflicted victim would usually die a slow and agonizing death.[20]

Miss Aramaki assembled the exhibit with assistance from the prefectural Health Section—Captain Jakofsky, the team's medical officer; Dr. Morita of the prefectural hospital; and Japan's and America's most noted parasitologists at the time, Drs. Sugiura Saburo and Donald B. McMullen.[21] Dr. McMullen was serving a two-year duty tour on the staff of the U.S. Army's 406th General Medical Laboratory in Tokyo, and he stayed frequently at the Yamanashi Military Government Team when working with Dr. Sugiura under the auspices of the Yamanashi Medical Research Institute in Kofu, Yamanashi Prefecture. The two scientists had been been experimenting for nearly a year on a way to curb the disease. On display were many laboratory specimens of infected human organs as well as descriptive posters and diagrams. There was a short motion picture, and lecturers from the prefectural Health Section gave detailed explanations on how to prevent the disease. After many thousands of adults and students had viewed the exhibit in team headquarters, it was shown in other prefectural towns. No health exhibit was more widely seen or appreciated by Yamanashi's citizens than this one. Doctors Sugiura's and McMullen's work finally succeeded in breaking the life cycle of the flukes, which greatly improved the health of Japan's farming families.[22]

June 1947 was highlighted by another photography contest of scenes in Yamanashi with a commercial firm providing monetary awards of 1,000 *yen* for first prize, 500 *yen* for second prize, and 100 *yen* for the next five best photos.

In late July and in August there were two other well-attended exhibits on nutrition. The first featured the preparation of imported foods, mostly American, and made available printed dietary information which was sold to housewives at very low cost. Display charts presented facts and figures on the amount of food sent to different nations either directly by the U.S. Government or under the aegis of the Licensed Agencies for the Relief of Asia (LARA). The second exhibit featured Japanese food and was arranged in cooperation with the prefectural Agricultural Association and Public Welfare Section. Posters described the vitamin content of various foods. Both exhibits were also shown in other areas of Yamanashi.[23]

Also very popular among young housewives, teachers, and middle school girls was an exhibit in September on the care of children of preschool age. This was followed by a most interesting exhibit of inventions by middle school students, with prizes awarded to all of the contributors. At a special ceremony in October, the team commander awarded fourteen new volleyballs as a gift from primary school children in America to schools in Yamanashi Prefecture. A map of the United States showed the location of towns and cities from where the volleyballs came. Numerous letters, hand-made cards, and photographs from American schoolchildren were also presented.[24]

Concurrent with the periodic exhibitions in the library of the Yamanashi Military Government Team were several held elsewhere that were organized by Yamanashi citizens. Especially engaging was the handicraft of primary school students shown in October 1947. Arranged by the local office of the Yomiura Newspaper Company and the prefectural Education Section, it was held in the prefectural assembly hall. Public attendance was very good. Then in November, there arrived from the United States several boxes of paintings by American students of various ages and several books on American art. Miss Aramaki assembled these items, with explanatory notes, for the final exhibit in 1947 in the team's library. As with previous art collections, this one was also shown in numerous other communities in Yamanashi.[25]

The New Japan People's Movement of 1948

The early months of 1948 found the adult education program still in high gear. In fact, the efforts by SCAP's adult education officials to further accelerate the program were, in my judgment, not realistic. Nonetheless, military government CI&E officers continued to monitor and assist in carrying out an extensive potpourri of programs and activities.

January witnessed another CI&E conference for the eight prefectural CI&E officers and their assistants at the Kanto Military Government Region headquarters on the outskirts of Tokyo. Although devoted largely to the impending changes in Japan's school reform program beginning April 1, 1948, four panels were devoted to adult education. One highlight was a presentation by Cora Lee, the women's affairs officer on the Nagano Military Government Team, who spoke on coordinating women's activities with other CI&E programs in her prefecture. Another participant was SCAP's Donald Typer, who once again proposed constructive programs for Japan's youth associations and students.

I gave a presentation on the purposes of the "New Japan People's Movement," recommended initially for the nation by the Japanese Diet in June 1947, and about to begin in Yamanashi Prefecture.[26] The movement's purpose was "to unite the public through meetings to advance the objectives of the new Constitution and reconstruction." Unlike previous programs for stimulating adult education, however, this one reflected the rising concern over the precarious economic viability of Japan as it would concentrate first on increasing economic production, and then on improving daily living, social education, and arts and religion. In Yamanashi, as in other prefectures, oversight of the movement resided in the prefectural Social Education Section.[27]

Upon my return to Yamanashi, one of my first tasks was to advise and assist prefectural officials in working out plans for the New Japan People's Movement. Details were sketchy, but I was informed by a SCAP CI&E official that this primarily Japanese initiative would have a stronger than usual informational component. In fact, in Yamanashi, team informational input was already underway, as can be seen by the large number of press releases my colleagues and I issued during January 1948, stressing the importance of citizen cooperation in several economic areas. The subjects and number of releases for the use of local newspapers and the local radio station were: rice collections, 6; tax collections, 4; electrical conservation, 3; price control and rationing of fish and vegetables, 3; and production of straw bags, 2. There was also one press release on each of the following subjects: black-market operations, land reform, labor management relations, and legal and government reform. Near January's end, in addition to the press step-up, I met with a member of the prefectural Education Section, representatives of all prefectural theater owners, and officials responsible for operating public address systems at Yamanashi's railway stations to obtain their assistance for the expanded adult education and information program. The Social Education Section quickly agreed to prepare slides for the use of Yamanashi's theaters, and for special announcements for the public address systems at railway stations. My assistant on labor education and I also met with prefectural and labor officials to plan ways to disseminate more useful information on democratic resolution of labor-management disputes.

February 1948 witnessed a continuation of the information program launched in January, with more press releases on the subject of tax collections, price controls and rationing of fish and vegetables, land reform, conservation of electricity, control of black markets, and improvement of labor-management relations. In addition, all theaters began showing, prior to the featured movie, slides on the aforementioned subjects plus a new one proposed by Captain Jakofsky: how to control venereal disease. All of these messages were broadcast periodically for the first time on all public address systems at Yamanashi's railway stations. Although citizens were exhorted concurrently in this information campaign to enhance their appreciation of the arts and religion, the deteriorating economy left little time for them to do so.[28]

The "information blitz" continued in March largely under the direction of a full-time civil information officer, Paul Patrick Judge, who joined the team the same month. With two degrees from Catholic University in Washington, D.C., he had taught school briefly before World War II. Throughout the war he had served as an intelligence analyst with the U.S. Army and, with the onset of the occupation, in SCAP headquarters. He had also acquired in an Army language school a modest speaking ability in the Japanese language. Very capable, Judge soon assumed responsibility for most of the team's information activity, although I retained a portion of the task for some facets of my civil education duties. By the time of his arrival, the impact of the New Japan People's Movement was declining, and in Yamanashi at least, despite repeated exhortations, the movement appeared to undergo a gradual, unpublicized demise. Nonetheless, Eighth Army headquarters issued additional directives and guidance to ensure no letup in the adult education information effort. It was now Judge's responsibility to keep the "information blitz" alive.[29]

Additional Youth and Women's Conferences

The arrival of Mr. Judge was more than welcome. With a sudden reduction in my information duties, I was free to give more attention to leaders of youth associations. Although I had met with several groups of them in January and February, much of the responsibility in providing them with guidance during the past year had been borne by Mr. Akaike, my Japanese consultant on youth associations and religion. A priority task at the moment was to work out final details for a special prefectural youth association conference scheduled for March 25 and 26. A guest participant would again be Donald Typer, SCAP's specialist on youth and student activities.

The two-day conference proved to be the largest held thus far by Yamanashi's young men and women, with more than 500 in attendance. Lectures and discussions focused on various issues: dealing with the wide age-range of members, planning interesting programs, and promoting financial support and coeducational activities within the associations.

Typer's ebullient personality came across even through his interpreter. Shortly after the second day's sessions began, he decided that
Yamanashi's youthful attendees were much too solemn. Some form of
entertainment was necessary. On the rostrum, he suddenly asked me:
"Do you know the words of 'Old MacDonald had a farm?'" I said yes.
"Well," he replied. "We are going to liven things up." My interpreter
quickly announced we would sing a famous American folk song in
which we would mimic the sounds of farm animals. The audience was
to guess what they were. Without further ado, the two of us launched
into an impromptu duet, mimicking the sounds of pigs, cows, chickens,
horses, and sheep. The hundreds of overly serious young men and
women roared their approval with applause and laughter for this display
of informality by two occupation officials. Our not very harmonic
rendition broke the ice and assured more relaxed lecture and discussion
periods on the final day of the conference.[30]

Despite their postwar poverty, a long-sought goal of prefectural
youth leaders was achieved, finally, in April 1948 when coming-of-age
ceremonies were held for seventeen young men and women who had
reached their twentieth birthdays. The popular ceremonies emphasized
"the responsibilities of young people to their families, community, and
nation upon becoming adults." They fitted in very well with the adult
education program.[31]

During the brief flowering of the New Japan People's Movement
in the first two months of 1948, Yamanashi's women leaders were
especially busy, holding no less than twelve separate conclaves throughout the prefecture. Except for occasional meetings with some of the
leaders, my role was minimal, underscoring their ability to arrange
conferences mostly by themselves, albeit assisted by the prefectural
Social Education Section. The agenda of one meeting in Kofu included a discussion on how housewives could conserve electricity and
fuel. Another was devoted to determining how to distribute a gift of
10,000 *yen* from women's organizations in the Osaka-Kobe area for
some of Yamanashi's families who suffered severely in the aftermath of
heavy rains and floods in September 1947.[32]

Three separate well-attended meetings in the prefectural assembly
hall in Kofu featured prominent citizens from Tokyo who spoke on
the new educational and legal rights as defined in the new Constitution
and new Japanese laws. The speakers were Dr. Obino, a lawyer, Dr.
Watanabe of Bunri University, and Mrs. Yamataka and Mrs. Ichikawa.

The last two were among the thirty-nine women who had won seats in the Japanese Diet during the April 1946 elections. In March, local unions, employer associations, and the prefectural Labor Relations Committee and government cooperated in arranging the first conference in Kofu devoted exclusively to the subject of women in the laboring force and their new working rights under Japanese labor legislation. The principal speakers, who addressed an audience of 800 Yamanashi women, were Setsuko Tanino, chief of the Women's and Minors' Bureau in the labor section of the Japanese government in Tokyo, and Golda Stander of SCAP's Labor Division.[33]

A breakthrough in advancing the status of women in Yamanashi in the education field also occurred in March when Mr. Yamaguchi announced the appointment of five outstanding women teachers to serve as principals of primary schools, beginning with the 1948–49 school year.[34]

I had been urging Mr. Yamaguchi for some time to make these historic appointments, although I left the selections up to him. Several weeks after the new school year began, initial reports indicated that the women were performing in a satisfactory manner. If there were negative reactions to these appointments, given Japan's cultural tradition, I was not apprised of them, nor did I expect any to be brought to my attention. I learned shortly that school principalships also had been awarded to women in other prefectures. Needless to say, SCAP education and labor authorities and women's organizations had been urging more appointments of this type for some time. As has been seen, during the April 1947 national, prefectural, and local elections, five Yamanashi women also won seats in village assemblies. Nationwide, 818 women won elective offices (see chap. 11).

The stepped-up pace in the area of women's education continued in May when Eleanor Lee, the Kanto Region's women's affairs officer, returned to Yamanashi to hold a series of meetings in six towns with local women leaders and groups. Meanwhile, in another significant development, Yamanashi's largest newspaper, the Yamanashi *Nichi Nichi*, began featuring a regular column "For and About Women," and Kofu's radio station started broadcasting a regular program of commentary on women. Both the columnist and the commentator were local woman leaders.[35]

The July 1948 Adult Conferences

With relatively little advance notice, all eight prefectural military government CI&E officers within the Kanto Military Government Region were summoned to attend still another conference at Urawa, the capital of Saitama Prefecture on June 7–8, 1948. Dr. Rollin Fox, the Kanto Region's CI&E chief, chaired the proceedings. The purpose, as in previous conferences, was to exchange views during lecture and discussion periods on our respective experiences in four basic areas: educational reform, adult education, teachers' unions, and labor education.[36] Five Japanese specialists in the area of school and adult education also gave presentations and participated in the discussion periods.

Generally, the similarities with respect to progress and problems in the main subject areas in the eight prefectures in the Kanto Region were greater than the differences.[37] Implicit throughout the proceedings, in my judgment, was a general recognition that, in light of Japan's still-deteriorating economic situation and its strong Confucian and other traditions, the prospect of developing western-style democratic political and social institutions, especially in rural parts of Japan, would take many more years.

On my return to Yamanashi, I prepared for two more adult education conferences like those of July 1947. Again the conferences would be scheduled to run for three days each. The first would be at Ichikawa on July 5–7, and the second at Yomura on July 8–10. Kofu was deliberately passed by since area citizens had already attended a variety of educational conclaves. At both towns on the opening day Mr. Yamaguchi delivered brief, appropriate comments. The proceedings then got under way.[38]

Once again, lectures and discussions covered familiar ground: the objectives of social education, youth associations, women's groups, PTAs, religion, libraries, recreation, health, and labor education. In addition, some new titles appeared on the agenda: Prospects in International Relations; Political Education; and How to "Democratize" Cities, Towns, and Villages. I spoke on five separate subjects. My team assistant Richard L. Zachry, who was designated labor education officer in early 1948 after my first assistant was transferred, spoke on unionism and the importance for labor and management to settle disputes through constructive collective bargaining. Although new in the area of labor, Zachry was a junior-college graduate and performed his duties diligently.

The liveliest discussions, with at least half of the questions directed to me or Zachry, were on the subjects of PTAs, social education, and democratic unions. The role of PTAs was especially germane as the Japanese Diet had just enacted on July 5 a School Board Election Law mandating the first step towards decentralizing control over Japan's educational system, a major SCAP objective. Control over the system would be transferred in phases from the Ministry of Education to prefectures, cities, towns, and villages, with school board members drawn primarily from the ranks of PTAs.

Yamanashi's adults did not look forward to assuming responsibility for their local schools. Despite my own reservations about the feasibility of American-style local school boards, especially in a rural prefecture with a small economic base like Yamanashi, I was duty-bound to assuage the concerns of the adults at the Ichikawa and Yomura conferences. Unlike large urban areas, there was little likelihood of radical Socialists and Communists of the Yamanashi Teachers' Union influencing the selection of board members. On October 5, 1948, or six weeks after I left Japan, the first national school board elections were held, but owing to the controversy about this drastic reform and also to the deteriorating economy, boards were established only at the prefectural level and in Japan's five largest cities. SCAP's CI&E Section reluctantly agreed to the postponement of the elections of additional boards in smaller cities and in towns and villages until 1950 and beyond.[39]

With respect to adult education, it was evident that the fairly new Social Education Committees created at the city, town, and village levels were not the best instruments to bring democracy to the populace. This was because city and town mayors and village headmen were inclined to appoint to them elderly and sometimes overly authoritarian individuals. With little enthusiasm for reforms in Japan, these individuals had asked very few women to serve on the committees. There was a strong consensus among attendees that it was far more rewarding to work with leaders of youth associations, women's organizations, PTAs, and other adult groups.[40]

This was not a new problem, but it was only now being aired openly. I had met with committee members in May and June 1948 and had concluded that their activities overlapped those of leaders of the adult organizations. The upshot of the discussion on this matter was a recommendation that members of local Social Education Committees henceforth should be selected only from the leadership of existing adult organizations in each community. I promised to relay the recommendation to SCAP's Adult Education Branch, which would convey it to the Ministry of Education.[41] This I did after returning to Kofu.

During a session on unionism and labor education in which I participated, a number of attendees also expressed more openly than heretofore their concern about the "radicalism" of many union leaders and their labor policies, especially at the national level. My recommended solution was the same I had offered many times to Yamanashi's teachers; namely, not merely to "rubber stamp" proposals drafted by union leaders but to ask many questions about what they were being urged blindly to endorse—in short, to learn to be more assertive at union meetings.[42]

Interestingly enough, prefectural members of the Japan Communist party held a competing series of meetings in Otsuki while the conclaves at Ichikawa and Yamura were underway during the first ten days of July 1948 (see chap. 16). Attended by several leading Japan Communist party officials from Tokyo, the proceeding at Otsuki was called officially a "Labor School Conference," albeit only one session was devoted to the subject of labor. Other Otsuki agenda items were titled: International Problems; The National Economy; Cultural Problems; Farm Problems; and Women's Problems. All of these were also discussed at Ichikawa and Yomura. About seventy-five citizens reportedly attended daily. The scheduling of the Communist-led sessions in Otsuki concurrently with the adult education conferences in Ichikawa and Yomura appeared to be more than coincidental. In my judgment, as well as that of my team colleagues and members of the prefectural Social Education Section, it was a deliberate effort to divert attention from the Ichikawa and Yomura sessions, where neither participants nor attendees expressed any enthusiam for the "Red" leadership of many trade unions.[43]

To summarize, the Ichikawa-Yomura conferences were conducted as efficiently as those held in Kofu and Otsuki exactly a year earlier. Citizen attendance ranged from 100 to 150 per day. The main shortcoming was the comparatively few women lecturers at both towns—only nine, compared with twenty-six men, some of whom obviously were selected by members of local Social Education Committees who, as has been noted, were appointed by village headmen or mayors of towns and cities. It demonstrated the difficulty, nearly three years after the occupation began, of altering the traditional attitude of Japanese males towards their distaff citizens.44

18

Additional Religion and State Problems

Abolishment of Neighborhood Associations

As discussed earlier, shortly after the onset of the occupation in September 1945 and through March 1947, the Yamanashi Military Government Team received frequent complaints from citizens in signed and unsigned letters and by occasional visits to the team's CI&E office about funds collected forcibly by officials of *tonarigumis* or neighborhood associations. Despite SCAP directives and postwar legislation prohibiting such collections (to ensure the separation of religion and the state), nonvoluntary fundraising to support local Shinto shrines and festivals and Buddhist temples had not ceased, giving rise to continued citizen complaints. It was observed, however, that some citizens objected primarily to the "bossy" behavior of neighborhood association officials, who collected funds based on a family's income, rather than to the request for funds *per se* and how they were used.

My awareness of the importance of neighborhood associations in Japan's culture had increased considerably by early spring of 1947. By then, as noted, Akaike Hajime was on my staff. Mr. Akaike was an elderly gentleman who had studied in the United States early in the century and had spent most of his career with the Japanese Young Men's Christian Association (YMCA). I appointed him my consultant on youth organizations and religion. As his first duty, I asked him to set forth his views on whether it was possible to make fundraising voluntary for neighborhood associations and their activities. His report of mid-April 1947 supported my emerging opinion about this particular problem:

All villagers or parishioners in a rural prefecture like Yamanashi feel protected by the local Shinto shrine. Because they live in a particular settlement, they cannot be members of another. Unlike Christians who select a church of their choice regardless of location, Japanese parishioners are bound by their settlements. Their duties are to hold festivals in the spring and autumn and to repair and maintain the local shrine. According to a very old custom, money is collected according to ability to pay.

The relationship between parishioners and the local Buddhist temple is similar. Priests hold mass for their ancestors and thus their relationship to the local Buddhist temple also cannot be broken.[1]

It was a problem, Mr. Akaike continued, "that can hardly be understood by foreigners." Furthermore,

SCAP's warnings about forcible contributions create an enormous problem for parishioners of local Shinto shrines and Buddhist temples, especially in areas where villagers look forward to the spring and autumn festivals. With few other amusements, shrine activities especially are very important to rural people. For SCAP to insist that all contributions for shrines and temples be voluntary will mean deficits so large they [shrines and temples] may eventually cease to exist.[2]

Mr. Akaike placed citizens who complained to military government and SCAP about forcible contributions into four categories: (1) those who disliked personally the individual officials of a *tonarigumi* or *burakukai*, or a *chonaikai-cho*, and desired, in Japan's new democracy, to get rid of them; (2) those extremely poor who could not afford presently to make contributions; (3) those who reported illegal fundraising to avoid getting into trouble themselves; and (4) some local political leftists and Communists who wished to change drastically Japan's traditional social, religious, and political institutions.[3]

Concluding that parts of SCAP's directives on the separation of religion and state (especially the directive of November 6, 1946, prohibiting neighborhood associations from collecting funds for any purpose) would not survive the occupation, I henceforth spent less time on this problem even after the Home Ministry, upon the order of SCAP, had ordered the abolishment of the associations on April 1, 1947. SCAP's decision to outlaw them was based primarily on continuing citizen complaints throughout Japan about the practice of most neighborhood association officials to collect funds for "religious purposes." In addition, SCAP also desired to end a common association practice of withholding scarce food rations from citizens who had refused to make a "religious" contribution, or who were repatriates from Japan's former colonies and possessions and had been adjudged not "legal" residents in the village, town, or city to which they returned.[4]

SCAP's abolishment of neighborhood associations, understandably, upset most Japanese, especially in rural areas. In Kofu, the mayor and two assistants came to my office to seek approval of new types of associations. Their proposal sought to maintain some semblance of traditional forms and underscored how citizens in Yamanashi believed they could not function effectively without them. I had no recourse but to counsel that whatever new types of associations they had in mind, any fundraising activity on behalf of local Shinto shrines and Buddhist temples would still have to be done on a voluntary basis. Nonetheless, the associations continued to function "unofficially" as evidenced by continued citizen complaints about solicitation of funds by former "bosses."

During the ensuing months, I let Mr. Akaike deal with the problem, although I sent reports on the most egregious violations to the prefectural Penal Affairs Office for investigation. I also continued to issue short press releases emphasizing the right of citizens to contribute funds voluntarily rather than forcibly in Japan's new democracy.[5]

Yamanashi's *Gokoku Jinja* Shrine for the War Dead

Mr. Akaike's valuable assistance notwithstanding, I still found it necessary to handle numerous religion/state problems on my own. In May 1947, a brief visit to a special Shinto shrine evolved into a discomfiting drama for me that was not without some humor. The visit was undertaken following a request from Dr. William K. Bunce, chief of SCAP's Religions Division. I was to observe "discreetly," if possible, the first "festival" for the souls of local war dead. The festival was a solemn occasion, to be held at Yamanashi's *Gokoku Jinja*, or "nation-protecting shrine." Bunce asked me to determine if the coming event would be accompanied by any resurgence of "militarism" or "ultranationalism." A brief explanation of this type of shrine is necessary.

On December 15, 1945, as an initial step to separate religion and state in Japan, SCAP issued a directive abolishing State Shintoism which prohibited official national, prefectural, or local government financial support for and worship of this unique type of Japanese religion, symbolized at its apex by Yasukuni Shrine in Tokyo. Established in 1869, a year after the Meiji Restoration began, the shrine was the national repository of the souls of all Japanese military personnel and of some civilians who had sacrificed their lives to bring about the Restoration. To these were added in subsequent years the souls of Japanese military and civilian personnel who had fallen in Japan's other wars, prior to and including World War II.[6]

In the years following the establishment of the Yasukuni Shrine, periodic ceremonies conducted by Shinto priests became increasingly elaborate and included the participation of not only the highest government officials but also the Emperor. According to some accounts, most of Japan's citizens developed an emotional bond to the shrine equal to their reverence for the Grand Imperial Shrine on the island of Shikoku and the Meiji Shrine commemorating the Emperor Meiji after his death in 1912. The will of servicemen was steeled by the knowledge that if they fell in battle, their souls would repose in the shrine. An oft-told tale about Japan's *kamikaze* pilots, who made suicidal attacks against American and Allied targets on land or sea during World War II, is that just before departing on their one-way missions they often consoled one another by saying: "We shall meet at Yasukuni."[7]

Less well known was the establishment throughout Japan after 1869 of smaller local shrines also embodying the souls of the war dead. Initially called *shokon-sha*, the "spirit-invoking shrines" contained the same souls of local servicemen and civilians consecrated in the Yasukuni Shrine in Tokyo, their presence there making it unnecessary for millions of citizens to undertake a long journey to the capital to pay obeisance to their departed family members. In 1939, as Japan's largely military leaders strengthened their hold on the populace, the *shokon-sha's* were renamed *Gokoku Jinjas* or "nation-protecting shrines" and were divided into two categories: designated and undesignated *Gokoku Jinjas*. The former, numbering forty-eight when the occupation began (21 were established after 1939), were fairly large and a few possessed imposing monuments located in prefectural capitals or near a military headquarters. They received, as had the Yasukuni Shrine, national government financial support. They too held periodic ceremonies or "festivals" for the war dead with the participation of local government officials.[8]

Undesignated *Gokoku Jinjas,* totaling ninety-nine, were located in more rural parts of Japan where citizens had fought mostly on behalf of the Meiji Restoration. They were invariably quite small, unimposing, and solely dependent on the financial support of local citizens for their maintenance. SCAP's directive of December 15, 1945, abolishing State Shintoism and forbidding henceforth any national, prefectural, or local government financial support for or participation in Shinto activities applied equally to the *Gokoku Jinjas*. The directive did not ban, however, private citizen ceremonies for the war dead at either the designated or undesignated shrines.9

Yamanashi Prefecture's *Gokoku Jinja,* established in 1944, was undesignated. I was aware of its presence. While on a brief visit to Tokyo a few months after assuming my CI&E duties, I asked a member of SCAP's Religions Division about the future status of this type of shrine. He said it was under constant study. He expressed two concerns. One was lest its abolishment and/or the prohibition against any citizen prayers or ceremonies for the souls of the war dead enshrined in them prove counterproductive. The other was the possibility, once the shock of defeat in the war abated, that the existence of these shrines might inspire a revival of nationalistic feeling, especially among millions of demobilized servicemen.

As there was no specific SCAP directive requiring periodic inspections of *Gokoku Jinjas,* I was under no obligation to maintain surveillance over the one in Kofu. Then, in late April 1947, a local newspaper reported that Yamanashi's *Gokoku Jinja* would hold its first postwar "festival" on May 5. This small news item also appeared in a national newspaper in Tokyo, impelling SCAP's chief of the Religions Division to ask me to observe "discreetly" the upcoming festival. I agreed to do so, although there was no way a military government official could observe anything "discreetly" in Yamanashi Prefecture.

Thus, shortly before noon on May 5, I motored with my interpreter to Yamanashi's *Gokoku Jinja.* There was no heavy vehicular or foot traffic on the road leading to the shrine. Upon my arrival, three greatly surprised, white-clad Shinto priests rushed towards my jeep and, with several bows and salutations, greeted me cordially. My interpreter explained I had read about the festival and, not having had an opportunity to witness such an event, felt it appropriate to come. The priests nodded agreeably. There was no indication they resented my appearance; indeed, they appeared unusually pleased to see me. The head priest escorted me to a small alcove where I signed the visitor's book, a common practice at many shrines and temples.10

Accompanied by the head priest, I strolled around the small, immaculately kept grounds, observing forty or so visitors eating their lunch and chatting with friends while their children played nearby. Everyone responded to my presence with bows and smiles. There was nothing mournful, militaristic, or ultranationalistic in their demeanor and all appeared to enjoy their outing. In response to my inquiry, the priest said there were presently 4,824 "souls" of local war dead in the shrine, including eight civilians. After spending about twenty minutes on the premises and chatting a bit more with the priests, I departed amid their profuse thanks for taking the time to visit their festival.

After returning to my office I composed a brief summary of my observations and, by day's end, learned from the head priest that about 350 to 400 visitors had come to the *Gokoku Jinja* during the day. I planned to send my report to Dr. Bunce in a day or two. It had been a very uneventful routine inspection. So I thought.

The next morning while I was still in the BOQ my interpreter phoned and asked me to come to the office immediately. "There is something in a newspaper that requires your prompt attention," she said. I dashed across the street to team headquarters and into my office. On my desk was a translation of a headline in a local newspaper which read: "Military Government Officer Pays Respects to Japan's War Dead." The story was detailed and mentioned my name and position. I was appalled! Equally upsetting was my interpreter's warning that highlights of the story might very well appear in some of Tokyo's national newspapers where SCAP officials would read it. Mr. Ito, the retired school principal and adviser on my staff, arrived at the office and said he had heard on the local radio station a report of my visit to the *Gokoku Jinja*. "What did the announcer say?" I asked. "Well, what I think he said," he replied diplomatically, "sounded like a mistake."

Barely twenty months had elapsed since the end of World War II. Many harsh feelings about Japan had not subsided. No member of the American or Allied forces in Japan could possibly contemplate paying respects to Japan's war dead so soon after the end of a bloody conflict. If the story appeared in a Tokyo newspaper, I envisioned General MacArthur firing me personally and sending me back to the United States on the next ship! I could not imagine how my visit to the *Gokoku Jinja* could have been so badly misconstrued. I made some quick decisions. First, I summoned the newspaper editor and the reporter who wrote the story and then called SCAP's Religions Division to inquire if any Tokyo newspapers had mentioned my visit to the shrine. The recipient of my call promised to inform me after scanning the main newspapers.

There was another potential difficulty; namely, the team's commanding officer. We were getting along splendidly and I had managed to avoid thus far any reason for him to circumscribe my freedom to conduct my CI&E activities as I believed necessary. Fortunately he had left Kofu for the day. I could not escape informing the team's executive officer, however. Surprisingly, he appeared more amused than concerned about the erroneous news story. So did several of my colleagues who, upon learning of my discomfiture, dropped by my office for some good-natured ribbing. "I didn't realize," said one, "you had forgotten so quickly about Pearl Harbor." I told him to "scram."

When the newspaper editor finally arrived he was accompanied by two aides, but not the reporter who had written the story. "Where is he?" I demanded. The editor said he was out of town and would not return until evening. In an aside, my interpreter reminded me of the Japanese sense of responsibility which dictated that the editor see me first. As usual, she was right. The reporter no doubt had been instructed to "disappear" for the day. Standing behind my desk for emphasis, I asked the editor if he knew why I had sent for him. Indeed he did. It was about the story of my visit to the *Gokoku Jinja*. When he first read it, he said, "it didn't look correct." It was a remarkable understatement. "Did the reporter write the story the way it appeared in the newspaper?" I asked. "General MacArthur wants an immediate explanation."

After expressing profound regret about the newspaper account, the editor explained how it happened to be written. Immediately after I left the shrine, the head Shinto priest excitedly called the newspaper office to report my appearance at the festival. He said the military government official had been very pleasant, asked about the number of souls of the war dead in the shrine and other questions, and signed the guest book. The Shinto priest said he felt highly honored that I had come to the *Gokoku Jinja* to pay my respects to the local war dead. As the editor completed his explanation, my interpreter whispered to me: "I believe he is telling the truth."

At this juncture I told the editor to print a correction in the next day's issue of his newspaper stating clearly that I was inspecting the shrine, not paying my respects to the war dead. As the editor and his aides fully understood, American and Allied personnel could not possibly pay respects to the war dead until a peace treaty was signed and the occupation had ended. Then, after discoursing for a few minutes on the importance of accurate reporting if Japan was to become a democracy, I bade the editor and his aides adieu. An hour or two later, a member of SCAP's Religions Division returned my phone call to state that some Tokyo newspapers had only reported my visit to Yamanashi's *Gokoku Jinja*. They said nothing about my paying respects to Japan's war dead. I was enormously relieved.

The corrected statement about my visit to the shrine appeared in the next morning's edition of the newspaper. Then promptly at 8:00 A.M., the reporter who wrote the story appeared in my office to convey his regret for having misunderstood the nature of my visit to the shrine. He appeared to be in his twenties and had obviously been briefed by the editor. He promised to be more careful in writing about members of the Yamanashi Military Government Team in the future. I also gave him a brief lecture about the importance of accurate reporting and sent him on his way. Presumably, the chief priest of the *Gokoku Jinja* must have been crestfallen when he read the next day about the true nature of my visit to his shrine.

I informed my commanding officer of the incident during the next staff meeting of team members, assuring him the reporting error had been corrected and I had "cleared everything with SCAP." "Let's hope they won't make the same mistake again," was his only comment.

Weeks later I learned by telephone from a member of SCAP's Religions Division that the future of the *Gokoku Jinjas*, designated and undesignated, was still undergoing review. I conveyed my opinion that, in the absence of any evidence of resurgent militarism or ultranationalism during private services for the war dead at these shrines, no action was necessary. SCAP's religious experts eventually decided the same. When the occupation ended on April 28, 1952, the *Gokoku Jinjas* were "still in business." SCAP's decision to permit private services for the war dead at these shrines had been a wise one.

The Unpopular Buddhist Priest

In September 1947, parishioners of a Buddhist temple, in an action rarely taken before the end of World War II, attempted to rid themselves of a young Buddhist priest who had inherited his position from his late father. When their local efforts to do so failed, they sent a petition to my office asking me to intercede on their behalf. It read in part:

> Why did the relatives of the deceased priest fail to consult with the parishioners before a successor was decided? The appointed priest, who had been

demobilized after the war, merely assumed the new position. But parishioners do not like him because of his undesirable behavior and because he took the priest position by an illegal method.

The temple is related to the "mother" temple in Kamakura but its officials show no sincerity in the dispute. The priest's actions are contrary to present democratic developments in Japan.[11]

A delegation of three parishioners also came to my office to plead their case. The details of their abrasive relationship with the new priest were so complicated my interpreter had difficulty comprehending them all. Consequently, I asked the parishioners to discuss their complaints with Mr. Akaike who, after their departure, composed a summary of the dispute.[12]

The summary contained three points. First, antipathy between parishioners and some of their Buddhist and Shinto priests was not uncommon. Since SCAP introduced the magic word "democracy," however, some parishioners were now emboldened to express more openly their dislike of a priest and to display more militancy in getting rid of him. Second, the Buddhist priest who was at the center of the controversy held his position by traditional "right of inheritance," having succeeded his father, who had died recently. Third, officials of the Buddhist sect based in Kamakura, as the petition stated, supported the priest's right to his sinecure. They considered irrelevant all complaints about his poor education and moral character. As I discerned no religion and state issue in the dispute, I concluded no action was warranted by military government.

I conveyed my decision to the parishioners through Mr. Akaike, but I counseled them to continue to assert their new "religious rights" in accordance with provisions of the new Constitution and other new Japanese laws, and to maintain their dialogue with the priest's superiors in Kamakura. I considered the case closed until late November 1947, when I received a letter from the controversial Buddhist priest.

Expressing shock about what had transpired recently, the priest wrote that there had been a few "consultative" meetings between himself and his parishioners, but they had come to no agreement. After the last meeting, he said,

we parted, expecting to meet again. Suddenly, on November 19, 1947, some parishioners came to my temple and told me leave on the 30th, as it was by order of the military government.

Is it true military government so instructed them? They are propagating that if I do not leave the temple by 30th inst., they will force it by violent act, and as it is in accordance with the order of military government, Japanese police will not be able to interfere.

If the parishioners do not like me so much, I would rather leave the temple but I have no other place to live as the temple is my domicile and no parishioner is authorized to drive me out. I did utmost to settle the matter peacefully but parishioners are taking every means to drive me out.[13]

Although the responsibility for funerals and other business had been transferred to another temple, he explained, the parishioners still wanted him to leave. Would military government assist him in his struggle to remain? He ended his letter by asking if he could meet with me.

I was not pleased to learn that the three parishioners had rendered my advice into an "order" (a not uncommon practice by some citizens who visited military government offices seeking assistance on a problem). Nevertheless, the priest's letter renewed my interest in the priest-parishioner conflict. I was curious to know more. So I acceded to his request to come to my office.

He arrived in my office several days later. Sitting in a chair before my desk was a most unpleasant-looking fellow with a surly countenance. I got quickly to the matter at hand, saying I had read his letter and regretted he might lose his domicile. I avoided mentioning whether I had "ordered" him to leave but said I had discussed with several of his parishioners their new religious rights under the new Constitution, specifically Articles 20 and 89, and also new Japanese education laws. Was he familiar with the religious provisions of these documents? He said he knew something about them but averred he saw no connection between the new Constitution and his right to continue living in the local Buddhist temple. I decided to give him a short lecture. The parishioners, I said, were trying to exercise their new religious rights in the maintenance and functioning of the temple. Many things were changing rapidly in Japan. State Shintoism had been abolished and there was now a more "voluntary" rather than "compulsory" relationship between parishioners and their Buddhist and Shinto priests. Also changes had occurred in how shrines and temples should be supported.[14]

The priest said there had been some misunderstandings between himself and the parishioners and he regretted they had not been resolved. He said he could not understand why the parishioners did not like him and wanted him to leave. He had no other abode. Are parishioners, I asked, responsible for supporting a priest they do not want? He gave a vague and rambling reply. In addition to the new Constitution, I cited several SCAP directives on religion, education, and government, all for the purpose of enabling Japan's citizens to manage more fully their own affairs. It was the duty of Buddhist and Shinto priests to learn about citizen's new rights in SCAP directives and Japanese laws and to abide by them. My visitor appeared unimpressed with my discourse and maintained an obstinate air. I began to understand why the parishioners were up in arms against his presence in the temple.

After several more minutes of unproductive discussion, the priest, realizing I was not supportive to his plight, took his leave, bowing stoically as he left my office. My interpreter, summarizing the essence of his comments, confirmed another allegation his parishioners had made: his lack of education was indicated by his very poor vocabulary. The vast majority of priests, she said, were better educated than he. Mr. Akaike, who had looked briefly into the case, had already opined the priest appeared to have no redeeming qualities.

I heard no more about the dispute for several weeks. Then one morning a parishioner phoned my office to report that the priest had left the temple and his whereabouts was unknown. A more suitable replacement would take his place. Thus, for the parishioners, "democracy" in a religious matter had triumphed!

A Funeral for Eight Soldiers

In October 1947, another religion/state case arose when I learned from Mr. Akaike, my assistant, of a plan by a village headman to hold a special funeral for eight soldiers from the village, including the headman's son, who had lost their lives during World War II. The headman, after conferring with the former chiefs of former local neighborhood associations decided to collect a small fee from all village families to pay for the funerals prior to the interment of the soldiers' souls in Yamanashi Prefecture's *Gokoku Jinja*.

Several citizens from the village came to my office to discuss the planned funeral services. Following their presentations, I had to inform them, regretfully, that their funeral plans would violate SCAP's directives in three ways: first, the headman was an elected official; second, all of the neighborhood associations had been abolished on April 1, 1947, by the Home Ministry on orders from SCAP; and third, any funds henceforth raised for political, social, religious, or other events had to be given voluntarily. As a consequence, the village altered its funeral plans. The case underscored again how difficult it was to abolish by fiat neighborhood associations, especially in a rural prefecture, because of their intrinsic role in citizens' lives.[15]

Nichiren Buddhist Headquarters Revisited

In November 1947, I undertook a second and longer inspection of the headquarters of Japan's well-known indigenous Buddhist Nichiren sect located a short distance from the town of Minobu in Yamanashi Prefecture. As mentioned earlier, the headquarters was known as Minobu *Kuonji*. Nichiren, the sect's thirteenth-century founder, had espoused a militant spirit among its many followers in succeeding centuries up to and during World War II. Although I had received no reports of militaristic or ultranationalistic behavior by Nichiren leaders or adherents since my first brief visit to the sect's headquarters in February 1947, I felt obliged to let officials of this particular Buddhist sect know that military government had not ceased its surveillance of its activities.

With the assistance of Mr. Akaike, I had obtained a report on the status of the Minobu *Kuonji*. It said the administration of all Nichiren temples in Japan were presently managed by a Religious Affairs Board in Tokyo, albeit the main spiritual and educational functions were centered in the Minobu headquarters. The superintendent (or chief administrator) was now seventy-nine years old. He had been appointed to his post in October 1943. In accordance with tradition, the superintendent was selected from a list of candidates from each Nichiren district in Japan. He had to be at least seventy years of age and, once appointed, served for life. He oversaw a staff of about twenty-five at Minobu. Nichiren adherents in the country were estimated to number about five million.[16]

Since the end of World War II, according to the report, Nichiren's leaders had renounced all forms of nationalistic militancy and support for war and would engage henceforth only in peaceful pursuits. Towards this end, Nichiren headquarters had established a "Mankind

Protection League" for the purpose of "maintaining permanent peace all over the world," and a full declaration of purpose would be made soon in English, Chinese, Sanskrit, and other languages. To implement its postwar goal, the league planned to establish a "Peace Research Society" and to cooperate with all learned organizations and spiritual circles. The league also planned to host a conference on the subject of permanent peace and to invite religious leaders throughout the world to attend.

My personal observations confirmed the report's statement that Minobu *Kuonji* did indeed conduct a rather extensive array of spiritual, educational, and charitable programs, at least locally. In education it operated a private kindergarten, a Sunday school, a Sozan Middle School, and a Sozan Technical College, the last consisting of a merger of two separate colleges in 1941, and a Youth Cultural Research Center. The Sozan Middle School (called Sozan *Gakuin* until 1935) possessed about 135 students who were taught by fifteen full-time and five part-time teachers. Students paid 30 *yen* tuition per month. The college enrolled seventy students, who were taught by twelve full-time and five part-time teachers, not all of them Nichiren priests. These students paid 50 *yen* per month tuition. Although many Sozan college graduates entered the Nichiren priesthood, others became public middle school teachers, government employees, or worked for commercial enterprises. Some trainees for the Nichiren priesthood also studied in the Buddhist Department of Rissho University in Tokyo. The schools appeared to be operating in full compliance with SCAP directives and Japanese postwar legislation governing the functioning of private and religious educational institutions.

During my inspection of the Sozan Middle School and the Sozan Technical college, I noted that

the structure of the buildings and teaching facilities were both above average in Yamanashi Prefecture. Students in both institutions appeared to enjoy a good balance between discipline and freedom in the classroom. This could be attributed to the fact that the students came from all parts of Japan and were above average in intelligence and maturity. Compared with other prefectural schools, the two institutions possessed an unusually large library totaling about 10,000 volumes.

One apparent shortcoming of the Sozan Middle School was a lack of interest by its faculty in Japan's new postwar education system. The school subscribed to very few education publications, nor did it possess other materials about the New Education although it clearly could afford to do so. This matter was brought to the faculty's attention. With the exception of courses on religion, the middle school students received the same education as boy middle school students in Yamanashi.[17]

The Youth Cultural Research Center had been founded very recently for the purpose of enabling Nichiren students to became better acquainted with young people in and around Minobu. The center occasionally sponsored lectures for young people. It did not function, however, like other prefectural youth associations, some of which engaged in a variety of activities. The Minobu *Kuonji's* most significant charitable program was the operation of a well-known leper colony, founded in 1906, and a hospital. Until SCAP directives decreed the separation of religion and state, and the new Constitution redefined the role of the imperial family, the leper colony was subsidized partially by funds from Her Majesty, the Empress of Japan. Under new postwar legislation, however, some public funds now helped to sustain the leper colony. Considerable funds also came from among Nichiren's five million adherents and the approximately 300 visitors per day who visited Minobu *Kuonji*. Presently, there were forty-nine leper patients, twenty-nine males and twenty females, who were cared for by four physicians and three nurses, although some were employed part time. Upon the death of a leper patient, his or her ashes were not returned to the families but were interred in the graveyard of the main Nichiren temple. The hospital treated all inhabitants of Minobu and vicinity and gave free medical treatment to indigents.

The extreme poverty of so many Japanese citizens during the early postwar years was very visible at or near Minobu *Kuonji*. According to one of the priests, fifty or sixty people arrived each month hoping to be employed as servants or janitors. Many, he said, were men of "hard living," spiritually at a loss and likely to become vagrants. There were also men who had enjoyed good positions before the war. Some visitors would linger because of the food shortage.

Among the average 300 visitors per day were many Nichiren adherents from all parts of Japan, including Hokkaido. Ocassionally, the faithful arrived in large groups, numbering as many as 2,000 notwithstanding the high cost of food and travel. For substantial numbers, their visit was a one-time pilgrimage to the headquarters of their Buddhist faith. Thirty-two temples surrounding the large temple provided lodging for most visitors. The aftermath of a disastrous, lost war impelled some visitors to seek solace by becoming a priest. For example, a former lieutenant in the Japanese Navy, who had fallen under SCAP's purge directive, now hated the world and was willing to work as a janitor in order to study for the priesthood. Another aspirant was a former important industrialist who had lost his wife, children, and all of his property in the American bombings.[18]

Physically, the Nichiren headquarters complex was quite large and impressive, although most of the temples and other buildings appeared drab and in need of fresh paint and repair. A priest said there were plans for the restoration of the buildings after many years of neglect due to the war.

A Conference on Religion and Education

In early 1948, several more religion and state matters required resolution. With many Japanese manifesting considerable curiosity about Christianity, there were several queries whether public school facilities could be used to study Christianity during nonschool periods such as evenings or on Saturdays in a few schools experimenting with a five-day school week. Another question was whether school bulletin boards could be used to advertise the time and place for Christian Bible classes. My policy was to forbid for the time being all types of religious activity in the schools for all religions: Shinto, Buddhist, and Christian.[19]

The foregoing and other religious issues were aired early in March 1948 during a two-day conference in Kofu on Religious Affairs and Education. The two main meetings drew an audience of about 400 each, attended by members of the prefectural Education and Social Education Sections, principal and teacher organizations, the Shinto, Buddhist, and Christian faiths, and numerous local citizens. At my invitation, Dr. Paul H. Viet, of SCAP's Religions Division also was present.[20]

Lectures and discussions focused on how to interpret the religious provisions of the new Constitution and the Fundamental Law of Education, the meaning of religious tolerance, how teachers should instruct students about different religions described in their social studies textbooks, and the type of religious or memorial services permitted in schools or on other public property. A special lecture and discussion session was also held for fifteen members of the Yamanashi Prefecture Religions Association which represented the three important faiths in

Japan, and for some faculty members and students of the *Eiwa Jo Gakko,* the only private Christian girls' school in the prefecture. Except for a meeting or two in my office with those arranging the conference, I played a minor role in the proceedings, gratified that Dr. Viet was on hand to represent SCAP's policies.

Some of the attendees subsequently said the various sessions enabled them to understand better the need to maintain a separation of religion from the state. In contrast, my intermittent discussions with principals and teachers who were not present disclosed many had not yet grasped the importance of the issue. The desire for some type of morals course within the educational curricula to curb unruly student behavior remained as strong as ever.

The Visit of Dr. Kagawa Toyohiko to Yamanashi

Another religion and state issue arose in June 1948 when Dr. Kagawa Toyohiko, Japan's famous Christian leader, announced he would visit Yamanashi Prefecture. An inveterate traveler and lecturer, he was on a nationwide speaking tour. The son of a nobleman, he became a Christian at age fifteen and in his youth worked on behalf of the poor in the slums of Kobe and Japan's then-nascent labor organizations. Well educated, he obtained a degree in divinity from Princeton University in 1917, and he wrote in subsequent years many books, novels, poems, and Christian tracts. A pacifist, he was imprisoned for his beliefs several times before and during World War II.[21] At war's end, his reputation soared to new heights under Japan's "Christian" conquerors and occupiers and he had been granted on one occasion a personal audience with General MacArthur, who openly encouraged, albeit unofficially, the spread of Christianity throughout Japan.

Notwithstanding SCAP's directives, the new Constitution, and other postwar Japanese legislation mandating the separation of religion and state, Dr. Kagawa appeared to have carte blanche permission to deliver his message on Christianity and democracy to his always large audiences, regardless of where he spoke. Thus it was with considerable interest that I learned he had delivered his standard lecture at two middle schools in Yamanashi Prefecture.

My office received no complaint about a possible religion and state violation occasioned by Dr. Kagawa's appearances. I chose not to take any action. Subsequently, I learned from Mr. Akaike, my assistant, that the two middle principals were aware that Dr. Kagawa's schooltime lectures were probably not in accord with SCAP directives and new Japanese laws, but neither wished to offend him because of his national and international stature. Assuming he was a friend of General MacArthur, they also did not wish indirectly to offend the Supreme Commander, who spoke frequently about the merits of the Christian faith.

One of the principals also noted that U.S. Army chaplains often held Christian services at the Yamanashi Military Government Team headquarters in Kofu for American and civilian personnel and invited local Japanese Christians to attend. Thus it appeared reasonable to assume military government would overlook a "technical" violation of the directives and laws requiring a strict separation of religion and state.[22]

I discussed this and other religious cases subsequently with William P. Woodard of the Religions Division of SCAP, who explained there was often no way to draw up a definitive rule on what was permissible on state property. In many parts of rural Japan, a school auditorium was the only place to hold a public meeting of any type. Also, on many religion and state issues, Japanese officials preferred to let Americans take the lead in defining the more complex problems.

Preserving Religious, Art, and Cultural Monuments

Military government CI&E officers were also expected to report on and proffer advice on preserving important prefectural religious, art, and cultural monuments. Japanese efforts to do so had been neglected in the years immediately preceding and during World War II. For Japan's most important national treasures, SCAP's Arts and Monuments Division (which was absorbed by the Religions and Cultural Resources Division in late 1947), generally took the initiative in dispatching American and Japanese specialists to examine the treasures and make recommendations on what was needed to ensure their preservation.

I had very little time to deal with this particular matter but received reports periodically on the state of Yamanashi's most important cultural properties. For example, in June 1947 following a visit to Yamanashi by a Japanese cultural official from Tokyo, I noted his counsel that "the majority of the objects and installations . . . are in fair or adequate condition. A few have deteriorated due to neglect or because of missing properties." Prefectural officials," I noted further, "will be consulted to determine what can be done to repair or recover the properties."[23]

On two occasions, a representative of SCAP's Arts and Monuments Division also visited Yamanashi to examine cultural properties, prepared reports on their importance and, contrary to the judgment of the Japanese cultural official just cited, urged immediate repairs. Because of the Yamanashi prefectural government's severe financial straits, it was not possible to do this immediately, although some of the cost would be borne by the national government in Tokyo.[24]

In late June 1948, an art and cultural specialist with the Kanto Military Government Region obtained a detailed estimate for rehabilitating one important Shinto shrine on which some minor repairs had been made. I then met with several officials of the prefectural Social Education Section to discuss the cost. I also met with officials in areas where seven other run-down cultural properties were located and asked them to make estimates for improving each one. Four were singled out as the most important. After receiving the estimates, I forwarded them to SCAP's Religions and Cultural Resources Division which, in turn, sent them to the office in the Japanese government responsible for maintaining Yamanashi's—and the nation's—most significant historical cultural holdings.[25]

19
Epilogue

Today, almost fifty years later, it remains clear that the summer of 1948 was a watershed in the efforts of American and Allied Forces to convert Japan into a western, and particularly an American-style, democracy. From July of that year until the official end of the occupation on April 28, 1952, there were volatile crosscurrents in General MacArthur's efforts to speed up reforms while attempting simultaneously to stabilize Japan economically and politically.

These crosscurrents were particularly manifest in the area of education. The program to ensure a 6–3–3–4 educational structure continued to move forward and the 1949–50 school year marked the beginning of compulsory education for all of Japan's boys and girls through the ninth grade and also coeducation in the classrooms. Earlier, with the onset of the 1948–49 school year, three-year upper secondary schools had been established to assure education for all students through the twelfth grade. Effective June 1, 1949, a revision of the School Education Law of March 1947 and other legislation reorganized higher education. By April 1951, there were 181 junior colleges (4 national, 24 public, 153 private), and 193 universities (71 national, 16 public, and 106 private).[1] The reorganization attempted to guarantee the existence of at least one national university in each prefecture, an objective strongly desired by all rural prefectures including Yamanashi. On paper, at least, it appeared that the 6–3–3–4 educational structure was now complete.

Unfortunately, the national and forty-six prefectural governments together did not possess the financial resources to enlarge all existing schools or to construct and equip fully all of the new ones needed at the primary, secondary, and the college and university levels. In fact, the capability of Japan's taxpayers to do so had grown progressively less, beginning in the last half of 1947 and through all of 1948, because of the inflationary economic spiral. School construction costs first doubled, then tripled. During 1948, several missions from

254

Washington (the most important headed by Undersecretary of the Army William H. Draper, Jr.), came to Japan to determine how to put the nation's economic house in order. The missions urged far-reaching measures which included balancing Japan's national budget, terminating programs requiring economic "deconcentration" of large industries and businesses, halting reparations payments and personnel purges, reducing occupation costs (which consumed one-third of the national budget), and reviving Japan's foreign trade. Washington agreed. So did General MacArthur, who finally announced on December 20, 1948, that a primary goal was to stabilize Japan's economy.[2]

Other events also impelled Washington authorities to undertake drastic measures to make Japan viable economically. There was a drive in the U.S. Congress to reduce the American cost of supporting Japan, estimated at $250 million a year.[3] In addition, the "Cold War" smoldering between the Soviet Union and the West since the end of World War II burst into the open in the summer of 1948 when the Soviets stopped all surface traffic into and out of West Berlin, triggering an American airlift for eleven months to keep the populace supplied until the Soviets relented on May 12, 1949. The American-financed Marshall Plan for the reconstruction of Western Europe had already begun, and in China, Communist armies continued to overrun the U.S.-supported forces of Chiang Kai-shek, China's non-Communist leader.

As a consequence, "reverse-course" economic measures were soon undertaken in an attempt to deflate Japan's economy. A special American emissary, Detroit banker Joseph M. Dodge, arrived in Tokyo on February 1, 1949, and remained three months to manage and expedite the implementation of the measures. His "Dodge Plan" succeeded in reducing the inflationary spiral, but its impact also created new hardships for virtually all of Japan's teachers, workers, and other citizens. More than 258,000 civil servants were dismissed. The Ministry of Education, which had been paying for teachers' salaries and for most of the new school construction, and had received 8.1 percent of the national budget during the 1948–49 Japanese fiscal year, found its share of the budget reduced to 6.3 percent for fiscal year 1949–50.[4] This slowed programs for the enlargement of existing schools and the construction of new ones for Japan's expanding student population under the 6–3–3–4 school structure.

The reverse-course economic measures also forced prefectures to reduce their spending. For example, Yamanashi Prefecture's annual budget had risen annually every year since the onset of the occupation. For the 1948–49 school year, it had appropriated 400 million *yen*, with 180 million *yen* or 45 percent, earmarked for education.[5] Its budget for 1949–50 was now also reduced. The same situation obtained in other prefectures. Reverse course also called for less spending on the occupation. One major manifestation of savings was General MacArthur's decision to deactivate, in November 1949, the Eighth Army's forty-five military government teams (renamed civil affairs teams in May of that year). Many of the civilians on the teams were transferred to the remaining eight civil affairs regions/districts.[6] This action reduced considerably the pressure (formerly applied by military government CI&E officers) on primary and secondary school teachers to end their traditional reliance on teaching by rote and to adopt other American-style democratic teaching methods.

As has been noted earlier, Japan's weakening economy threatened to delay plans to establish upwards of 10,000 prefectural, city, town, and village school boards throughout Japan. The purpose of these plans was to decentralize control of education, as in America at the time, in order to reduce the power of the Ministry of Education. Following enactment of the School Board Election Law on July 5, 1948, the first elections were held on October 5, of that year. Economic and other circumstances resulted, however, in limiting the first election to members of boards of education only at the prefectural and five major city levels. Eighth Army headquarter's military government office in Yokohama warned at the time that most Japanese citizens were neither ready nor willing to assume responsibility for their local schools. There was danger Communists and other radicals might dominate the boards in large cities. In addition, most towns and especially villages did not possess the economic resources to support primary and secondary education, including teachers' salaries. (This was especially true in a rural prefecture like Yamanashi.) Despite Eighth Army's warning, SCAP's Civil Education officials insisted on continuing with the decentralization process, even if the Ministry of Education would have to continue providing most of the financial support for the schools, and even if the elections of board members in all smaller cities, towns, and villages could not be completed until 1952.[7]

Not surprisingly, educational decentralization's strongest supporters were Japan's Communists and radical Socialists, especially those within the large Japan Teacher's Union (*Nikkyoso*). *Nikkyoso* members were determined to reduce the power of the Ministry of Education, which they viewed as a "reactionary" institution. They saw an opportunity to elect teachers and other citizens sympathetic to their views and thereby to dominate many school boards, especially in urban areas. Such domination, which was a generally acknowledged threat, would give them more control not only over teachers' salaries and benefits but also over the content of textbooks, particularly those on history, geography, and social studies which, no doubt, would then be suffused with Marxist overtones.

Inevitably, the rising tide of economic distress caused by inflation throughout Japan in 1948 (and which led to the Dodge Plan in 1949) redounded to the benefit of Japan's Communists. For example, Nosaka Sanzo, the head of Japan's Communist party, had come to Yamanashi Prefecture in May 1948 to hold meetings, to tap the discontent of teachers, workers, and other citizens, and to demand the overthrow of the Japanese government, then headed by Ashida Hitoshi. In early July, Communist party leaders in Tokyo were again in Yamanashi to hold a Communist-style "Labor School Conference." Similar Communist activity throughout Japan, plus an increase in demonstrations, walk-outs, and strikes by unions which proved costly to both the national and prefectural governments, impelled General MacArthur gradually to institute measures leading to what became popularly known in 1949 as the "Red Purge."[8]

The first measure leading to the Red Purge was imposed on July 22, 1948, when the Supreme Commander directed the Japanese government to amend the National Public Service Law to prohibit the right-to-strike of all government workers, which included the members of *Nikkyoso*.[9]

The government complied quickly by issuing a cabinet ordinance to this effect by the end of the month, although the National Public Service Law was not formally amended until near the end of the year. *Nikkyoso's* leaders—about one-fourth of its central executive committee were Communists or fellow travelers—protested strongly against the strike ban. So did most officials of SCAP's Labor Division, with the result that its chief, James Killen, who had replaced Theodore Cohen as head of the division in the spring of 1947, resigned. Killen believed that the ban contravened Article 28 of the new Constitution permitting all of Japan's workers, including those in government, to organize and bargain collectively with their employers.[10] The upsurge in Communist activities indicated that the Labor Division's accelerated labor-education program, in which CI&E military government personnel participated from January 1947 onward, and who attempted to convince unionists to resolve their labor problems with government and management by arbitration, conciliation, or mediation, had had no effect on Marxist-oriented union leaders.

Another facet of the Red Purge was aimed at college and university students and professors. Growing Marxist influence on campuses had coalesced in September 1948 into the All Japan Federation of Student Self-Government Associations (*Zengakuren*)—with considerable assistance from the Japan Communist party. Very militant, *Zengakuren* opposed the Ministry of Education—and the Japanese government—on a variety of academic and nonacademic matters ranging from constantly increasing tuition costs to courses of study. By early 1949 the new organization claimed to have 300,000 members in more than 145 colleges and universities.[11] SCAP's Civil Education Division watched this development with growing apprehension, but waited until mid-1949 before launching a frontal attack against *Zengakuren* members and Marxist professors. Meanwhile, the political influence of the Japan Communist party had been strengthened during the general election of January 1949, when thirty-five Communists won seats in the House of Representatives, a postwar high.[12]

On July 19, 1949, Dr. Walter C. Eells, adviser on higher education in SCAP's Civil Education Division, in an address before students and professors at Niigata University, publicly denounced Communist influence in Japan's institutions of higher learning. "Communism is a dangerous doctrine," he declared, "since it advocates the overthrow of democratic governments by force." Further: "The basic reason for advising exclusion of Communist professors is that they are not free. Their thoughts, their beliefs, their teachings are controlled from the outside." His address triggered a storm of protests. In subsequent weeks and months he carried his anti-Communist message to other universities. At Tohoku and Hokkaido universities, student heckling forced him off the stage.[13]

Shortly after Dr. Eells began his attacks on Communist teachers in Japan's universities, General MacArthur ordered the dismissal of all Communists in government and in other sectors of Japan's society. This stage of the purge began following a secret meeting on September 7, 1949, in Tokyo between the Minister of Education and all prefectural superintendents of education. The Supreme Commander had specifically ordered, the minister informed them, summary dismissal of all Communist teachers. As a result, 1,010 teachers were fired. More firings in other positions followed. The number of those removed in the areas of education, information, media, and industry soon totaled 20,997. *Nikkyoso*, which had been wracked by ideological differences for some time—primarily between Communist and moderate Socialist factions—was now further weakened, especially at the prefectural level, although it managed to stage a comeback politically in 1951 and 1952.[14]

General MacArthur shortly took additional measures against the Communists and, with the outbreak of the Korean War in June 1950, he suspended publication of the Japan Communist party's newspaper *Akahata*. The suspension of other Communist publications followed. *Akahata* did not resume publication until May 1, 1952, three days after the occupation ended.[15]

Thus the Dodge Plan of 1949, the financial concerns of the U.S. Congress, international events, and the outbreak of the Korean War combined to hasten the occupation's end. Also contributing was President Truman's decision to dismiss General MacArthur on April 10, 1951, for his failure to adhere to administration policy in prosecuting the Korean War. MacArthur was replaced by General Matthew B. Ridgway.[16] A peace treaty, formally ending a state of war between Japan and the United States and forty-seven other nations, was signed in San Francisco on September 8, 1951. After the treaty and other security arrangements were approved by the U.S. Senate in March 1952, General Ridgway ended the occupation officially on April 28, 1952.[17]

Postoccupation events in education are another story. Suffice it to say that considerable reversion has taken place. The Ministry of Education gradually has reassumed control over most educational matters. Most of Japan's citizens have readily acceded to other changes: a new "morals" course reentered the educational curricula in September 1959; the "examination hell" for students, which SCAP military government educational reformers tried to eliminate, has been maintained as an integral part of Japan's educational system. Particularly intense are examinations that determine whether students will be admitted to desirable "university track" rather than "vocational track" upper secondary schools.

Further, teaching by rote, with some modifications, has not lost its
favor as the preferred method of instruction, especially in the primary
and lower secondary schools; the Ministry of Education has regained
final approval for the content of textbooks; and only prefectural and
municipal boards of education have been retained, their members now
appointed by prefectural governors and mayors, respectively. Despite a
substantial increase in students enrolled in higher education, the system
remains very elitist, with Tokyo University enjoying its prewar preem-
inence. The status of Japanese women in their relationship with men
is still not commensurate with that of their American and European
counterparts. Japanese women's salaries for identical work is invariably
less than salaries for men. In the area of religion, neighborhood associations still function, especially in rural areas, and their members see
no harm in supporting their local Shinto shrines and Buddhist temples
in accordance with the ability of families to pay.

Not all reforms have been completely discarded, however. Educational opportunities for all boys and girls, compared with the years
prior to 1945, have been greatly enhanced, and more than 90 percent
receive education through the twelfth grade. More than one-third
continue into higher education. No major nation today has a higher
literacy rate. There is far more coeducation in the classrooms than there
was before 1945. The political enfranchisement and new legal rights
of women have endured, and more women teachers have found their
way into classrooms in the primary and secondary schools, colleges and
universities, and into other professions. They continue to be elected
to seats in the National Diet and in prefectural, municipal, town, and
village assemblies. Women's organizations have flourished, and women
dominate the activities of PTAS.

Religious freedom remains in effect. Although there has been a
rise in nationalistic feeling in recent years, State Shintoism has not
reemerged. At the local level, the heads of neighborhood associations
(*tonarigumis* and *burakukais* and the *chonaikais*) are now selected more
democratically than they were in the past.

With Japan's economic recovery, triggered by large U.S. procurement orders and the establishment of a Japan Defense Force following
the outbreak of the Korean War in June 1950, and especially from
1960 onward, many labor unions gradually have taken on more of
the trappings of enterprise unions. Leaders of *Nikkyoso*, representing

primary and lower secondary teachers, once noted for their political radicalism, have become more moderate in their activities.

Overall, student and political Communists have shrunk in numbers. Freedom of the press has been maintained.

Most significant of all, Japan's new democratic Constitution of May 3, 1947, which was written by the occupation authorities and which replaced the Meiji Constitution of 1890, has never been revised or amended.

Notes

Chapter 1. Assignment to Japan

1. The first bombing of Japan, on 18 April 1942, sought to divert, if possible, the formidable Japanese navy in the Pacific. Sixteen B-25 bombers, led by Lt. Col. James H. Doolittle, took off from the aircraft carrier U.S.S. *Hornet*. Some of the planes dropped bombs on Tokyo and the others struck targets in Yokohama, Yokuska, Nagoya, and Kobe. After the bombings, one plane was forced to land near Vladivostok in the Soviet Union, and its crew was interned there. Of the eighty crewmen on the mission, three died in crash landings in China and eight bailed out and were captured in Japanese-held parts of China. Of those eight, three were executed by a firing squad near Shanghai and the other five were given life sentences. One of the five men died in prison; the four survivors were released at war's end. See Carroll V. Glines, *Doolittle's Tokyo Raiders* (New York: Van Nostrand Reinhold, 1964), pp. 360–74, 408–9.

2. D. Clayton James, *The Years of MacArthur*, vol. 3, *Triumph and Disaster, 1945–1964* (Boston: Houghton Mifflin, 1985), pp. 4–5.

3. The International Tribunal, which completed its work on 12 November 1948, tried twenty-eight alleged Class A war criminals. Of the twenty-five who survived the trial, seven were hanged and the rest were given lengthy prison sentences. About 5,100 Class B and Class C military and civilian leaders were tried for alleged war crimes in Yokohama by Eighth Army military commissions. Of these, half received life sentences and 900 were executed. Another 5,000 defendants were tried in China and Southeast Asia, including the Philippines. About 3,000 received various prison terms and 700 were executed. See James, *Years of MacArthur*, vol. 3, pp. 93–102; and W. G. Beasley, *The Modern History of Japan* (New York: Praeger, 1963), pp. 281–82.

4. Early in the occupation, the cost of supporting American and Allied forces in Japan was estimated to consume about 20 percent of the Japanese national budget. By 1948, the cost was estimated at one-third of the national budget. See James, *Years of MacArthur*, vol. 3, p. 230.

5. Wilson Le Couteur, *To Nippon, the Land of the Rising Sun: A Guide Book to Japan* (Tokyo: Nippon Yusen Kaisha, 1899), p. 39; *Encyclopedia Americana*, vol. 15, int. ed. (Danbury, Conn.: Grolier, 1988), p. 779.

Chapter 2. The Yamanashi Military Government Team

1. Lt. Col. Henry Hille, Jr., Corps of Engineers, "Eighth Army's Role in Military Government in Japan," *Military Review* 22, no. 11 (Feb. 1948), pp.

9–14; Weekly Reports, YMGT Detachment, 32nd Mil. Govt. Hqs. and Hqs. Co., (APO 343), Jan.–Feb. 1946.

2. Hille, "Eighth Army's Role," pp. 10–11.

3. Ralph J. D. Braibanti, "Administration of Military Government in Japan and the Prefectural Level," *American Political Science Review* 43 (April 1949), pp. 252–53.

4. Hqs. 32nd Mil. Govt. and Hqs. Co., APO 343. Subject: *Orders*, 1 Feb. 1946.

5. Ibid., Subject: *Unit Occupational Reports*, Feb. 1946.

6. This figure fluctuated in subsequent months. For example, in December 1946 it dropped to 1,888. Then after Eighth Army in July 1947 authorized a maximum of 605 civilians to serve on the teams, total authorized military and civilian personnel reached 2,495. Before July 1947, civilians were sometimes additions to authorized team military strength. Afterward, military strength was usually, but not always, reduced to accommodate additional civilians. Recruiting qualified civilians was a slow task, so it is doubtful that the authorized figure (605) was ever reached. For discussion, see Layton Horner, *The American Occupation at the Prefectural Level*, M.A. thesis, University of Denver (Dec. 1949), pp. 14–18.

7. Braibanti, "Administration of Military Government," pp. 253–56; Horner, *American Occupation*, pp. 15–17.

8. Horner, *American Occupation*, pp. 15–17.

9. Ibid., p. 6.

Chapter 3. The Team's Task: Demilitarization and Education

1. War Department Pamphlet No. 31–369, *Civil Affairs Handbook: Japan. Prefectural Studies: Yamanashi-ken* (24 Sept. 1945), p. 1.

2. Ibid., chapter 2.

3. Ibid.; *Records of Kofu Air Raid*, Kofu City publication (6 July 1974). Data provided by Hosaka Chushin in letter to author, 26 August 1987.

4. D. Clayton James, *The Years of MacArthur*, vol. 3, *Triumph and Disaster, 1945–1964* (Boston: Houghton Mifflin, 1985), pp. 88–92.

5. William F. Nimmo, *Behind a Curtain of Silence: Japanese in Soviet Custody, 1945–1956* (New York: Greenwood Press, 1988), pp. 115–18; and also William F. Nimmo, editor, *The Occupation of Japan: The Grass Roots*, Norfolk, Va.: General Douglas MacArthur Foundation, 1991, p. 124.

6. *Report of the United States Education Mission to Japan* (30 March 1946), p. 24.

7. It was evident by late 1946 that SCAP's Education Division had already decided not to require the Japanese government to adopt *romaji* to replace Japan's traditional method of writing. Rather, studies were under way on how more *romaji* might be taught to assist adults and students in making the transition to the study of English and European languages, thus opening the door to reading classical writings on western history, philosophy, and literature which inspired democratic ideas and ideals.

8. *Report of U.S. Education Mission*, chaps. 3 and 4.

9. Harold S. Quigley and John E. Turner, *The New Japan* (Minneapolis: University of Minnesota Press, 1974), chap. 8.

10. Initially called the "Imperial Education Association" or *Teikoku Kyoikukai* when it was founded in 1883, the association was theoretically a federation of autonomous local, prefectural, and cultural associations, albeit in reality it was an instrument of the Ministry of Education designed to unite teachers in support of national education policy. About 1920 it became increasingly a progressive force in education, but with the rise of militaristic governments in the 1930s it became an instrument for teaching ultranationalism and militarism. In 1944 it became the "Great Japan Education Association" or *Dai Nippon Kyoikukai*. In 1946 during the occupation, the association's former relationship with the Ministry of Education was severed. Reorganized, the word "Great" was dropped from its name in early 1946 and the former leadership was purged, but it had to compete with two postwar education associations—the moderate *Zenkyo* and the Communist-influenced *Nikkyo*. The Japan Education Association's reputation was sullied by its wartime role, and its leadership remained very conservative. Most of its prefectural affiliates had little influence on postwar educational reform. See further, Benjamin C. Duke, *Japan's Militant Teachers: A History of the Left-Wing Teachers' Movement* (Honolulu: University of Hawaii Press, 1973), pp. 25–27, 35, 37, and 39ff.

11. War Department Pamphlet No. 31–369, pp. 86–95.

12. Report, Yamanashi Detachment, 32nd Military Government Company (APO 343), *Summary of* CI&E *Activities*, April–July 1946, pp. 2–6.

13. Ibid.

14. Although SCAP's directive barring former officials of the IRAA and other organizations from public office did not provide for exceptions, I soon discovered, as did some of my CI&E colleagues, that many officials had joined the IRAA under pressure from Japan's ruling military leaders and were essentially "paper members," i.e., they performed no particular additional duties on behalf of the IRAA.

15. Headquarters, Yamanashi Military Government Team (APO 201), Kofu, Yamanashi, *Semi-Monthly Occupational Activities Reports to Commanding General, Headquarters, Eighth Army* (hereinafter, YMGT Report or Reports), 16–31 July 1946, 1–15 and 16–31 August 1946.

16. YMGT Report, 16–30 November 1946.

17. Ibid., 1–15 and 16–30 July 1946, 1–15 and 16–31 August 1946, 1–15 and 16–30 September 1946; monthly summaries of YMGT activities, July and August 1946.

18. YMGT Reports, 1–15 and 16–31 August 1946, 1–15 and 16–31 October 1946.

19. Ibid., 1–15 and 16–31 October 1946.

Chapter 4. The First School Inspections

1. YMGT Report, 1–15 November 1946.

2. Author's notes, 24 November 1946.

3. YMGT Report, 16–30 November 1946; author's notes, 25 November 1946.

4. YMGT Report, 16–30 November 1946.

Chapter 5. Other Initial Duties

1. My own files include documents and photographs showing how the films were burned under the supervision of an Eighth Army lieutenant on 23 April and 2, 4 May 1946.

2. YMGT Report, 1–15 November 1946; author's letters to friends, 11, 24, and 26 November 1946.

3. YMGT Report, 1–15 November 1946.

4. Ibid.

5. Ibid.

6. Ibid.; author's letter to friend, 20 November 1946.

Chapter 6. Democracy's Pangs in the Classroom

1. YMGT Report, 16–31 January 1947.

2. *Japan Year Book, 1946–1948* (Tokyo: Foreign Affairs Association, 1948), pp. 220–27; Jacob Van Staaveren, "The Educational Revolution in Japan," *The Educational Forum* 17, no. 2 (January 1952), pp. 232–33.

3. *Report of the United States Education Mission to Japan* (30 March 1946), p. 33.

4. YMGT Report, 16–31 January 1947; author's letter to friend, February 1947.

5. YMGT Report, 16–31 January 1947.

6. The low voltage also made it impossible at times for members of the YMGT to get clear reception on their radios. The problem was partially overcome by attaching small Japanese transformers to the radios. Occasionally this proved hazardous. If there was a sudden increase in voltage, transformers turned on "high" would catch fire, requiring fast action by the team member.

7. YMGT Report, 16–31 January 1947; Monthly Report, February 1947.

8. The American baseball stars, assembled under the flag of the Philadelphia Athletics and their famous coach Connie Mack, for their post-season tour were transported, after their arrival at Yokohama, to Tokyo in a special railway car provided by the Emperor. They were billeted in the Imperial Hotel and paraded down the Ginza. Their first four games against Japanese baseball teams were played in Tokyo before crowds totaling 200,000. Ruth and his colleague were besieged by autograph seekers wherever they went and were showered with gifts. Although the Americans won every game, Japanese fans did not seem to mind. They marveled at Ruth's batting prowess and were amused by his antics on the field. He played every inning. Then–U.S. Ambassador to Japan Joseph Grew said that Ruth and his fellow players were better ambassadors than

he and his colleagues. One Far East diplomat predicted that the baseball tour would offset "war talk" at an upcoming naval conference in London.

Ruth's legacy in Japan was considerable. After the 1934 baseball tour, the Japanese government sponsored a Babe Ruth Day to encourage boys to play baseball. His visit to Osaka was commemorated with a plaque. During World War II a frequent war cry of Japanese soldiers against Americans was: "Go to Hell, Babe Ruth! Americans, you die!" After war's end, Ruth's reputation quickly regained its luster. In 1954 a Japanese newspaper polled its readers on famous people of the twentieth century. Only one foreigner made the list— Babe Ruth. See further Karl Wagenheim, *Babe Ruth: His Life and Legend* (New York: Praeger, 1974), pp. 48, 226, 448–85.

9. Jacob Van Staaveren, "Hosaka's New Learning," *Portland Oregonian* (5 December 1948); D. Clayton James, *The Years of MacArthur*, vol. 3, *Triumph and Disaster, 1945–1965* (Boston: Houghton Mifflin, 1985), pp. 480-85.

10. SCAP belatedly took cognizance of a "national holiday problem" and persuaded the Japanese government to enact on 5 July 1948 a National Holiday Law reducing from twelve to nine the number of national holidays and to eliminate celebrations formerly associated with State Shinto and the Imperial Court. Henceforth, the nine national holidays were: New Year's Day, Adults' Day (Jan. 15), Vernal Equinox (Mar. 24), Emperor's Birthday (April 29), Constitution Day (May 3), Autumnal Equinox (Sept. 24), Cultural Day (Nov. 3), and Labor Thanksgiving Day (Nov. 24). See further, *SCAP Non-Military Activities in Japan*, no. 34, July 1948, pp. 341–42.

11. YMGT Report, February 1947.

12. Ibid., March 1947.

Chapter 7. Secondary, Normal, and Medical Schools

1. *Japan Year Book, 1946–1948* (Tokyo: Foreign Affairs Association, 1948), p. 471.

2. War Department Pamphlet No. 31–369, *Civil Affairs Handbook, Japan Prefectural Studies, Yamanashi-ken*, 24 September 1945, p. 4.

3. YMGT Report, March 1947.

4. Ibid.

5. Ibid., 1–15 January 1947.

6. Ibid., March 1947.

7. Ibid., 1–5, 16–31 January 1947, February 1947, March 1947 (sections on Public Health Activities).

8. Ibid., February 1947.

Chapter 8. Yamanashi's Teachers' Union

1. *Yamanashi Prefecture Centenary History* (late Showa period), p. 1,104. Cited in letter to author from Hosaka Chushin, 27 June 1987.

2. Donald R. Thurston, *Teachers and Politics in Japan* (Princeton: Princeton University Press, 1973, pp. 52–60.

3. YMGT Report, 1–15 October 1946.

4. SCAP directive, "Removal of Restrictions on Political, Civil, and Religious Liberties," 4 Oct. 1945, in *Japan Year Book, 1946–1948* (Tokyo: Foreign Affairs Association, 1948), Appendix, pp. 10–12; Thurston, *Teachers and Politics*, pp. 52–60.

5. Joe Moore, *Japanese Workers and the Struggle for Power, 1945–1947* (Madison: University of Wisconsin Press, 1983), p. 14.

6. *Japan Year Book, 1946–1948*, Appendix, pp. 230–36, 247–50.

7. Ibid., Appendix, pp. 24–34.

8. Thurston, *Teachers and Politics*, p. 55; YMGT Report, *Activities of Education Associations*, 10 January 1948.

9. YMGT Report, 1–15 January 1947.

10. Ibid., 16–30 November 1946.

11. Ibid., 1–15 November 1946; Thurston, *Teachers and Politics*, p. 55.

12. YMGT Report, 1–15 November 1946.

13. Ibid.

14. Ibid.

15. Ibid.

16. Moore, *Japanese Workers*, p. 42.

17. YMGT Reports, 1–15, 16–31 December 1946; Theodore Cohen, in *Remaking Japan: The American Occupation as New Deal*, edited by Herbert Passin (New York: Macmillan, 1987), pp. 277–83.

18. YMGT Report, 16–30 December 1946; author's notes, 30 December 1946.

19. Benjamin C. Duke, *Japan's Militant Teachers: A History of the Left-Wing Teachers' Movement* (Honolulu: University of Hawaii Press, 1973), pp. 59–62.

20. YMGT Report, 16–31 January 1947.

21. Ibid.; author's notes, 17 January 1947.

22. Cohen, *Remaking Japan*, pp. 85–86.

23. Author's files include transcripts of four of the papers presented by SCAP officials at the conference: Richard Deverall, chief of the Education Branch, Labor Division, "Aims and Methods of Information Work with Trade Unions"; Thomas Dunleavy, chief and field liaison officer, Labor Division, "Aims and Methods of Information Work with Government Officials"; Miriam Farley, economic affairs information officer, CI&E, "A Suggested Local Information Program"; J. V. Fields, assistant economic affairs officer, CI&E, "Aims and Methods of Information Work with Employers."

24. YMGT Report, 16–31 January 1947.

25. Duke, *Japan's Militant Teachers*, pp. 59–62; Tokyo, *Japan Times*, 20–31 January 1947.

26. Cohen, *Remaking Japan*, pp. 283–85.

27. Ibid., 293–95; Duke, *Japan's Militant Teachers*, pp. 63–64.

28. YMGT Report, February 1947.

29. Ibid.; author's letters to friends, February 10, 12, 1947.

30. YMGT Report, February 1947.

Chapter 9. Teaching Democracy to Japan's Adults

1. *Report of the United States Education Mission to Japan* (30 March 1946), p. 47.

2. Ibid.

3. Jacob Van Staaveren, "Adult Education for Japanese," *Portland Oregonian* (12 December 1948); memo, *Adult Education*, prepared by Adult Education Branch, CI&E Section, Hqs. SCAP, Tokyo, Japan, 26 February 1947.

4. YMGT Reports, 1–15, 16–31 January 1947.

5. Ibid.

6. Ibid., 16–31 January 1947.

7. Ibid., March 1947.

8. Memo, *Women's Education*, prepared by Women's Education Branch, Education Division, CI&E Section, Hqs. SCAP, Tokyo, Japan (n.d., but about September 1946).

9. Basil Hall Chamberlain, *Things Japanese: Being Notes on Various Subjects Connected with Japan*, 4th ed., rev. and enl. (London: Kelly and Walsh, 1902), pp. 453–54.

10. YMGT Report, February 1947.

11. Memo. *The Citizens' Public Hall: An Outline of Its Creation and Management*, prepared by the Adult Education Branch, Education Division CI&E Section, Hqs. SCAP, Tokyo, Japan, 1 July 1946.

12. YMGT Reports, 1–15 November 1946, 1–15 January 1947.

13. Ibid., YMGT Special Report, "Record of Exhibitions Held by the Yamanashi Military Government Team," December 1946–September 1947.

14. YMGT Report, August 1947.

15. YMGT Special Report, "Record of Exhibitions."

16. YMGT Report, February 1947; "Record of Exhibitions."

17. Ibid.

18. YMGT Report, March 1947; "Record of Exhibitions."

19. YMGT Report, March 1947.

Chapter 10. The Conundrum of Religious Freedom

1. William P. Woodward, *The Allied Occupation of Japan, 1945–1952, and Japanese Religions* (Leiden: E. J. Brill, 1972), pp. 285–86.

2. Ibid., pp. 291–99.

3. Ralph J. D. Braibanti, "Neighborhood Associations in Japan and Their Democratic Potentialities," *Far Eastern Quarterly* 6 (February 1948), pp. 136–64.

4. YMGT Report, 16–30 November 1946.

5. Citizen's letter to YMGT, 29 October 1946.

6. SCAP directive, "Sponsorship and Support of Shinto by Neighborhood Associations" (SCAPIN 1311), 6 November 1946 (text is in Woodward, *The Allied Occupation*, pp. 299–300).

7. YMGT Report, March 1947.

8. U.S. Army, Service Forces Manual M 3 54–15, *Civil Affairs Handbook, Japan, Section 15, Education*, 23 June 1944, p. 13. The *Handbook* also asserts (p. 13) that the East and West Honganji Buddhist sects of Shinshu needed watching. Their hereditary abbots, the *Otani*, were related by marriage to the Imperial family and were wealthy. "Otani Kozui, in particular, has been a leading advocate of Greater East Asia and has used the wealth and religious organization at his disposal to promote Japanese propaganda and infiltration throughout Asia under the guise of trade and religion. Buddhist missions and missionaries require special attention." In addition, the *Handbook* warns, some adherents of Zen Buddhism "bear watching," albeit this particular sect was relatively weak.

9. Hugh Byas, *Government by Assassination* (New York: Alfred A. Knopf, 1942), pp. 25–30, 53–62.

10. YMGT Report, 1–15 October 1946; author's notes, November 1946.

Chapter 11. Political Interlude: Surveillance of the April 1947 Elections

1. SCAP directive, "Removal of Restrictions on Political, Civil, and Religious Liberties," 4 October 1945, in *Japan Year Book, 1946–1948* (Tokyo: Foreign Affairs Association, 1948), Appendix, pp. 10–12.

2. SCAP directive, "Removal and Exclusion of Undesirable Personnel from Public Office," 4 January 1946, in *Japan Year Book, 1946–1948*, Appendix, pp. 17–19.

3. D. Clayton James, *The Years of MacArthur*, vol. 3, *Triumph and Disaster, 1945–1964* (Boston: Houghton Mifflin, 1985), pp. 132–34.

4. Harold S. Quigley and John E. Turner, *The New Japan: Government and Politics* (Minneapolis: University of Minnesota Press, 1956, repr. 1974), p. 246.

5. James, *The Years of MacArthur*, pp. 117, 148.

6. SCAP, *Summary of Non-Military Activities in Japan*, Tokyo, April 1946, p. 4; YMGT Report, April 1946, p. 1.

7. *Japan Year Book, 1946–1948*, p. 82; James, *The Years of MacArthur*, pp. 48–49, 117–18; Sir Esler Dening, *Japan* (New York: Praeger, 1961), pp. 105–6.

8. SCAP, *Summary of Non-Military Activities*, April 1947, p. 18.

9. *Japan Year Book, 1946–1948*, Appendix, pp. 44–79, 129.

10. Ibid., p. 33; Quigley and Turner, *The New Japan*, pp. 102–9; YMGT Report, March 1947, p. 3.

11. Layton Horner, *The American Occupation of Japan at the Prefectural Level* (M.A. thesis, University of Denver, Denver, Colorado, 1949), pp. 14–20.

12. YMGT Report, March 1947, p. 4.

13. YMGT Report, *Summary of Non-Military Activities*, April 1947, p. 1.

14. Author's notes, 8 April 1947; YMGT Report, April 1947, Annex G, subject: *Election Reports*, pp. 1–3.

15. YMGT Report, April 1947.

16. Ibid.

17. Ibid.

18. Ibid., *Japan Year Book, 1946–1948*, p. 175; SCAP, *Summary of Non-Military Activities*, April 1947, pp. 26, 32–33.

19. YMGT Report, April 1947, Annex G, pp. 1–3.

20. Ibid.; SCAP, *Summary of Non-Military Activities*, April 1947, pp. 21–22.

21. YMGT Report, 16–30 October 1946, p. 8.

22. YMGT press releases, May 1947.

23. SCAP, *Summary of Non-Military Activities*, April 1947, p. 17.

24. Ibid.; *Handbook of Data on Japanese Women in Political Life: In Commemoration of the 40th Anniversary of Woman Suffrage in Japan*, 2nd ed. (Tokyo: Fusae Ichikawa Memorial Association, 1987). English translation in McKeldin Library, University of Maryland, College Park, MD.

Chapter 12. Inauguration of the Educational Structure

1. YMGT Report, May 1947.

2. Ibid.

3. SCAP leaflet, *The Community School*, Education Division, 6 pp., circa February 1947. The basic content and objectives of the social studies courses came directly from John Dewey, *Experience and Education* (1938). The book was variously quoted and summarized in the above SCAP leaflet, which was translated into Japanese and widely distributed. The possibilities of community resources to provide student experiences, the leaflet suggested, include "field, orchard, or forest; at seashore and mountain; in mines, sawmills, and factories . . . wharf or railway station; at construction projects; at reservoir and power plants; at the telephone exchange or the fire department; at the market or bakery; at the post office. The list of resources varies from community to community, but in any locality there are available many experiences which will provide the basis of understanding of the natural and social environment."

4. YMGT Reports; April and June 1947.

5. Ibid., June through October 1947.

6. Ibid., May and December 1947.

7. Ibid., January 1948.

8. Agenda, Headquarters IXth Corps CI&E conference at Headquarters Kanto Military Government Region, Tokyo, 13–15 January 1948; letter to friend, 23 January 1948.

9. YMGT Report, January 1948.

10. Ibid., February 1947.

11. Ibid., April 1947.

12. Ibid.

13. Ibid.

14. Ibid., November 1947.

15. Ibid.

16. SCAP, *Summary of Non-Military Activities*, February 1948, no. 29, p. 294 (July 1948) no. 34, p. 337; YMGT Report, May 1948.

17. YMGT Special Report, *Correspondence Schools*, prepared by CI&E office, 21 June 1948.

18. YMGT Report, June 1948; author's notes, June 1948.

19. YMGT Report, May 1948.

20. Agenda, Kanto Military Government Region Conference of Military Government Education Officers at Maebashi, Gumma-ken, 22–23 March 1948, and at Urawa, Saitama-ken, 7–8 June 1948; author's notes on conference, 7–8 June.

Chapter 13. Further Reforms in Teacher Training

1. YMGT Report (CI&E office) to CG, Hqs. IXth Corps, APO 309 (Attn. CI&E office), subject: *Normal Schools*, 22 October 1947.

2. Ibid.

3. YMGT Report, August 1947.

4. YMGT Report (CI&E office), *Normal Schools*, 22 October 1947.

5. YMGT Report, October 1947.

6. YMGT Report, February 1948.

7. Ibid.

8. Ibid., May 1948.

9. Ibid., June 1948.

10. Ibid.

11. Ibid., July 1948.

12. Ibid.

13. Ibid.; YMGT Report (CI&E office to CI&E office, Kanto Military Government Region), *Activities of Education Associations in Yamanashi Prefecture*, 10 July 1948.

14. Agenda, Kanto Military Government Region Conference of Military Government Education Officers, Urawa, Saitama-ken, 7–8 June 1948.

Chapter 14. Private Schools and the School for the Handicapped

1. YMGT Report, October 1946.

2. Richard Hanks Mitchell, *The Korean Minority in Japan* (Berkeley and Los Angeles: University of California Press, 1967), pp. 100–14.

3. YMGT Report, June 1947.

4. Ibid., August 1947.

5. Mitchell, *Korean Minority*, pp. 107–8.

6. Ibid.

7. Ibid.

8. Ibid., pp. 114–15.

9. *New York Times*, 26, 28 April 1948, p. 1.

10. SCAP, *Summary of Non-Military Activities*, May 1948, no. 32, p. 383.

11. YMGT Report, May 1948.

12. Mitchell, *Korean Minority*, pp. 116–18.

13. Ibid.

14. YMGT Report, 16–30 November 1946, June 1947.

15. Ibid., August 1947.

16. Ibid., November 1947.

17. Morris Fishbein, editor, *Fishbein's Illustrated Medical and Health Encyclopedia*, Home Library ed., vol. 1 (New York: H. S. Stuttman, 1977), p. 41.

Chapter 15. The School Lunch Program

1. SCAP, *Public Health and Welfare Technical Bulletin* (APO 500), June 1948.

2. The contributing agencies were the American Friends Service Committee, Catholic Welfare, Church World Services, Brotherly Service Committee, Christian Science, Salvation Army, YMCA, YWCA, American Federation of Labor, and Congress of Industrial Organizations. Reported in *Nippon Times* (1 December 1946).

3. *Japan Year Book, 1946–1948*, p. 479.

4. YMGT Report, March 1947.

5. Ibid., April, August, and November 1947. By the end of 1947, 4,500 schools throughout Japan were receiving LARA food for school lunches to feed about 4 million students. The school lunch program continued for many more months with expenses paid out of the U.S. Aid Counterpart Funds after the discontinuation of LARA funds and funds from Government and Relief in Occupied Areas GARIOA. See *Japan Year Book, 1949–1952*, p. 656.

6. YMGT Special Report, *Civil Education Activities*, prepared by CI&E office, YMGT to CO, YMGT, June 1948.

7. SCAP, *Public Health and Welfare Technical Bulletin* (APO 500), June 1948.

Chapter 16. Expansion of the Labor Education Program

1. YMGT Report, May 1947.

2. Ibid.

3. Memo for Record, J. Van Staaveren, YMGT CI&E officer, subject: *Silk Mills*, 13 June 1947.

4. Ibid.

5. YMGT Report, June 1947.

6. Ibid., June and July 1947.

7. The new law outlawed the closed shop and secondary boycotts; made unions liable for breach of contracts or damages resulting from jurisdictional disputes; imposed a 60-day cooling-off period for called strikes; authorized an 80-day injunction against strikes affecting national health or safety; prohibited political contributions by unions, "featherbedding," and excessive dues; established a conciliation service outside the U.S. Department of Labor; and required union leaders to take a non-Communist oath. (Author's notes, July 1947.)

8. The team commander's concern had been heightened by the hour-long English-language program broadcast every evening by Radio Moscow. The broadcast boomed clearly into Kofu from a transmitter presumably located in Siberian Vladivostok. A man and a woman (nicknamed "Moscow Joe" and "Moscow Mary" by team members) always depicted America as a fear-riven society where only one "progressive" political leader, Henry A. Wallace, stood up to a "reactionary" U.S. Congress which had enacted a Taft-Hartley "slave labor" bill that "severely oppressed" all workers. Wallace headed a new Progressive party, backed strongly by American Communists, during the 1948 national political campaign. Nonetheless, Truman won a second term in office in November of that year. (Author's notes, July 1947.)

9. Memo, J. Van Staaveren, YMGT CI&E officer to Lt. Col. Burton E. Stetson, CO, YMGT, no subject, 3 September 1947.

10. Benjamin C. Duke, *Japan's Militant Teachers: A History of the Left-Wing Teachers' Movement* (Honolulu: University of Hawaii Press, 1973), pp. 69–70, 75.

11. Ibid., pp. 75–77.

12. YMGT Report, September 1947.

13. Ibid., October 1947.

14. Ibid., December 1947.

15. Ibid.

16. Ibid.

17. Ibid., February 1948.

18. Ibid., March 1948.

19. Ibid.

20. Duke, *Japan's Militant Teachers*, pp. 78–79; YMGT Report, May 1948.

21. YMGT Report, May 1948.

22. Ibid., June 1948.

23. Ibid., July 1948.

24. Ibid.

25. Duke, *Japan's Militant Teachers*, pp. 79–80.

26. Memo, J. Van Staaveren, YMGT CI&E officer to Lt. Col. Burton E. Stetson, CO, YMGT, subject: *Civil Education Activities*, November 1946–July 1948, July 1948.

Chapter 17. Expansion of Adult Education Programs

1. YMGT Report, April 1947.

2. Ibid.

3. Ibid.

4. Ibid.

5. Ibid., June 1947.

6. Ibid., March and July 1947.

7. Ibid., April, May, and June 1947.

8. Ibid., May 1947.

9. Agenda, subject: *Outline of Courses to be Offered During Three Half-Day Adult Education Institutes in Each Prefecture* in July 1947, 21 April 1947.

10. YMGT Report, July 1947.

11. Ibid.; author's notes, July 1947.

12. YMGT Report, September 1949.

13. Ibid.

14. Ibid.; author's notes, September 1947.

15. YMGT, September 1947.

16. Ibid., October 1947; author's notes, October 1947.

17. YMGT Reports, October and December 1947; author's notes, December 1947.

18. YMGT Reports, October and December 1947.

19. YMGT Report, November 1947.

20. Ibid.; Special Report, subject: *Record of Exhibitions Held Under the Auspices of* YMGT, December 1946–September 1947 (hereafter, *Record of* YMGT *Exhibitions*).

21. In 1946 Dr. Donald B. McMullen (1903–67), was awarded the Medal of Freedom, America's highest civilian award, for his work in the Philippines during World War II on schistosomiasis. His successful research in Japan during the occupation led to a meeting with Emperor Hirohito. From 1958 to 1963 he headed the schistosomiasis advisory team of the World Health Organization which counseled nations in the Middle East, Africa, and Latin America on the prevention of parasitic diseases.

22. YMGT Report, May 1947; *Record of* YMGT *Exhibitions*.

23. YMGT Report, June, July 1947; *Record of* YMGT *Exhibitions*.

24. YMGT Report, September 1947; *Record of* YMGT *Exhibitions*.

25. YMGT Reports, October and November 1947.

26. Agenda, Hqs. IXth Corps, subject: *Civil Information and Education Conference of the Kanto Military Government Region*, 12–14 January 1948.

27. YMGT Report, January 1948; author's letter to friend, 25 January 1948.

28. YMGT Report, February 1948.

29. Ibid., March 1948.

30. Ibid.

31. Ibid., April 1948.

32. Ibid., January, February 1948.

33. Ibid., January, March 1948.

34. Ibid., March 1948.

35. Ibid., April, May 1948.

36. Agenda, subject: *Kanto Military Government Region Conference of Military Government Officers and* CI&E *Chiefs*, Urawa, Saitama-ken, 7–8 June 1948; author's notes, June 1948.

37. Author's notes, June 1948.

38. Agenda, Social Education Section, Yamanashi-ken, subject: *The Program of the Social Education Conference* (in Ichikawa and Yomura), July 1948.

39. Harry W. Wray, "Decentralization of Education in the Allied Occupation of Japan, 1945–52," in *The Occupation of Japan: Educational and Social Reform*, edited by William F. Nimmo (Norfolk, Va.: General Douglas MacArthur Foundation, 1980), pp. 155–56.

40. YMGT Report, July 1948; author's notes, July 1948.

41. Author's notes, May, June, July 1948.

42. Ibid., July 1948.

43. YMGT Report, July 1948.

44. Ibid.; Agenda, Social Education Section, Yamanashi-ken, subject: *The Program of the Social Education Conference* (in Ichikawa and Yomura), July 1948.

Chapter 18. Additional Religion and State Problems

1. Memo, Mr. Akaike Hajime, Consultant on Youth Organizations and Religion to J. Van Staaveren, CI&E Officer, YMGT, no subject, 15 April 1947.

2. Ibid.

3. Ibid.

4. Operational Directive, Hqs Eighth Army, subject: *Food Distribution*, April 1947; SCAP, *Summary of Non-Military Activities*, April 1947, no. 20, p. 36.

5. YMGT Reports, May 1947; author's notes, June 1947.

6. YMGT Report, July 1947; William P. Woodward, *The Allied Occupation of Japan and Japanese Religions* (Leiden: E. J. Brill, 1972), p. 132.

7. Woodward, *The Allied Occupation*, pp. 151–58.

8. Ibid.

9. Ibid.

10. YMGT Report, May 1947.

11. Petition by parishioners of Kissoji Temple, author's notes, 17 September 1947; YMGT Report, November 1947.

12. Report on Rinzai priest by Mr. Akaike, November 1947.

13. Letter, Buddhist priest to YMGT, 22 November 1947.

14. Author's notes, November 1947; YMGT Report, November 1947.

15. Memo for Record, subject: *Funeral for War Dead*, 14 October 1947.

16. Report on Minobu Kuonji by Mr. Akaike, October 1947, and materials from SCAP's Religions Division; Memo for Record, subject: *Interview with Nichiren Priests*, November 1947.

17. YMGT Report, November 1947.

18. Memo for Record, subject: *Interview with Nichiren Priests*, November 1947.

19. Author's notes, February and March 1948.

20. YMGT Report, March 1948.

21. *New York Times*, 24 April 1960.

22. Memo for Record, Mr. Akaike on Dr. Kagawa, 27 June 1948.

23. YMGT Report, June 1947.

24. Author's notes, June 1948.

25. Ibid.

Epilogue

1. *Japan Year Book, 1949–1952* (Tokyo: Foreign Affairs Association, August 1952), p. 657.

2. D. Clayton James, *The Years of MacArthur*, vol. 3, *Triumph and Disaster, 1945–1964* (Boston: Houghton Mifflin, 1985), pp. 226–33, 251–52; Theodore Cohen, in *Remaking Japan: The American Occupation as New Deal*, edited by Herbert Passin (New York: Macmillan, 1987), pp. 410–13; Benjamin C. Duke, *Japan's Militant Teachers: A History of the Left-Wing Teachers' Movement* (Honolulu: University of Hawaii Press, 1973), pp. 85–86.

3. Cohen, *Remaking Japan*, p. 410.

4. Duke, *Japan's Militant Teachers*, p. 86.

5. Memo by J. Van Staaveren, CI&E officer, YMGT, subject: *Civil Education Activities*, 19 July 1948.

6. James, *Years of MacArthur*, p. 85.

7. Toshio Nishi, *Unconditional Democracy: Education and Politics in Occupied Japan, 1945–1952* (Stanford: Hoover Institution Press, 1982), pp. 211–12; Duke, *Japan's Militant Teachers*, pp. 110–11.

8. YMGT Reports, May and July 1948; Duke, *Japan's Militant Teachers*, pp. 78–81; Nishi, *Unconditional Democracy*, chap. 11.

9. Duke, *Japan's Militant Teachers*, p. 79.

10. Ibid.; Nishi, *Unconditional Democracy*, chap. 11.

11. Janet E. Hunter, *Concise Dictionary of Modern Japanese History* (Berkeley and Los Angeles: University of California Press, 1984), p. 256; *Japan Year Book, 1949–1952*, pp. 658–59; Nishi, *Unconditional Democracy*, pp. 226–27.

12. *Japan Year Book, 1949–1952*, p. 222.

13. Duke, *Japan's Militant Teachers*, pp. 88–89.

14. Ibid., pp. 90–91, 111–12.

15. Nishi, *Unconditional Democracy*, p. 250.

16. James, *Years of MacArthur*, pp. 591–96; William L. Langer, editor, *An Encyclopedia of World History*, 4th ed. (Boston: Houghton Mifflin, 1963), p. 1,284.

17. Langer, ed., *Encyclopedia*, p. 1,284.

Glossary

Akahata	Newspaper of the Japan Communist Party
Benjo	A toilet
BOQ	Bachelor officers' quarters
Burakukais	Groups of *tonarigumis* or neighborhood associations in rural areas
CI&E	Civil information and education
CO	Commanding officer
CPH	Citizens' Public Halls
Chonaikais	Groups of *tonarigumis* in an urban area
Chonaikai-cho	The chief of a *chonaikai*
DAC	Department of the Army civilian
Daigaku Kosen Kyoso	Teachers' Union of Universities and Specialized Colleges
Choren	League of Koreans in Japan
ESS	Economic and Scientific Section
Eiwa Jo Gakko	Christian Girls' School
Gokoku Jinjas	Nation-protecting shrines
Hibachi	A brazier for burning charcoal in a room
Hiragana	One of two indigenous Japanese alphabets
Hoanden	A shrine near the entrance of a school which contains a portrait of the Emperor
IRRA	Imperial Rule Assistance Association
Kanji	Chinese characters used in Japanese writing
Kakemona	An ornamental hanging scroll, vertical, featuring a painting or a specimen of calligraphy
Katakana	One of two indigenous Japanese alphabets
Ken	Prefecture
Kyozenren	National Federation of Teachers' Unions
LARA	Licensed Agencies for the Relief of Asia
Nikkyoso	Japan Teachers' Union
Sanbetsu	Congress of Industrial Unions of Japan
Sen	A former Japanese coin worth one-hundredth of a Japanese *yen*
SCAP	Supreme Commander for the Allied Powers
Shokan-sha	Spirit-invoking shrines

277

Tonarigumi	A neighborhood association consisting of about six to thirteen households headed by a chief
TQC	Teachers' Qualification Committee
YMGT	Yamanashi Military Government Team
Zengakuren	All-Japan Federation of Student Self-Government Associations
Zenkyokyo	Council of All-Japan Teachers' Union

Selected Bibliography

Bunce, William K. *Religions in Japan: Buddhism, Shinto, Christianity.* Rutland, Vt.: Charles E. Tuttle Co., 1955.

Byas, Hugh. *Government by Assassination.* New York: Alfred A. Knopf, 1942.

Chamberlain, Basil Hall. *Things Japanese: Being Notes on Various Subjects Connected with Japan.* 4th ed., rev. and enl. London: Kelly and Walsh, Ltd., 1902.

Cohen, Theodore. In *Remaking Japan: The American Occupation as New Deal.* Edited by Herbert Passin. New York: Macmillan, 1987.

Duke, Benjamin C. *Japan's Militant Teachers: A History of the Left-Wing Teachers' Movement.* Honolulu: University of Hawaii Press, 1973.

Hall, Robert King. *Kokutai No Hongi: Cardinal Principles of the National Entity of Japan.* Translated by John Owen Gauntlett. Cambridge: Harvard University Press, 1949.

Handbook of Data on Japanese Women in Political Life: In Commemoration of the 40th Anniversary of Woman Suffrage in Japan. 2nd ed. Tokyo: Fusae Ichikawa Memorial Association, 1987. (English translation in McKeldin Library, University of Maryland, College Park.)

Hunter, Janet E. *Concise Dictionary of Modern Japanese History.* Berkeley and Los Angeles: University of California Press, 1984.

James, D. Clayton. *The Years of MacArthur.* Vol. 3. *Triumph and Disaster, 1945–1964.* Boston: Houghton Mifflin, 1985.

Japan Year Book, 1946–1948. Tokyo: Foreign Affairs Association of Japan, December 1948.

Japan Year Book, 1949–1952. Tokyo: Foreign Affairs Association of Japan, August 1952.

Langer, William L., editor. *An Encyclopedia of World History.* 4th ed. Boston: Houghton Mifflin, 1962.

Le Couteur, Wilson. *To Nippon, the Land of the Rising Sun: A Guide Book to Japan.* Tokyo: Nippon Yusen Kaisha, 1899.

Manchester, William. *American Caesar: Douglas MacArthur, 1880–1964.* Boston: Little, Brown, 1978.

Mitchell, Richard Hanks. *The Korean Minority in Japan.* Berkeley and Los Angeles: University of California Press, 1967.

Moore, Joe. *Japanese Workers and the Struggle for Power, 1945–1947.* Madison: University of Wisconsin Press, 1983.

Nimmo, William F. *Behind a Curtain of Silence: Japanese in Soviet Custody, 1945–1956.* New York: Greenwood Press, 1988.

——, editor, *The Occupation of Japan: Educational and Social Reform.* Norfolk, Va.: General Douglas MacArthur Foundation, 1980.

——, editor. *The Occupation of Japan: The Grass Roots.* Norfolk, Va.: General Douglas MacArthur Foundation, 1991.

Nishi, Toshio. *Unconditional Democracy: Education and Politics in Occupied Japan, 1945–1952.* Stanford: Hoover Institution Press, 1982.

Oppler, Alfred C. *Legal Reform in Occupied Japan: A Participant Looks Back.* Princeton: Princeton University Press, 1976.

Passin, Herbert. *Society and Education in Japan.* New York: Teachers College Press, 1965.

Quigley, Harold S., and John Turner. *The New Japan: Government and Politics.* Minneapolis: University of Minnesota Press, 1956. Reprint. Westport, Conn.: Greenwood, 1974.

Reischauer, Edwin O. *Japan: Past and Present.* New York: Alfred A. Knopf, 1946.

——. *The Japanese.* Cambridge: Belknap Press, 1977.

Sansom, G. B. *Japan: A Short Cultural History.* Rev. ed. New York: D. Appleton Century, 1943.

Schaller, Michael, *The American Occupation of Japan: The Origins of the Cold War in Asia.* Oxford: Oxford University Press, 1985.

——. *Douglas MacArthur: The Far Eastern General.* Oxford: Oxford University Press, 1989.

Swearingen, Roger, and Paul Langer. *Red Flag in Japan: International Communism in Action, 1919–1951.* Cambridge: Harvard University Press, 1952.

Thurston, Donald R. *Teachers and Politics in Japan.* Princeton: Princeton University Press, 1973.

Ward, Robert E., and Yoshikazu Sakamoto, editors. *Democratizing Japan: The Allied Occupation.* Honolulu: University of Hawaii Press, 1987.

Woodward, William P. *The Allied Occupation of Japan, 1945–1952, and Japanese Religions.* Leiden: J. J. Brill, 1972.

Newspaper and Journal Articles

Braibanti, Ralph J. D. "Administration of Military Government in Japan at the Prefectural Level." *American Political Science Review* 43 (April 1949).

——. "Neighborhood Associations in Japan and Their Democratic Potentialities." *Far Eastern Quarterly* 7 (February 1948).

Hille, Lt. Col. Henry. "Eighth Army's Role in Military Government in Japan." *Military Review* 22, no. 11 (February 1948).

Van Staaveren, Jacob. "Hosaka's New Learning." *Portland Oregonian* (5 December 1948).

——. "Adult Education in Japan." *Portland Oregonian* (12 December 1948).

———. "The Educational Revolution in Japan." *Educational Forum* 16, no. 2 (January 1952).

———. "Enforcing SCAP's Religious Directives on a Military Government Team." *Annals of the Southeast Conference of the Association for Asian Studies* 10 (January 1988).

Wray, Harry J. "Decentralization of Education in the Allied Occupation of Japan." In *The Occupation of Japan: Educational and Social Reform*. Edited by William F. Nimmo. Norfolk, Va.: General Douglas MacArthur Foundation, 1980.

Government Publications

Note: Government publications listed below are housed in Archive II of the Washington National Records Center at College Park, Maryland.

General Headquarters. Supreme Commander for the Allied Powers. Civil Information and Education Section. Education Division. *Education in Japan* (15 February 1946).

———. Supreme Commander for the Allied Powers. Civil Information and Education Section. Education Division. *Digests of the More Important Ministry of Education Orders and Directives Issued Since the End of the War.* (10 May 1946).

Headquarters, Eighth Army. *Orders to Military Government Units/Teams* (January 1946–July 1948).

Report of the United States Education Mission to Japan. Submitted to the Supreme Commander for the Allied Powers. Tokyo (30 March 1946).

Supreme Commander for the Allied Powers. *Summaries of Non-Military Activities in Japan.* Tokyo (September 1945–August 1948).

U.S. Army Service Forces Manual M 354-1. *Civil Affairs Handbook: Japan.* Section 1. *Geographical and Social Background.* (22 July 1944).

———. *Civil Affairs Handbook: Japan.* Section 15. *Education* (23 June 1945).

War Department Pamphlet 31–369. *Civil Affairs Handbook: Japan. Prefectural Studies: Yamanashi-ken* (24 September 1945).

Yamanashi Military Government Team. *Occupational Activity Reports to Commanding General, Headquarters, Eighth Army.* Kofu (December 1945–September 1948).

Yamanashi Prefectural Government Records. Kofu (September 1945–September 1948).

Unpublished Sources

Horner, Layton. *The American Occupation of Japan at the Prefectural Level.* M.A. thesis. University of Denver. 1949.

Van Staaveren, Jacob. Letters, journals, and other memorabilia, August 1946–August 1948. Author's files.

Yamanashi Military Government Team. Letters from citizens of Yamanashi Prefecture, October 1946–July 1948. Author's files. See also Archive II of the Washington National Records Center at College Park, Maryland.

Index

influence, 102–3 passim; Education Institute, 172–76; contract provisions, 208–11
Yamanashi Prefecture Religions Association, 250–51
Yamanashi Teachers' Qualification Committee, 49, 69, 72
Yamanashi Technical College, 212
Yamanashi's Education Association, 176–78
Yamanashi's *Gokoku Jinja* (shrine for war dead): inspection of, 238–43
Yashiro Ii, 109
Yokohama: author's arrival in, 7–8
Yoshida Shigeru, 23, 103
Yoshie Katsuyasu, 95, 196–97

Young Men's Christian Association (YMCA), 50, 116–17, 119
Young Women's Christian Association (YWCA), 117–18, 223–24
Youth associations, 65–67, 116–20, 217–19, 222–24, 229–30; Funatsu, 66
Youth Cultural Research Center (Nichiren): inspection of, 248–49
Youth schools, 91–92; abolished, 164

Zachry, Richard L., 232–33
Zengakuren, 215, 258
Zenkyokyo, 206–7